More Praise for *Dancing with the Octopus*

"*Dancing with the Octopus* is a brave and authentic picture of the tailwinds of trauma, the limits of human forgiveness, and what it takes to maintain hope in a world bent on breaking us. Highly readable and deeply moving." —Rachel Louise Snyder, award-winning author of *No Visible Bruises*

"Bravely looks at her family trauma and the hope of restorative justice—combining wit, drama, and deep self-reflection to investigate the aftershocks of a devastating crime." —*Oxygen*, "The Best True Crime Books of 2020 for Holiday Gifting"

"A gripping account of one woman's confrontation with the terror and heartbreak of her past. Harding combines true crime and family saga to illustrate the aftershocks of trauma and the courage, tenderness, and humor that recovery requires." —Melissa Febos, author of *Girlhood*

"This moving story of grit and resilience will resonate with readers long after the final page is turned." —*Publishers Weekly* (starred review)

"A gripping memoir, *Dancing with the Octopus* is both a heartbreaking reconstruction of a crime and a powerful account of healing from trauma." —*Electric Literature*, "Most Anticipated Debuts of the Second Half of 2020"

"Harding's writing is exquisite, often funny . . . This book is personal, deeply and bravely thoughtful, and creatively expressed . . . It can serve as a tool for the politically engaged." —*New York Journal of Books*

"Darkly humorous . . . Harding draws a complex web of interlinked experiences to show how suffering can set up shop for good in a family and a town. *Dancing with the Octopus* joins a host of recent true crime memoirs dedicated to grounding crimes in a wider framework of social and familial contexts." —*CrimeReads*, "Most Anticipated Crime Books of 2020"

"An incredible book . . . Debora writes with a lightness of touch that belies the heavy lifting in a work of such magnitude and power." —Philip Selway of Radiohead, on Twitter

"This is a fantastic memoir . . . beautifully written and it's an excellent example of trauma's long hold on people . . . An incredible look at depression and parenthood and forgiveness . . . It is excellent." —*Book Riot*'s *All the Books* podcast

"Compelling . . . Harding is completely honest, whether describing her wariness, defiance, bewilderment, self-doubt, or the truths she eventually discovered about herself and her parents . . . Her unsparing and candid observations allow readers to really get to know this strong, determined survivor." —*Booklist*

"Debora Harding writes with a stunningly original mixture of insight, wit, and humanity about a life packed with so much drama, loss, and resilience that you can't believe it's not an epic work of fiction." —Kate Weinberg, author of *The Truants*

"In this compelling and unflinching memoir which switches between past and present, Harding . . . unravels the impact of this random act of violence and of her dysfunctional childhood. It's a tale of trauma and PTSD, but also of recovery through the healing power of restorative justice, and of enduring love." —*The Bookseller* (editor's choice)

"A searing literary work that will help many of us see trauma in a different light. In strong and powerful prose Debora Harding shows us what it means to move forward through grief." —Julia Samuel, author of *This Too Shall Pass*

"Gripping . . . You are drawn in straightaway." —BBC Radio 2

"Extraordinary, so powerful, and like nothing I've read. Astonishing book. It deserves to be the most massive hit." —Kate Mosse, author of *Labyrinth*

"I have just finished reading *Dancing with the Octopus* . . . You are lucky! The electricity of this true crime memoir awaits you." —Lemn Sissay, author of *My Name Is Why*, on Twitter

"Debora Harding's book is a beautiful and exacting monument to resilience and recovery." —*The Telegraph*

"It's as gripping as any thriller and as moving as any novel you're ever likely to read." —Paul Chahidi, actor, on Twitter

"A powerful true story about a violent crime, a dysfunctional family, resilience, reckoning, and recovery." —BBC *Woman's Hour*

"With remarkable narrative skill, Harding untangles the lingering effects of family dysfunction and criminal trauma. This is a page-turner with a deep heart and soul, full of forgiveness but demanding of accountability." —*BookPage*, "Best Books of 2020: Memoirs"

"A sharp, compelling recollection of abuse, gaslighting, and the process of trauma . . . Ultimately, *Dancing with the Octopus* is a book about *telling* and the power of *retelling*—an act carried out with wit, grace, and humor by an author of her own narrative truth." —*Cambridge Review of Books*

"An often-wrenching but clear-eyed look at the crime, Harding's life, and the hard work of therapy and recovery." —*Omaha World-Herald*

"Her book is more than a heartbreakingly disturbing account of childhood abuse in the United States, in the vein of Tara Westover's *Educated*. A third, parallel strand explores her love for her kind, devoted father and carefully extracts moments of real happiness from the chaos of her early life. Having braced myself for misery, I found these sections the most impressive part of the book." —*The Guardian*

Dancing with the Octopus

a memoir of a crime

Debora Harding

BLOOMSBURY PUBLISHING
NEW YORK · LONDON · OXFORD · NEW DELHI · SYDNEY

BLOOMSBURY PUBLISHING
Bloomsbury Publishing Inc.
1385 Broadway, New York, NY 10018, USA

BLOOMSBURY, BLOOMSBURY PUBLISHING, and the Diana logo are trademarks
of Bloomsbury Publishing Plc

First published in the United States 2020
This edition published 2021

This memoir is a work of nonfiction. However, the names of certain individuals have
been changed to protect their privacy, and dialogue has been reconstructed to the best
of the Author's recollection. With respect to Charles Goodwin, please see a statement
at the end of the text of this book.

ISBN: HB: 978-1-63557-612-2; PB: 978-1-63557-784-6; EBOOK: 978-1-63557-613-9

LIBRARY OF CONGRESS CATALOGING-IN-PUBLICATION DATA

Names: Harding, Debora, author.
Title: Dancing with the octopus : a memoir of a crime / Debora Harding.
Description: New York, NY : Bloomsbury Publishing, 2020.
Identifiers: LCCN 2020005048 (print) | LCCN 2020005049 (ebook) |
ISBN 9781635576122 (hardback) | ISBN 9781635576139 (ebook)
Subjects: LCSH: Harding, Debora. | Kidnapping victims—Nebraska—Biography. |
Abduction—Nebraska.
Classification: LCC HV6574.U6 H37 2020 (print) | LCC HV6574.U6 (ebook) |
DDC 362.88 [B]—dc23
LC record available at https://lccn.loc.gov/2020005048
LC ebook record available at https://lccn.loc.gov/2020005049

2 4 6 8 10 9 7 5 3 1

Typeset by Westchester Publishing Services
Printed and bound in the USA

To find out more about our authors and books visit www.bloomsbury.com and sign up
for our newsletters.

Bloomsbury books may be purchased for business or promotional use. For information
on bulk purchases please contact Macmillan Corporate and Premium Sales Department at
specialmarkets@macmillan.com.

For my husband, Thomas
You are the most beautiful of humans

Life would be tragic if it weren't funny.

—STEPHEN HAWKING

In Which the Clock Starts Ticking

Lincoln, 2003—The truth began to emerge when I saw Charles Goodwin sitting at a white Formica table in a Nebraska prison canteen, waiting for his parole hearing. I wasn't expecting to recognize him in a crowd, but when I observed his dark brown eyes scanning the room, I felt the pulse of memory kick in, and when it did, a passage of history, a quarter of a century, all but disappeared.

It wasn't the first occasion I'd struggled with a disproportionate sense of time. I certainly didn't expect that when I learned to read a clock, it would turn into an exercise of such great profundity or that this would be my first major concession to there being a science and order to our universe. One has to learn to add multiples of 5 all the way to 60, often at an age when you are barely able to count to 10. Then you have to learn that 60 minutes equal 1 hour, 24 hours equal 1 day, 7 days make up 1 week, and 365 days make up a year, which is the time it takes the earth to orbit the sun, with the exception being the fourth year, when we leap ahead by a day.

For the earth to orbit the sun twenty-five times seems an enormous distance to travel. But for me, time often operates with rules disconnected from the workings of the universe—randomly bending with an emotional weight of metric tonnage proportion before disappearing into one black hole.

In Which I Study the Object of My Attention

Lincoln, 2003—Charles Goodwin had spent twenty-five years in Nebraska state prisons. He appeared to be in his element, not overly anxious. His hands, folded, rested on a thick hardback book whose title was *Revelation: A Book of Judgment.* Perched on top were a spiral notebook and pen.

His looks were pleasant enough, his hair closely shaven. He was wearing a plain white T-shirt, baggy jeans, and neutral-colored sneakers. There was nothing in him of the aggressive body language that was common in this environment. He appeared fit, no doubt from hours spent in the prison gym, but he hadn't acquired that machismo bodybuilder look.

About fifty prisoners sat or stood around, waiting their turn to appear in front of the parole board. None lacked for company—parents, a wife, friends, a few even had kids to broaden the audience, so the energy of the room had the backstage buzz of a school Christmas pageant.

But my offender, and it would be correct to call him "my"—though every ounce of me recoiled at the idea that he might consider me "his"—sat alone, displaying a casual but respectful patience, wearing a look of friendly approachability, as if he were waiting there just for me in the same way he'd been that afternoon, twenty-five years ago, when our paths happened to cross.

But before I go further, let me explain how we first met.

In Which a Portent Arrives

Omaha, 1978—When you're struggling to make your way up a long hill, in sleet driven by twenty-mile-an-hour winds, and you can't close your jacket because the zipper won't work, and you have no hat or gloves, it's easy to become thoroughly pissed off.

It was the day before Thanksgiving. Classes at my school, Lewis and Clark Junior High, had been dismissed an hour early due to the severity of an ice storm warning issued by the National Weather Service. The roads were filling quickly with cars, families eager to beat the storm to their destinations before the start of the nation's four-day holiday.

I decided against taking the school bus home, after hearing the district wrestling tournament was going ahead. Not because I was a sports fan, but because I assumed if the tournament wasn't canceled, then my youth church choir practice wouldn't be either, particularly as it was the last rehearsal before Thanksgiving, the most popular service of the year. Our church sat across the parking lot from my school, a convenience that made the decision all the easier.

With two hours to spend before choir practice, I stopped by to see my favorite science teacher, Kent Friesen, hoping that our weekly math tutorial was still on. When I arrived in his classroom, I found a bag of popcorn waiting on his desk with an apology note saying he had been asked last minute to serve as a referee for the tournament. After munching down the treat, I headed back to my locker, where I bumped into a friend who said he was going to J. C. Penney to buy tickets to an upcoming Kiss concert. I decided I'd tag along with him. The Crossroads Shopping Mall sat only five minutes away at the bottom of the hill and I could spend the next hour looking for ideas for Christmas presents. The sky was hideous, the color of a deep purple bruise, when we emerged from the doors of our school, but I had yet to realize the speed with which Mother Nature could move.

Only an hour later, as I was returning, the sleet was freezing nearly as fast as it hit the ground, and the landscape was turning glacial. It would be safe to say, because I had never been exposed to the difficulties imposed on navigation in such a storm, I grossly underestimated its challenge. In addition to my eagerness to make it to choir rehearsal, I was undeniably swayed to persevere by the mindset I had inherited from my father—if you let a winter storm in Nebraska stop you, you'd never walk out the door.

Unfortunately, I wasn't the only one thinking that way.

In Which Charles Goes for Retail Therapy

Omaha, 1978—Charles Goodwin, seventeen years old and ten days free from the Kearney Youth Development Center, turned sideways in front of the department store's full-length mirror, assessing a pair of new Levi's. At first, he wasn't convinced about the brown stitching down the legs and back pockets, but now he thought the trim lent a nice tailored look.

He moved closer to the mirror, checking out what he thought was his best asset—his smile; at least it had been before that guy broke his jaw. Now every time he looked at his reflection, he was trying to correct the once-perfect symmetry of his face.

Next on the shopping list was proper outdoor gear. He found himself some tan steel-toed work boots with good traction on the sole and a light-brown hooded parka with large pockets. And then to finish the look, he wanted a balaclava. He tried a black one, but it had no character; instead, he settled on one that was red with black embroidered around the eyes.

Last but not least, he needed a knife. The Montgomery Ward sports department would have a wide selection. After surveying a few in the glass display case, he went for a fishing fillet knife with a wooden handle. It would cost a bit more, but it balanced nicely in his grip.

With his purchase list complete, Charles walked back through the mall and pushed his way out the glass doors at the back of the Brandeis department store. That's when he spotted a van sitting by the loading dock. The engine was idling, with no driver in sight. In fact, there wasn't a soul to be seen. His eyes went back to the van. He couldn't believe what an easy pickup it would be, like it had been planted there just for him.

So, being the seasoned carjacker he was, he looked around one last time, walked up to the van door, jumped in, and put the stick in reverse. As he backed out, he felt that sweet relief of an addict surrendering to his poison.

In Which I Contemplate Prairie Weather

Omaha, 1978—At fourteen years old, I was entering the plateau of what might be called real adolescence, but there were days when I still felt like a kid, and for a kid in the Midwest, a winter storm was the herald of good things to come: school cancellations, playing in the streets, and the opportunity to earn vast amounts of cash. But most glorious was a world blanketed in white, brilliant snow.

Within hours of a storm's end, forts sprung up, caves were hollowed out with underground tunnels to connect them, snowmen were built, stockpiles of snowballs were stacked—and all this created with the knowledge that if lucky, these sculptured creations would last for a week. Out of all the benefits, the most splendid by far was the sledding. After a snowfall, the best place to be if you lived in Omaha was Memorial Park, which offered panoramic views of the city.

But it wasn't snow I was navigating that afternoon—this was an ice storm, and as I headed toward my church, keeping my balance was becoming increasingly difficult. The air was heavy, its weight dampening the noise of traffic, and the cars on the road weren't having an easier time moving through the frigid muck. I watched as one became stuck, its wheels spinning furiously. The driver reversed and tried again, this time a little faster. Another car fishtailed its way through the deepening slush.

After much effort, I finally managed to get up the hill to the church parking lot. When I reached the side entrance of the choir annex, I found a note tacked to the door, flapping in the wind, runny with red ink. *Choir practice canceled due to bad weather.* How unfortunate.

I wore a cross fixed on a necklace, which I'd reach for if I needed a little emotional buoying, like I did at that moment. The storm was growing worse by the minute. As I slid my cross along its chain, I caught sight of the line of yellow school buses across the parking lot. The wrestling tournament was still under way, which meant the building would be open and I could find a way to get myself home.

So I headed in that direction.

In Which Charles Lands His Dream Job

Omaha, 1978—Later, Charles was driving and leaned over the steering wheel to check out the sky. It had this color to it, like nothing he had ever seen. And the weather outside couldn't make up its mind. One minute it was raining, the next squalling with snow. He hadn't been sure how the van was going to handle on the road, but he felt a sort of manly pride as he steered it through traffic.

He was heading back over to 5025 Castelar Street to take care of some unfinished business. The new knife sat on the seat next to him. He wanted to pay his respects to the punk who attacked him at school. He had gone by the house earlier, one of those ranchers, even knocked on the door. The kid's mother answered. Said he wasn't home. Charles noticed she was pretty. Even thought for a split second it would serve that kid right if he took his revenge by slicing her face; actually, he thought about doing more than that. He assured her he'd be by again.

As Charles approached the boy's neighborhood, the rain turned to sleet. Left turn, right turn. Just as he was about to pull into the driveway, he spotted a police car sitting there. Damn, she must have made a call. Or was he just being paranoid? That was the second time he'd gotten himself all jacked up for nothing. He steered himself accordingly, right on by. Might as well head over to Lewis and Clark Junior High a little earlier, to surprise his cousin. She was a cheerleader, and there was a district wrestling tournament.

The drive only took fifteen minutes, but during that time the roads had turned into almost solid ice. He pulled in around back near the school buses, so he could catch his cousin Crystal coming out of the gym. But she sure was taking a long time. Drumming his fingers on the steering wheel, he noticed the needle indicating the gas tank was near empty. He checked his pockets—two dollars and a few loose coins. Not good. He wasn't seeing a paycheck until Friday, from his new job at Godfather's Pizza. It was one of the conditions that his father, a minister at the local Baptist church, had given him if he was going to move back home. When Charles asked him what he expected him to do in the meanwhile for cash, the Reverend told him to figure it out.

That's when the movie sprang to mind, the one that he and his brother had gone to see last year. These guys kidnap a banker's daughter and hold her for ransom. He tried to remember the name—maybe *60 Seconds*? The guys had names like Dirty Larry and Mo. He needed money like that. His next thought was why not, why not do the same thing? He didn't need a banker, just a family man with money in his account, plus a kid. And if he got enough, he could split, go to California like he'd always wanted to.

And then, like the universe had had the same idea, he spotted a girl off in the distance, walking away from the church. He turned the engine on, revved her up, and said something to the effect of, "She looks good enough to me."

In Which I Meet a Masked Man

Omaha, 1978—My first thought as he pulled up in front of me, blocking my path, was that he had a question, perhaps needed directions, but then I saw the ski mask. And then I met his eyes.

The speed with which he jumped from his vehicle (I will now call him Mr. K, for *kidnapper*) and the dexterity with which he positioned his large fillet knife to my throat were most worthy of respect. I might say my next thought was to grab the blade, but one does not think in these situations, one just does. I caught his fist and pulled the weapon halfway down the length of my chest, before I felt my feet skidding out on ice underneath me and reflexively released his arm. I fell against Mr. K. "YOU WANT ME TO CUT YOUR FUCKING FACE?" he yelled.

At this stage, you might imagine, there was much screaming, yet I can't say I in fact did scream. He yanked my arm behind my back and, twisting my shoulder, shoved me toward the driver's seat. My head landed near the accelerator pedal, and he kicked at my legs. I struggled to turn sideways and kicked back. He shouted, "I WILL KILL YOU," with such violence and force he left no doubt as to his sincerity, and then he told me to crawl over the floor in front of the passenger's seat.

Finally, he jumped into the driver's seat, moved the gearshift in first, and off we went.

In Which I Contemplate the Powers of Wonder Woman

Lincoln, Nebraska, 2003—I was no longer a fourteen-year-old girl but a thirty-nine-year-old woman standing alongside my husband, as I looked at Charles Goodwin in the cafeteria at the Lincoln Community Corrections Center. I couldn't remember his face because he'd worn a ski mask the entire time we were together, so I wasn't exactly sure what I was looking for— perhaps a demonic bird with evil eyes. But when I spotted him looking up, there was no doubt.

"That's him," I said, my heart pounding in my throat with an odd exhilaration— a mixture of fear, anger, and wonderment that he was real and not a specter of my hallucinating mind. My husband brought me back to earth by nudging me with the *Omaha World Herald* he had rolled in his hand. "Show me. Where is he?"

"The one at the table, by himself." I nodded in Goodwin's direction.

If I am honest, I was almost disappointed to find him looking so cheerful and friendly, so clean, so averagely midwestern, so . . . well—normal.

I wanted nothing more than to act with beautiful simplicity—to stride up to him with my new feelings of boldness, feet planted wide, hands on hips, and proudly proclaim, "Ah ha! Bet you didn't expect to see me, victim back from the dead." But that wouldn't have been wise.

Especially because it was likely he'd be walking free from prison the next day, leaving the institution that had raised him from a seventeen-year-old boy to a forty-three-year-old man; the same time it had taken me to grow from a fourteen-year-old girl to a fully formed Wonder Woman.

Sort of.

They say with severe crimes there's no avoiding the aftermath. What they don't say is how post-traumatic stress can become a disorder because of your childhood family, the one you're trying to survive.

I will now tell you about my childhood. Do not be scared.

In Which I Think on My Cornhusker Roots

Omaha, 1969—I can see the day my parents moved us to Omaha, as clear as water in a toilet bowl. I was five years old. We were sitting in the driveway—Mom, Dad, my two sisters, my dog, and me—waiting for the keys to be delivered to our new house.

Our raised ranch, with a double garage, was nestled alongside eight others in a field overlooking Lee Valley, the name of our budding suburb. The view from our suitcases was unimpeded as far as the eye could see: hundreds of barren plots marked off in a checkerboard fashion, with neon orange mini flags and string. Interstate 680 lay in the distance, with its constant drone of vehicles traveling east and west.

My parents, with the excitement of being first-time homeowners, had forgotten it was Sunday and church services weren't over until one P.M., so our real estate agent had yet to arrive. As we stood waiting, the heat reflected off the newly cemented road. Zorro, our cocker spaniel mutt, dropped on my feet. I looked around for a tree I could climb. Not a one in sight. I noticed my younger sister Gayle, age three, wilted on the fresh-rolled turf like melted bubble gum; then, at last, I spotted some entertainment—my sister Genie, age seven. I inched my foot toward her, the oldest bored sibling move in the book. Before I even made contact with her, Mom saw and reached over to backhand me, but my father swooped in from the left and took my hand.

"Let's take Zorro for a walk and have a Chautauqua."

A Chautauqua was the name for special talks my father and I had, where he would impart wisdom. Later on I learned he got the name from the salons hosted by pioneers, the first being near Lake Chautauqua, which once belonged to the Native Americans in New York. Here was the wisdom my father imparted that day:

"Half of Nebraska's farmers are Indians," he said as we walked, "and they were such good farmers that the United States government gave them land, but not any land, the most difficult land in the country to farm. This is because they thought if anyone could work miracles out of that soil, the Indians could. And that is how Omaha got its name—from one of the great Nebraska tribes."

Anyone hearing that story might think Dad was minimizing the tragic violence inflicted on Native Americans, but that wasn't Dad's way. Instead, he was always looking for the positive spin on a helpless situation, no matter what emotion had to be ignored. I listened, I registered: Indians, great farmers, U.S. government, very smart and generous. Omaha, Indians.

"But the most important thing about Nebraska," Dad continued as we looked over the distant cornfields that disappeared into the horizon, "is the Cornhuskers football team. In fact"—he jabbed his finger in the air—"there isn't a better college football team in the country. And that's the truth."

And there was indeed some truth to this. The Nebraska Cornhuskers were on the way to a two-year national championship winning streak in 1970 and 1971.

He looked at me then, to make sure I understood, really understood, the value of the real estate we had landed on. "Yeah," I said, my eyes opening wide with enthusiasm. And to punctuate the deep meaning of the moment, he put his arm around my shoulder, and the three of us—Dad, Zorro, and I—looked out at what was to become the view from my bedroom window, where the sinking sun would hypnotize me to sleep for the next eight years.

"Those Cornhuskers," Dad added, looking dreamily out at the cornfields, squeezing my hand.

"Yeah, those Cornhuskers," I said dreamily back as I spotted a huge oval water tower farther beyond the golden-tasseled stalks. Dad told me it belonged to Boys Town, a juvenile detention center founded by Father Flanagan, who believed there was no such thing as a bad kid, just a kid needing one person to believe in him.

My father and I didn't know it, but Mr. K was in the landscape even then. At the time we were standing there, he was eight years old, living on the other side of Omaha in a nice middle-class neighborhood, maybe eating Cheerios.

Reality surfaced like a whale, with Gayle running around the corner, hollering that a neighbor had arrived with a pitcher of iced lemonade and chocolate chip cookies. Shortly after introducing ourselves, we heard the strained sound of shifting gears as the semitruck with a Mayflower logo pulled all our earthly belongings up the hill. My childhood in Lee Valley was about to begin.

In Which I Think Respectfully on Postnatal Depression

Omaha, 1970—Not long after we settled into life in Lee Valley, we had a family conference where Mom announced she was pregnant again and, after what felt like five years because I was so damn excited, my baby sister Jenifer arrived.

By that time, Genie and I were trained in the art of running a household. This isn't so unusual in families short of an extra pair of adult hands—the older kids just pick up the slack. By the age of six, I could clean the kitchen, wash the clothes, vacuum, and change my baby sister's diapers. When Dad was home, he took over most of the jobs, though it was never really clear he understood whose load he was easing. He would pull up at the end of a workday, or most often a workweek; we'd run down the hill, Zorro chasing after us, and leap on him. Sometimes we would even tackle him to the ground.

"Here comes Jesus Christ," Mom would say on cue.

Once inside, Dad would perform his Tevye from *Fiddler on the Roof* routine, thrusting one hand up in the air, then he'd put one wrist behind, snap his fingers, and sing "If I Were a Rich Man" while thrusting his hips side to side, stomping a beat, Zorro running in circles around him barking. He was better than Chaim Topol in that role, the way he expressed the sweet and bitter pain of life so well.

And if he was home on a Friday, he would clap his hands and tell us to pile into the car for a trip to the Dairy Queen. After getting our double-dipped ice-cream cones, we detoured over to the new apartment complex behind the strip mall where Dad would drive around in circles until we were dizzy. Genie, Gayle, and I would laugh so hard it sucked the oxygen out of any misery.

One winter morning, Dad had gone off to work and Genie, Gayle, and I went off to school—as was the normal routine, leaving Mom at home alone with the baby. We'd been standing at the bus stop for what must have been twenty minutes and had started doing the Virginia Reel, a barn dance strategy we used for keeping warm, when a neighborhood parent yelled at us from her front door. Hadn't we heard? School had been canceled because of the two feet of snow we were do-si-do-ing in. Trudging back to the house, I became excited thinking about the fort I was going to build, where I was going to run the tunnels, and wondering whether we had carrots in the fridge for the snowman—normal Nebraska blizzard kid thoughts.

Those thoughts evaporated when we came through our front door and I heard the baby crying. Mom was deaf in one ear because when she was sixteen, her half brother accidentally shot her with a popgun and burst her eardrum. Nothing could wake her up, and to tell you the truth there was no benefit to doing it.

I went to get the baby, reached down in her crib and found she was sopping wet because she was wearing one of those cotton diapers that leaked all over the place. So I grabbed some dry cloths and wiped her down, but she didn't like it. She started kicking like a frog and waved her strong little angry fists while her face blew up into the color of a cherry. It made it impossible to get the safety pins into the diaper, and I didn't want to stick her, so I was making funny faces, and just then I heard Mom stomping down the hall, yelling, "What the hell is going on!"

The next thing I knew Genie, Gayle, and I were getting hustled out the basement door into the unheated garage. She didn't give us any time to collect our coats, hats, and gloves. Footwear would have been nice, too. We weren't sure what we were meant to do next. We hoped she'd cool off quick enough and let us back into the house. It wasn't clear what we'd done wrong.

After fifteen minutes, we started thinking about going to a neighbor for help. But I had the next thought—if she wasn't angry now, we'd hate to see her when a neighbor showed up at the door. So we distracted ourselves the best we could by taking turns riding our Big Wheel tricycle around the garage floor and playing hopscotch and four square with a ball. More time passed. Gayle started crying. She was four years old. The cold was hurting. Genie picked her up while I started banging on the door as hard as I could. Nothing. We had to consider other options. I rolled up the garage door and started looking at which neighbor's house we could go to when I heard Gayle start shouting— "Dad is coming, Dad is coming!" I remember thinking she must be hallucinating, until with my own eyes I saw him down the hill, pushing his way, one leg at a time through the deep snow, the car parked behind him. We waited for him to reach the garage, then monkey-tackled him. He hugged us, grabbing Gayle and me, each under an arm, Genie on his back, carrying us into the basement and telling us to please sit, while he went upstairs to see what was wrong with Mom.

I remember him coming back down and saying how sorry he was, as he blew on our toes and warmed up our feet with his hands, saying, "Damn, you could have gotten frostbitten," and you could see he was a man sick with worry for his children and for his overwhelmed wife, who clearly wasn't coping. But it was all okay because Dad was home. And when Dad was home Mom was as different as a blackbird is to a vampire. Both have wings, but one sucks your blood.

In Which the Aftermath Comes Knocking

London, 1992—You might say, for me, the first major fault line made its appearance when I arrived at the door of a hard-earned adult-made happiness.

I was twenty-eight years old and had recently moved to London to join my husband-to-be. Given both nature and nurture, I viewed myself more a prime candidate for prison or a mental asylum than good marriage material, but Thomas assured me he had vetted me well. I had just unpacked my luggage when a postman arrived at the door with a medium-size box. I opened it to find the most unusual bearer of messages—a large stuffed frog with a note in its mouth.

Call home. Mom in hospital. Seems to be doing fine. Will be home soon. Love Dad.

I had time to puzzle over the MacGuffin's meaning with our six-hour time zone difference. It wasn't unusual for Dad to use humor to lighten a heavy emotional situation. But when I finally reached him, he sounded odd, asked me about the English weather and was more interested in talking about the Queen Mother than getting to the point. I asked him to please just tell me what happened.

"Your mother was in the hospital."

I reminded him the frog arrived ahead with the message, and then asked if it had been serious.

"Well . . . serious . . . yes and no." He told me they'd gotten into an argument six weeks earlier; Mom went psychotic and tried to stab him with a kitchen knife. After he wrestled the knife from her hand, she locked herself in the bathroom.

"They gave me a choice to press charges or call the ambulance and have her committed . . ."

"Hi, honey!"

Evidently, Mom had been standing next to him. This term of endearment, addressed to me, was definitely out of character. She then told me about her time in the hospital. I won't go into too much detail, but phrases like "triggered a childhood wound," "discovering her child within," "daily group therapy," and "art therapy" were used. I kept waiting for mention of "anger management," but there was nothing that suggested the homicidal rage behind Mom's attack was even an issue. By the end of the conversation, I was more concerned for Dad. One thing was clear. Whatever drugs she was on, they were doing a fine job of elevating her mood.

Later that night, as Thomas and I were putting clean sheets on the bed, I shared the news headline from back home but had a hard time doing it with a straight face. Thomas didn't think I was serious. I assured him unfortunately I was, and half-joked he might want to back out of our relationship now. While he stuffed pillows into cases and I grew more frustrated in my attempts to get the duvet into its cover, I shared it wasn't that far out of character for Mom . . . but I was particularly troubled by her total lack of concern for Dad. What if he hadn't stopped her? Thomas, seeing I wasn't getting anywhere with my duvet efforts, took the wad of bedding out of my hands, disappeared into its cover sheet with the enthusiasm of Tigger pouncing on Winnie the Pooh, and emerged with the quilt perfectly fitted into corners. "It could be a cultural difference," he suggested.

That night, as I was falling asleep, the words from a Sesame Street song, "One of these things is not like the other," kept popping into my mind alongside alternating images: the knife-wielding masked abductor of my childhood and my knife-wielding psychotic mother. It went straight back to the kid in me, setting off all kinds of peculiar effects.

In Which I Make an Unusual Friend

Omaha, 1978—I was now screaming, trapped on the van floor in front of the passenger seat, with the tip of the knife sharp between my neck and skull.

"Shut the fuck up bitch before I kill you!" Mr. K shouted again, in a tone that left no doubt he would be willing to execute his threat.

To convince me, he applied pressure to the skin. I tried to calm down, but found it difficult to bring the spasms wracking my ribs under control. He yelled louder, "SHUT THE FUCK UP OR I'LL KILL YOU!" which was completely unnecessary, as he'd just said this, and it didn't help the situation at all. I gulped, choking down the spasms. "I'm trying," I whispered. He acknowledged the change of attitude, and I felt a tiny shift in the pressure of the knife.

We drove for what felt like ten minutes, my cheek cold against the floor from the dirty sleet on the bottom of his boots. I felt my body slightly shift with the turns of the van. During this time I began to breathe more normally.

Mr. K turned on the radio, tuning into a classic rock station. A gentle ballad in a minor key from the rock group Kansas played. *Dust in the wind / All we are is dust in the wind.*

It occurred to me that if I strained my eyes to the right, I could gather more information. I took in the tops of trees, telephone lines, street signs, anything that would help me determine the location and direction in which we were moving.

It was then that Mr. K offered to take the knife away if I kept quiet.

"Yes," I said. You can imagine my relief.

"What?" he said.

I was not sure how to interpret his question. It may be that he wanted me to understand that he was strong, an adversary to be contended with, and my yes didn't reflect the proper register of fear. Or it may have been that he sincerely did not hear me and was concerned to know which option it was I preferred—the knife at the back of my head and screaming or removal of the knife and silence. So I chose to respond with a somewhat louder yes that conveyed a mixture of both great respect and fear. May I tell you, it did not take much acting effort.

I felt the knife lift and was able to breathe again without fear of being cut. We passed more time listening to music. This time it was Little River Band's single "Lady." *Look around, be a part / Feel for the winter, but don't have a cold heart.*

The stanzas in these songs could have been a compilation tape for the drive, so appropriate were they to the situation, but no, it was just a classic rock station.

In Which I Consider the Nature of Dreams

London, 1992—A couple of days after Dad's frog arrived, the night terrors began. I was lying there asleep, eyes wide open, waiting for a trip wire to blow, my nerves tuned into a sensorily perceived threat in the room, nondescript yet palpable. Thomas tried to wake me, soothe me by talking, but this only alarmed me further, and I jumped out of bed, awake but unable to step out of the dream. It was like a director had called a cut in action, but whatever the source of the malevolent feeling was, it hadn't cleared the room.

I'd been having night terrors all the way back to adolescence, but realized I had never had anyone witness one. My unconscious strategy for dealing with them was to avoid sleep altogether. All-nighters, often twice a week, had been a part of my lifestyle as long as I could remember. I had plenty of excuses. There are never enough hours in a day for a workaholic. And then there was my manic thirst for knowledge. Once I got on a reading bender, I hated to stop. And often, just the stimulation of the day made it impossible to sleep.

But a mutual bedtime was a nonnegotiable term for Thomas. Sharing life together should include going to bed at the same time, in the same bed. He wasn't unreasonable, though: he understood there would be exceptions.

After the start of the new nightmare season, I decided to stop at a local book-store and check out the self-help section. I found information on night terrors; while not that common, they weren't rare. It was a form of lucid dreaming. Children were more likely to experience them, and most grew out of them; scientists didn't know why. Nothing suggested that they were anything to be worried about. Relieved at the findings, I shared my research with Thomas over Marmite and toast, a newly acquired taste for me. We now understood why his attempts to wake me up were counterproductive. We both decided to trust the experts and assumed the terrors would just run their course.

But I couldn't let go of the fact I was interrupting his sleep. I decided to try analyzing my dreams. Perhaps the night terrors were nothing other than a neurological digestive problem, an overload with all the new information I had to process given the transatlantic move, and writing them down would help. I decided on a narrative analysis—I'd track the following items:

- Time (date and age in my life the content pulled from, which was not always obvious)
- Time in the dream (which proved interestingly nonimportant, and usually a mystery)
- Location (rather straightforward, but still sometimes not clearly discernible)
- Theme (was it concerned with my childhood, my family life, my health, my impending marriage?)
- Length (was it one of those all-night marathon dreams, or was it a series of short ones? medium-length ones?)
- Structure (nested: a dream within a dream? linear: a straightforward narrative? nonlinear? meta?)
- Character (family? animals? friends? workmates? famous figures?)

After keeping a log for a month, I tallied the results. Nightmares made up about 30 percent of my overall sleep. Night terrors, less than 5 percent. I took comfort in the insight the exercise offered. I thought storytelling was the reserve of those who practiced the craft, but there was no refuting it. Humans are biologically wired with the need, but most of us do it unconsciously. It helped me reframe my attitude: it wasn't the product of my dysfunctioning mind after all.

But it still couldn't remove the anxiety of the 5 percent of the dreams that felt traumatizing. These dreams didn't feel like dreams, but like another human being was breathing in the room. I never "saw" the object of my fear, only sensed an abstract figure in the dark.

As more time passed, I began to fear the oppressive force sitting in the room was the shadow of myself, a reflection of my own violent nature. This wasn't a comforting thought.

In Which I Play with Fire

Omaha, 1969—Mom claimed that she was of the "School of Tough Love," like it was a parenting association that charged membership fees. In fact, you would have thought it's where she picked up some of her child-rearing techniques, like washing my filthy mouth out with soap. I still can't look at a bar of Irish Spring without wanting to puke.

Her really bad freak-out episodes, like the day she shoved us in the garage, didn't happen frequently, but she didn't need many of them to instill fear in all of us.

And it didn't stop any of us from being normal kids who wanted to push boundaries; if anything, it made us more rebellious. I was just dumb when it came to being caught.

To give you an example, one day a friend and I decided we wanted to play Neanderthals in the field next to my house. I spent some time digging out an area of dirt that would act as a cave, and then we decided to add a fire component. I borrowed a matchbook from Mom's collection she kept in a glass jar and remember igniting that match was absolute magic. And I also remember the disappointment when the wind snuffed each flame out.

Somehow word got back to Mom, and in the next memory I'm standing on my bed, looking at this weird cruel smile on her face, pleading with her. She laughed, then beat my legs with a belt so bad I had to cover them up at school the next day. I deserved a punishment. I did. But her anger was like a never-ending rope.

Gayle and I liked to push the limits in the morning by watching hours of the forbidden "boob tube" while she slept in, Saturday morning's *H.R. Pufnstuf* being one of our favorites, and *Scooby-Doo* another, until we'd hear her fear-raising footsteps when she'd get out of bed and rush to switch it off.

You might say those morning sessions gave me my first taste of adrenaline from risky behavior.

In Which My Body Learns a New Trick

London, 1992—After Thomas and I settled into our flat, we took a quick trip across the English Channel to visit his sister and her husband in Paris. While there, we went to see a movie in the Latin Quarter, near Les Deux Magots, the café where Simone de Beauvoir and Jean-Paul Sartre used to smoke Gitanes, drink absinthe, and discuss the meaninglessness of life.

The film—*A Woman Under the Influence*—was directed by an American, John Cassavetes, who was known for his highly charged camera effects. The main character, played by Gena Rowlands (in the performance of a lifetime), is a wife, a mother, a woman struggling to do her best; she has to work at it so hard her mental health unravels. I found it absolutely tragic, deeply unsettling.

After the film we went for a bite to eat. I felt shaky, listened as the others discussed the film's docudrama style, the effects of the handheld camera, assessed the power of the color tones and sparse set. It was rare for me not to offer an opinion—but the harder I tried to formulate a coherent thought, the more it eluded me. The interest I felt a minute before disappeared. I felt nothing. An emotional lens closed, yet I became acutely aware of any sensory impression—the noise in the restaurant, the animated voices of Thomas and his sister and brother-in-law, the dull neon lights of the café. All these pieces were distinctly layered, as if I could separate one sensation from the other and tape them together at different speeds. Every word spoken rang with volume but no meaning.

The feeling of being detached felt terrifying, though strangely I felt no change physically with all this sharp sensitivity—no quickened heartbeat, no shortness of breath, no queasiness in my stomach. I stood up, left the table as if sleepwalking, while being held in a strange but comforting space of consciousness, and found the stairs to the street, knees weak, cold of the steel door handle bar on my hands. Blast of traffic. Icy wind. Blurred city lights. I watched the traffic signal turn green. No thought, concern for anything except to cross. The world had gone completely flat, and somewhere inside a hypnotic wave was sweeping across my soul.

Uh oh.

The last thing I felt was my foot falling short of the curb. Yells, sound of hissing brakes, screams in a foreign language. Hands under my armpits, my legs scraping against cement, knowing there to be pain, feeling it but with no emotion, no care. Voices surrounded me. Thomas was with me, his sister and her husband behind him. My knee was burning, my shoe had fallen off, my foot was freezing.

Several minutes later, control of my right arm came back first. I moved my hand, my fingers. I touched Thomas's arm, and then found my voice. He lifted my head, asked me if I was okay. I opened my eyes. A few curious onlookers stood a few feet away. A bus hissed and moved on.

Thomas hailed a cab, helped me into the car. My sister and brother-in-law grabbed the taxi behind us. As we pulled out, I leaned my forehead against the back seat window, wet with moist steam. I felt the rumble and bump of the brick streets as we drove across Paris. The evening darkness was a visual delight, illuminated lights—pulsing reds, fluorescent greens, warm yellows, electric blues—my vision razor-sharp. I could see the pastries I had admired throughout the day, so perfect you could taste them through glass:

mannequins poised as if to move; Thomas's hand cupped like a whorled shell over mine as we drove without a word.

An hour later I had my full strength, complete mental clarity, and the spell was gone. Other than a few scrapes here and there, no substantial injuries. It was as if nothing had happened at all. A blank moment, a short blink where life suddenly stopped but the pulse continued.

In Which We Take a Family Vacation

Florida, 1974—Our first family road trip was to Disney World, in Orlando, Florida. Besides it being our dream-come-true destination, it was the first time Dad was ever given a paid vacation. We kids had no idea of how he intended logistically to get us to Florida, until he pulled into the driveway in our Chevy station wagon with wood paneling down the side, towing a mini collapsible RV.

A bunch of the neighbors congregated as he demonstrated how this little trailer was a marvel of engineering. When you unhinged the heavy plastic lid, a canvas tent popped up, with a kitchen and two double beds on each side. And then you just tucked everything back in when it was time to travel. A bunch of us kids jumped in and out, and Dad let us sleep there overnight while it was parked in the driveway.

Before we left for the 1,400-mile, 22-hour drive, I noticed Mom brought her own style to the sleeping arrangements by folding down the seats in the back of the car and sewing little drapes for all the windows. Zorro and our cat, Linus, along with her three kittens and a litter box, accompanied us as well.

Once we hit the road, I pulled out the travel bingo cards with the red cellophane tabs and started looking for telegraph poles, trucks, billboard signs, and road markers until we reached the state of Missouri. Then we all started keeping track of how many different state license plates we could spot, and when we grew bored of that, Dad taught us how to count from one to ten in what he said was Cherokee.

Next came the family sing-along, including rounds of "Row Row Row Your Boat," "Daisy, Daisy, Give Me Your Answer, Do," "John Jacob Jingleheimer Schmidt," and "The Old Lady Who Swallowed a Fly." Then we started counting cars, farms, anything we could. When the elbowing and kicking started for territorial control in the car, Mom had us drink Dramamine-laced orange juice, and my sisters and I passed out.

We arrived at about four-thirty P.M. at the Magnolia Springs State Park, not too far from Savannah, Georgia, and were surprised to find nobody at the main gate to greet us. There wasn't a box or anywhere else to deposit the fee, but neither was there anyone to prohibit us from entering, so onward we went.

"Look, kids, it's Camper Heaven." Dad was wearing a baseball cap with moose antlers on it, so when he bobbed his head around it looked like he had on radar antennae. He was clearly enjoying the moment. I bobbed my head in support.

Nirvana it was. Over one thousand acres of moss-covered cypress trees, a twenty-eight-acre lake, natural clear springs, and history galore. My father slowed down in order to read the interpretive signs.

"Wow, girls. During the Civil War, the park served as, quote, 'the world's largest prison,' unquote. Bet we have a few ghosts running around here, eh?" And then he turned around with a silly mwahahahaha, which provoked even a guarded laugh from Genie.

We had our faces plastered against the windows. It was all too good to be true.

"Hey, where are all the people?" I asked him.

"Ah, they just don't know a good thing when they see it." We drove around the park for a few more minutes, looking for the perfect campsite. There were two RVs parked next to the restroom facilities.

"Bummer," Dad said, "we aren't the only ones." He finally pulled into a site a good distance from our neighbors and popped up our little half-hexagonal home. We kids jumped out of the car and unloaded pillows and blankets from the back like little Berenstain Bears. Then Mom and Dad pulled out their neon orange-and-green plastic woven chrome folding chairs, a six-pack of Schlitz beer, and a large bag of potato chips. Mom sat down to enjoy her beverage while Dad set up the barbecue grill, and my baby sister Jen toddled around. I asked Dad for a guzzle of his beer, a routine sharing in our family, and then Gayle, Zorro, and I went to play in the meadow with overgrown grass and weeds. Genie was perched on a picnic table several empty camp-sites away, reading *Gone with the Wind* for the fifth time.

Suddenly, our little oasis was interrupted by several gunshots. Zorro scam-pered under the car. Frightened, I looked over at my father. He just waved while he threw a match on kerosene-doused charcoal briquettes, and the flame combusted into fire.

"Firecrackers!" he cupped his hand to his mouth and yelled.

Gayle, Zorro, and I were still shaken, but we overcame our fears and started playing a game of Red Light, Green Light. After dinner, we were all tucked down in our camper beds when a set of headlights cut through the darkness. Zorro barked and Dad went out, in his nice respectful manner, to greet our guest.

"Good evening, sir." We heard a state sheriff introduce himself in a southern drawl, and then he asked my father to see his driver's license.

"Certainly. If this is about the camping fee . . ."

"The camping fee?"

"Yes, we tried to leave a camping fee when we came in . . ."

"Well, sir, there was no one at the gate because the park is closed. There's been a fugitive criminal on the loose for several days now, and we believe he's been hiding in the park."

"Oh, that's not good."

"Can you tell me who's in the trailer tent?"

"My wife and four girls."

"Do you mind if I just flash the light in there, sir?"

"Go ahead."

A meaty face under a cowboy hat peered through the camper door. Zorro leaped up and gave a nervous growl. The sheriff just rubbed her head.

"Hi," Gayle said, never the shy one.

"Howdy," he responded, tipped his hat, and backed out again. We heard him ask Dad what time we arrived in the park.

"About four P.M."

"Did you hear any gun shots?"

"We heard firecrackers."

"Oh, no. No, those weren't firecrackers. The criminal we're looking for attacked a woman tonight." He looked at my father's driver's license. "Mr. Cackler. He raped her, tried to murder her, and is now on the loose, somewhere in this park. You didn't happen to see anyone, did you?"

"Do you mind if we step away from the trailer?" Dad asked politely, not changing his tone of voice at all.

"That won't be necessary. I see you're all settled down there. Here's my business card. If you see anything fishy, you just give me a call. There's a telephone over there by those bathrooms. You'll be moving on tomorrow morning, first thing, right?"

"Yes."

"Well, enjoy the rest of your stay, Mr. Cackler. You on your way to Disney World?"

"Yes."

"Lucky kids."

We listened as the sheriff climbed into his car and backed out. I wasn't sure how the business card was going to help us out if that rapist/murderer showed up at our site. Dad opened the door and came in.

"It's okay, girls, it's safe," he said reassuringly. "The sheriff just stopped by to collect the camping fee."

He kissed each of us goodnight I pulled my blankets up and struggled to get comfortable again. Ten minutes passed. The wind began to blow. Long trails of Spanish moss, hanging from the huge oak trees above us, swept against the screen windows of our trailer tent. The moon cast gothic shadows onto the roof and floor of the caravan. Suddenly, my mother lurched up and screamed. My father was out of bed as fast.

There, on the floor, sat an insect the size of a squirrel. Dad did his best to keep us calm. He switched on the small battery-operated camper light, which launched the armored beetle into the air. I jumped up and started knee-huffing it across the mattress, shrieking. The beast buzzed around the trailer, and Gayle and Jenifer joined the hollering. Dad chased the giant insect around with a pot until he finally smashed it. Bang. Splat. Crunch.

Swish went the headlights. Flash went the red. The sheriff was back. Dad, sweaty and breathless, almost tripped down the portable pullout step as the door slammed behind him. He assured the officer that everything was okay. "Only a cockroach, sir," he explained.

I went back to sleep, assured that the police car had not been far. I admired the way Dad had been there to smash that insect. I kept that little piece of truth in the back of my mind, for a bit of security.

Genie said the next day in private that she couldn't believe that my father expected us to believe that crap about the camping fee. We had heard what the sheriff said. We had also heard the gunshots. I understood her point, but Dad was firmly in the camp of positive thinkers, and this would be no time for an exception. His gods were Norman Vincent Peale, Dale Carnegie, and Zig Ziglar. He'd always be dropping a few quotes from that crowd, like "Change your thoughts and you change the world." Genie said you can deny the facts, but no matter how you dress them up, they're still facts.

"Like, if you're standing in front of a werewolf, you better run?" I suggested.

"Yes, if a werewolf was in fact real, you dummy," she said, stomping away.

In Which I Mimic Anna O

London, 1993—I was sitting with my fiancé and his family at Passover, listening to the hypnotic lull of Hebrew prayers, in awe of the service, of a strength of connection that could bring so many together—forty-five Londoners, on a weeknight no less. I was moved to be invited to the ceremony. Thomas and I were both so laissez-faire about our issues of faith that it hardly occurred to me I was marrying into a Jewish family.

Across the street at 20 Maresfield Gardens sat Sigmund Freud's house, where he spent his last year of life after being forced to leave Austria in 1938. It had been turned into a museum. At the head of our table sat my husband's grandmother, "Granny," with her sister and twin brothers—who also escaped from Nazi Germany in 1938. The windows were open. Fresh-cut daffodils stood in vases on the table. The golden light of a spring evening was still with us.

As I looked around that table at the older generation and thought about their strength and resiliency, the enormity of their tragedy moved me deeply. And the more I cast my look of admiration at these survivors, the farther in distance they grew—or perhaps the room was just overheated. Suddenly, I felt my whole body slouch, and the folding chair collapsed underneath me. Uh oh. My head hit the floor.

The room went quiet. Fortunately, Thomas's uncle, a physician seated on my right, gently moved my body into a more comfortable, modest position, telling everyone it was okay, that I'd be fine in a moment. And then I felt my limbs twitch. I tried not to grow more anxious, mortified with the shame of needing assistance, aghast at my feeling of helplessness. All I have to do is lift a finger, I coached myself. But I couldn't. So I surrendered and felt my mind drift into what I can only describe as that state between consciousness and unconsciousness, while I remained hyperalert to everything going on around me. After several moments, I began to feel strength return to my body, as if someone had pushed a reset button. I tried moving a pinky again. The muscle responded. I gathered the courage to open my eyes.

Thomas's uncle smiled at me. "There is a little pill this big," he said with a pinch of his fingers, "that will stop that from happening again," and he snapped his fingers, like a hypnotist disrupting a trance. "She's fine," he announced, assisting me to a standing position. "Let us continue."

In Which I'm Thankful for Public Institutions

Omaha, 1970—My kindergarten teacher was Mrs. Wood. I loved her. She had a cool short haircut that curved stylishly around her ears, and wore dresses cut mid-thigh in the 1970s fashion. Most important, her mood remained stable, predictable. She never raised her voice no matter how crazy and loud things became in class, and she made me feel like the teacher's pet— though I suspect she had a way of making every kid feel that special.

One day at nap time, I reached out and pulled the hair on my classmate Diane's leg. She wore bobby socks with patent leather shoes and suspenders on her skirt. She was such a perfect student in class and didn't play with any of us on the playground, so I could sense she was especially loved at home. The next day, I rolled my rug out next to Diane's and pinched her hard on the arm. I saw tears roll down her cheeks, though she was trying to hide that it hurt. The following day Mrs. Wood called me into the hallway and crossed her arms, obviously displeased.

"Debbie, did you really pinch Diane?"

I dropped my head, crushed. "I cannot tell a lie." Mrs. Wood had just read the class a story about George Washington and his refusal to tell a lie, and there was nothing more I enjoyed in the world than making her happy.

"I just don't know what would get into you, to make you do that!" Mrs. Wood said, pleading for it not to be true. "You need to go see Mrs. Bow." A chill went through my body. Mrs. Bow was the school principal.

"Yes. But don't worry." Mrs. Wood averted her eyes before looking at me again. "She might seem scary, but she's a very nice person. I'll take you to her office." She put her arm around my shoulder and made small talk as we walked through the halls with their shiny floors. When we reached the principal's office, Mrs. Wood steered me to the secretary's desk, her hands on my shoulders. The secretary buzzed the intercom and announced my presence.

I didn't have to sit for long before the principal opened the door and gestured for me to enter. Mrs. Bow pointed to the couch and took a chair opposite, crossing her ankles under her seat. I might add that her dark-brown beehive hairdo and her blue eye shadow and heavy eyeliner enhanced her already imposing presence. She looked like an Egyptian queen.

"Debbie," she said. "I don't want you worried, but it is important we have a talk." I was surprised at the friendliness of her voice. It gave me the courage to look up. "I understand you pinched Diane?"

I nodded.

"And pulled the hair on her legs?" She paused. "Did she do something to you? Something to upset you?"

I thought about it. Diane had done nothing to me. So why did I hurt her? It was as if Mrs. Bow and I were two scientists trying to figure out human nature. "No, she didn't do anything to me."

"I see," she said. Then she leaned in a little and looked me in the eye. "Can I ask you a very important question?"

"Yes."

"How do you think Diane felt when you pinched her arm and pulled the hair on her leg?"

I wasn't sure what to say. After a few awkward seconds I guessed. "Sad?"

"Well, I don't think sad is the only thing she might have felt. Let's think a little more about how Diane might feel. Let's do a little exercise by imagining we are Diane. We're lying on our rug resting, and suddenly someone pinches us. We ignore it. But the next day, the same girl pinches us so hard we cry. How do you think we feel at that point?"

"Angry, so angry we would want to pinch her back?"

"Yes, but you see, Diane doesn't like to pinch people because she knows it hurts." The calm of Mrs. Bow's voice made me feel safe. "Now," she said. "I want to show you something very special." She leaned over to a table next to the couch and picked up a hand mirror and held it out to me. I took its long handle, and found it weighed heavy in my hand. "Now, what do you see?" she asked, encouraging me to look at myself. "Do you see the person who did these hurtful things to Diane?"

My eyes fixed themselves in an unfocused stare. No way was I looking.

"Don't be scared," she said. "I know you have a good heart. So that child in the mirror? Is she a good child?"

I nodded, but I felt like a slug being covered in salt.

She leaned over and patted my knee. I wiped the tears streaming down my cheeks.

"You'll only see the good Debbie when you look in that mirror because only the good Debbie exists, isn't that right?" She smiled. "I am so confident that you have stood up to that monster, that I do not feel it is necessary to call your mother." Need I share what a relief that was?

Meanwhile, as I was getting my lessons in empathy at age five, Mr. K was having his first big scare at age eight. He was hanging out with some friends on a bridge that crossed the interstate in east Omaha when one of the boys challenged him to throw a large rock onto a windshield below.

Without thinking, he did it. He didn't see the driver, and it didn't seem to do any damage or slow the traffic down, but he couldn't help but ask himself: When had he become the kid who would throw a rock at a passing car? He could have killed someone. It scared him. At the same time, he tasted some kind of charge that was delicious.

In Which I Ponder Dad's Benign Pets

Omaha, 1971—Dad would find activities to get my sisters and me out of the house on the weekends so that Mom had space. He was particularly good at finding municipal parks with fabulous adventure playground sets—the kind with monkey bars and slides and chain-link bridges. They'd look like forts, or castles, or even a rocket ship. Occasionally we'd hit Peony Park and catch the amusement rides, or we'd go to the Henry Doorly Zoo. It was on a visit to the animals that Jenifer stood up in the baby carriage and fell over the push bar, smacking her two front teeth out. We ended up at the emergency room. I'd never seen Dad look so sick to his stomach.

On one of those weekends, we experienced a poetic moment that I would return to again and again, sensing in it a deeper meaning.

We were on our way home from one of our municipal park runs. Dad turned into the Old Mill Plaza, a new strip mall not far from our house, and pulled up in front of its decorative feature. He got out of the car to inspect a huge wooden wheel that churned water at the center of a fake pond. When he came back, he appeared to be talking to someone sitting on top of the car.

Gayle rolled the window down and asked him who he was chatting to.

He pointed, like wasn't it obvious? "The octopus we picked up in Florida, the one who's hitched a ride with us."

"Oh, him." Gayle started giggling.

"Now come on down here, you old octopus. If you stay on top of that car any longer, you're going to get all dried out. Here's a nice garden for you to live in." Dad hesitated like he was listening for a moment. "Yes, I understand you don't want to go, but we can come back and visit you here every day."

He cupped his hand around his ear and leaned toward the car. By then, Gayle, Jenifer, and I were all laughing so hard our stomachs hurt. "Yes, I know you are going to miss the family, but this garden is a much better place to live." Then he turned to us.

"Look, girls. He's hobbling there right now on all eight legs. And he's waving. Ah, he's so sad," and then my father looked sad, too. That made me sad, and I waved at the octopus.

Every time we drove by the Old Mill after that, Dad would roll down his window, honk the horn, and wave. Sometimes he'd pull into the parking lot and start driving around in a circle. We'd ask him what he was doing, and he would say, "Why, we're dancing with the octopus."

Of course, now I know there to be a heavy influence of the Beatles' hit song "Octopus's Garden" in Dad's strange parable. But back then, that feeling— *warm below the storm, in our little hideaway beneath the waves*—was due entirely to Dad's creative genius for comedy and faith in life.

I'm now going to put the octopus in a glass box on a shelf above my desk because remembering that sad abandoned octopus sucks.

In Which I Consider Macro Memories

Omaha, 1971—People who live outside the Midwest like to make jokes about us. They'll say things like, "Do you guys have indoor plumbing in Nebraska? I heard you use cornhusks as toilet paper." And I'll laugh along with them because this self-effacing humor is a trait among my people.

I am now walking down 107th Street with the help of Google Earth to our house in Lee Valley. I'm in front of it. It's just as I remember. A raised ranch with a double garage, on a sloping hill. The shutters are still black, but where the wooden clapboard once was a dark olive green, it is now a dull beige. And it still has a gable roof, which could mean it's never been hit by a tornado, of which there is always a chance in the Midwest.

An American flag hangs to the right of the front door, where it always hung while we lived there. I even see the black cherry tree that Dad planted almost fifty years earlier. Okay, I have no idea if it's the same tree, but I'm a romantic, and I know there was a tree in that exact same spot, so I think it's safe to assume.

It's lovely to think that back then, that tree had yet to be imprinted with the memories of all the people who have come and gone since: all the children who leaned against it playing hide and seek, counting back from one hundred, a crazy amount of time to find a hiding place because you could run two blocks by then. All the people who have walked their dogs past that spot would have seen that tree, too, and maybe they'd be thinking they could guess the seasons of the year by the amount of leaves on its branches, and the color of those leaves, too—or maybe that's just a thought you have when looking at trees from Google Earth.

I don't have specific memories of our play performances, which we'd abridge from the Disney soundtrack albums we'd listen to on our record players (our favorite was *Peter Pan*), or of playacting *Little House on the Prairie*, or statue maker, or Red Light, Green Light. My memories aren't separated into neat units that way—rather, they merge into a collage of general feeling that blended years of experience and morphed into a landscape picture in my mind.

But I do remember this one episode at age seven. Mom, who was in a notably good mood, asked me if I wanted to join her at the Crawleys' across the street to see their chickens. When we arrived, there were about ten adults gathered around a wooden crate inside the two-car garage. I gave consideration to the possibility of a cockfight because I had once heard of this phenomenon. But then I noticed the meat cleaver.

I watched as Mr. Crawley reached into the crate and pulled out a particularly loud squawker. Mr. Lewis, another neighbor, was standing right next to him and held a stopwatch. Mr. Crawley brought the meat cleaver down on the neck, and the chicken's head fell into a basket. Mr. Lewis dropped the stopwatch and grabbed the body. But the bird jumped out of his hands before he could get it to the floor.

That chicken started running around the garage with its head cut off, bumping into the walls and then a structural pole. I looked over at its head, in the basket, while its body was running around the garage with blood spurting out of its neck cavity. Bump, run, bump, wham, spurt, spurt, spurt went the chicken.

Mom leaned over and whispered that even though the chicken no longer had a head, it still had a heart, and that's why the blood was pumping through its arteries with that fountain effect.

Maybe she was trying to tell me, if you had a head on your shoulders, make sure you use it; or, even if you're bleeding everywhere and you can't see, as long as you're moving, you're still alive.

Anytime I feel like giving up, all I have to do is picture that chicken and remind myself it ain't *that* bad.

Here's another memory that involves the Crawleys. I went outside one morning to ride my fine gold-painted Schwinn three-speed bicycle and noticed a trail of Pabst Blue Ribbon beer cans organized like footsteps leading across the street. The beginning of the march started at our open garage door, then made its way across the driveway, over the road, and up the sidewalk to the front door of the Crawleys' house.

I remember it for this reason—because it was funny. And I knew it was my father's humor. I couldn't imagine the time it must have taken him to line up those beer cans, and how big the smile on his face would have been as he chuckled his nasally hee-hee-hee when he was imagining the reaction of the neighbors when they discovered his high-art installation in the morning.

When I came running back into the house, the screen door banging behind me, I remember telling my mother, and she said, "Your father was drunk last night," like it was a character defect that he should be checked into jail for, and all I could think was I wish she was like that when she was drunk.

I'd never seen Dad drunk. But I knew it happened because he'd told me the story of how trying to sneak a six-pack of beer into a girls' dormitory got him kicked out of college.

In Which My Father Learns to Fear God

New York, 1959—My father, James Travis Cackler, went to college to become a minister. His god was not one he feared, though this would change as life went on. He enrolled in a private university on the East Coast and worked hard for three years before making the mistake that would define our lives.

A group of college girls enticed him into their residence hall for a party—okay, so maybe he wanted to go—though boys were not allowed. He climbed through a dormitory window and was the life of the party until he drank so much he blacked out. When he woke up the next morning, he found himself face flat in vomit.

Because he was raised a midwesterner with good manners, he knew it wouldn't be nice to leave the mess for someone else, but he couldn't find paper towels. The only thing he could find was an industrial vacuum cleaner, so this is what he used.

What he didn't realize was that a girl was watching him as he did this, who fancied herself a spy. He didn't find out until he discovered a note in his student mailbox from the university president asking him to come to tea.

It's safe to assume he was scared, but he didn't tell me this.

The president told him that he was banned from the school forever because he went into the girls' dormitory. My father was now cast into the wilderness of a society for which he was not prepared. He didn't say he would never become a minister because of this, but instead told me the following: "Never blame other people for things you do not make come true."

Because he felt terrible about the authorities kicking him out of college, and how it was going to crush his parents when they found out, he made an executive decision to join the army. My father considered joining the army just as honorable as finishing his college education and becoming a minister.

But his parents, Katherine and Arlo, were devastated when he told them the news. They didn't think the army was a good solution to being kicked out of college and didn't understand why he didn't speak to them first. They viewed higher education as a morally good force in society for one simple reason—it encouraged the discipline of human thought.

Well, Dad didn't stay away very long.

Six months after he enrolled in the army, he was assigned to a major. When the Major's seventeen-year-old daughter arrived fresh from California, my father was attracted to her long brunette hair and brown eyes, her marvelously shaped legs, and the dark lure of her nervous energy. She was attracted to his fast fingers on the keyboard.

I'm not sure of this exactly, but the romance must have developed quickly, as it often does when you want things that you are not meant to have. It was against regulations for my parents to be dating (as my father was the Major's clerk, and my mother the Major's daughter), though it became apparent that this is exactly what they were doing before my mother discovered she was pregnant.

My father asked the Major for an honorable discharge from the army in order to marry my mother. According to everyone, my grandfather was proud and happy to have him as a son-in-law.

When I asked my father why he married my mother, he said he didn't want a child of his given up for adoption; he wanted his baby to stay with her natural parents. To appreciate this, it helps to know another important piece of information about my father.

My grandmother Katherine had a good friend who worked at the Salvation Army in the 1940s. This friend watched as my grandmother lost two of her children, aged two and eight, both sons, to polio. So one day she arrived at Katherine's home in Des Moines, Iowa, with a present and rang the doorbell. Katherine said she opened the door, and there was this beautiful six-week-old baby smiling at her, with huge merry eyes and bouncy health. "Surprise," her friend said. "Look what I have for you."

Katherine said she was not even looking for a baby, but my father just arrived and it felt right. Her friend brought his papers, diapers, clothes, and a basket for him to sleep in.

So that's why he didn't want anyone playing ding-dong ditch with his baby.

Mom's view of the marital situation was clear. She didn't feel saved at all at the young age of seventeen. According to her, my father had ruined her life by getting her pregnant and talking her into marriage.

Dad didn't seem to think she meant it because he'd just laugh lightheartedly whenever she said this. I wasn't so sure.

In Which Mr. K Introduces Himself

Omaha, 1978—One minute, five minutes, ten minutes passed. The position on the floor wasn't growing any more comfortable. Left turn, right turn, right turn, left turn. Mr. K was a considerate driver and used his indicator to signal his direction. The windshield wipers sounded as if they were struggling to clear the sleet.

I felt my mind sink into a meditative state, my unconscious guiding me to a place of safety it already knew. I was still on my stomach with my neck twisted to one side. After more time passed, maybe another five minutes, I sensed another shift of energy in the van, and it occurred to me I might risk asking to move into a more comfortable position. I gathered the courage to speak.

"May I turn my head?" I asked politely.

"Yeah."

As I did so, I observed Mr. K's choice of wardrobe. His blue jeans had fashionable brown beading down the legs, and he was wearing tan suede workman boots. His legs were of medium build. Proximity to the pedals suggested while he was not short, he was not particularly tall. Perhaps five foot eight.

I evaluated my options. Could I grab his legs? Given the condition of the icy roads, that might not achieve anything but a traffic accident. Could I go for the passenger door? Hard to get up from the floor between the seats that fast. Instead, I comforted myself with positive thinking and trusted that my time would come. I remembered the cross on my necklace. I boldly asked if I could move my arm.

"Yeah."

I clasped the cross in my hand, thankful for its reassurance, and found myself descending into a state that felt like sleep. Several moments later I was brought back to the moment by his voice. I lifted my head slightly so I could hear. The change in tone was encouraging. He was apologizing.

"I didn't mean to scare you. I just had to shut you up, you understand?"

I nodded to indicate I understood.

"I'll let you sit in the passenger's seat if you won't do anything funny."

"Okay." It was almost as if the calmness in my voice came from somewhere outside me.

I slowly pulled myself into the passenger's seat, looking for the knife as discreetly as I could.

"So what's your name?" Mr. K asked, as if he were about to introduce himself.

"Debbie," I said, as friendly as I could be. She surprised even me, this girl who was speaking.

"What's yours?"

"Charles," he said without hesitation, apparently eager to be friends. "Well, Debbie, I guess this is your lucky day. I'm not going to hurt you."

"Oh," I said with genuine gratitude, spotting the knife, now resting on his thigh.

In Which I Contemplate the Nature versus Nurture Question

Omaha, 1971—Behind us lived the Burnett kids. There were three of them, and they had a mother who liked being at home. I noticed that whenever I was over, their house smelled of French toast and freshly baked Nestlé Toll House chocolate chip cookies. Mrs. Burnett wasn't the type to be overly concerned with her appearance. She was the size you'd expect a housewife to be who cooked three decent meals for her kids a day, and wore slippers rather than shoes. She was a happy person, but not too, and she didn't dote on her children. She just provided safe warm space for her Michael, Bridgette, and Sue. Their hair was always brushed, their faces washed, their clothes were clean, and their socks matched. I just knew something was right because those kids liked being at home. They would play outside together quite happily on their own, with or without other kids. Then I'd observe Mrs. Burnett calling them back in for lunch. They would disappear for a good while. Then come back out. And when they felt bored, they could go inside, and she would hold the side screen door open for them. Because of this, I decided that I didn't like those Burnett kids and I would get even.

So one day when they went inside for lunch, I snuck into their garden, where their Barbie camper sat, and stole all their Barbies—about five of them. I ran across the street to a neighbor who had a really mean dog, a dog so mean they had to keep it in a fenced-in yard. I ripped the Barbie dolls' heads off and threw them over the fence. Then I came back and threw the Barbie bodies into the Burnetts' yard. I was in such a fit of rage I didn't know what I was doing. But then I sensed the enormity of the act and grew terrified. How could I fix this? Who could I tell? How could I possibly explain it?

A week went by before I saw Mrs. Burnett at our front door. I rabbited behind a bush, and it was clear, after my mother came out on the porch, that Mrs. Burnett had figured out the identity of the Barbie killer. This is how I knew Mom was angry: her lips. She had this habit of knitting them together before agitation took hold of her.

I realized that I was going to have to leg it. She'd kill me, and that wasn't hyperbole. My father was out of town, so there was no chance of him lifting the mood. I bolted. Dashed as fast as I could with only one vision in mind— widening that gulf between Mom and me, slowing only to gulp air, until I reached the Old Mill Shopping Center where Mr. Octopus lived. I was thankful for the floodlights that lit up the water, since it was dark by then. I was seven years old and three miles from home.

But when I got there, there was no sign of Mr. Octopus. Frightened and exhausted, I sat next to the pond and watched the mill go round and round, water kerplunking down like pixie dust briquettes, and thought I might sleep on the grass in front of the pond, but realized I was tired and quite frankly terrified and that even if Mom was going to kill me, I didn't want to be woken up by some stranger-creepy-guy, and then I became more scared of staying than I was of going home. I started making my way back, and as I crept up the hill toward our house, sprinting from bush to bush for cover, thinking I could at least fall asleep in one of the neighbors' yards, I spotted two police cars in the drive.

One officer was speaking into a radio attached to his shoulder and the other scribbled down notes while talking to my mother. I figured the policemen were there because I had stolen the Barbies, so they were going to take me to prison. I considered surrendering but told myself to stop being ridiculous. Of course they weren't there to arrest me—they were there to find me. I decided to slip in the house through the backdoor and sneak into my room and act like I had been sleeping all along.

Tiptoeing across the living room Pink Panther–style, I thought I was in the clear until Pat Maddox, another neighbor, opened the door and Zorro came running at me, body-slamming herself at my feet, thumping her tail, hardly able to sit. Pat didn't say anything. She just waved her hand and signaled for me to join her in the bathroom.

Zorro followed us in as Pat shut the bathroom door. When she asked why I had run away and I told her it was because I was afraid my mother was going to kill me, she looked concerned. So did Zorro, who pricked up his ears.

She said, "No, Debbie, your mother won't kill you, I promise you. She has been worried sick," and when she said that, the door opened and there stood my mother. Pat went quiet. Mom flashed a curt smile and praised my dramatic talent. She called the police officers over and said that I had something to tell them. All eyes were on the prize. The officers made it as easy as they could for me to admit my shame.

It was one of those incidents that came up when I began to question my memory. Was it a good thing I ran with fear for my life, or was it the dramatic flourish of my pea-sized brain distorting guilt, self-pity, and fear of punishment into a threat that didn't exist?

Mom wasn't the only person who scared me that night. I didn't know what made me act like that, and it made me feel sick. What kind of kid did that sort of thing?

In Which We Receive Good News

Omaha, 1972—Mom went out one night and came home with a solution, unwittingly, that was going to help my soul. By the time she pulled her car into the garage, Genie and Gayle had already made themselves scarce, but I felt confident because my extrasensory perception must have been working well that night. Zorro stopped barking and took a half-seated position next to me. After hearing the crunch of snow up the front steps, I opened the door for her and offered to take her bags.

After shaking the snow from her jacket and hanging it in the closet, Mom reached her arms out to me. "Oh, Debbie, I have such great news. Hug me!" I did my best to accommodate this unusual request while Zorro watched on full alert. "Come here," Mom said, walking toward the living room. "I have something special for you."

And that's when I noticed the flared bell-bottom jeans. I had never seen her wearing anything but polyester slacks with elastic waist bands, so let me tell you these were worthy of real contemplation. The denim was printed with images of fans at a concert, flower children of all shapes and colors wound up and around her legs, through her crotch, and across the front and back panels right up her butt.

"Sit down," she encouraged me. "This is a very important night in our lives." Again—the smile of peace. Zorro lay down at my feet. Next she took a record album from her shopping bag, which solved the mystery of the artwork on her jeans. *Pat Boone Sings the New Songs of the Jesus People.*

We spent the next half an hour listening to songs that put me in a surprisingly groovy mood. They had lyrics that stuck in my head, like *One book and it's the Holy Bible that'll take you to the promised land.* After we had played the whole record, Mom shared the good news she was waiting to tell me.

"I've found Jesus," she said, followed by a bliss-shaped smile. And then she reached into her bag and pulled out a little box. "And look, I bought you and each of your sisters a present."

I took the box, one of those curious "why, thank you" looks on my face, and tried to match her eagerness. "Go ahead! Open it!" she encouraged me. I raised the lid, and there sat my gold-plated cross necklace, inserted into a plush cushion.

"Oh, Mom," I said, not sure of the appropriate response. "It's so beautiful."

I don't remember ever having attended church, but even if we had, it wouldn't have helped my confusion over the statement "I've found Jesus." She continued, "I went to a Bible study tonight, and I was with a group of people, and they helped me ask Jesus into my heart." She made it sound like she had invited him to dinner and was shocked when he walked in the door. After she explained it further, telling me something like it was insurance against going to hell, she sent me to bed.

I couldn't remember ever seeing Mom as happy as she was that night, so lying there under my Snoopy-themed bed cover, I thought that if asking Jesus into her heart made Mom that happy, then maybe if I did it too—it might keep her that way.

I repeated the words she used. Then waited to see if the same transformation came over me. Sure enough, I felt a rush of happiness take over my whole body, a power not to be underestimated in a child with the most unhappiest Mom.

A couple of weeks later, Mom broke her normal practice of not allowing any of the kids from the neighborhood in the house (she said four kids were more than enough for her nerves), and hired a Bible teacher whose name was Mr. Good. We all took it for granted that this was his real name. He was like a Tupperware party hostess, but instead of plastic food containers he sold Jesus, wore a cardigan sweater, and had short hair parted to the side and plastered with Brylcreem. He was slim and trim, spoke quietly, and had a permanent ever-so-slight smile on his face, like he'd been well dosed at an outpatient clinic.

The best thing about the Good News Club, however, was that whoever memorized the most Bible verses would receive little gifts—like a laminated bookmark that featured a picture of Jesus with a lamb in his arms, or little plastic figurines of prophets in the Old Testament. I set my aim on the whole collection.

My relationship with God never became one I feared. His personality was in line with the character depicted in the Broadway musicals *Godspell* and *Jesus Christ Superstar*—generous with the gift of life, the world, and all its beauty. My relationship with Jesus was a different thing though, closer. He was hip, like the Hummel Park summer camp counselor I once had a crush on named Maurice.

My grandmother Vivian, when she heard how I felt about Jesus, sent me a five-by-seven portrait of him, the *Head of Christ* painted by Warner Sallman of Chicago in 1940. The artist used sepia oil colors and depicted Jesus with long waves of brown hair, a trim beard, olive skin, a long delicate nose, high cheekbones, and eyes that radiated calm benevolent love—in short, a humble yet handsome presentation. I put it by my bedside so I could talk to him every night.

From then on, I worked hard to adhere to Christ's directive of "do unto others as you would want them to do unto you" through a regular spiritual practice. It consisted of a good-morning check-in and a good-night review, when I would consider my behavior for the day. I would imagine it seen through the eyes of the Lord and, if laden with particularly heavy shame, would get down on my knees alongside the bed and lower my head.

More often than not, I'd carry out an informal chat while I looked up at the ceiling, or out the window, or at the large poster I had of a male lion. Sometimes I spoke out loud, but more often the conversation took place inside my head, as I looked at that picture of Jesus.

I often wondered later if that's why I took to therapy so naturally. There are remarkable similarities to the practice: the process of self-examination and confession, the running self-monologue. The same ritual, really, but with a plug-and-play human.

Mom found a liberal Protestant church to attend soon after, and my parents became youth group leaders, which meant we had a bunch of hippie teeny-boppers at our house who wore things like bell-bottom jeans and go-go boots. It was by far the most peaceful two years of our family life. But after a fallout with the minister's wife, whom Mom felt had become jealous, Mom said she didn't need to go to church to be near God, and Sundays became her "me time," so Dad took us to church on his own.

I loved standing next to him during service. He'd put his arm around my shoulder as we sang. His favorite hymn was "Onward Christian Soldiers." I can still hear his gentle, deep voice. And even though he hadn't been able to become a minister, because he snuck through that girls' dorm window with a six-pack, he got to enjoy teaching Sunday school. And he'd always plan for a stop at Dunkin' Donuts. He'd say, "Let's go get us a dozen before we go home," like he was a cowboy tipping his hat.

When Dad went on the road, my passion for Christ would grow. I no longer felt alone when I went to sleep at night. Mom didn't show any interest in my faith after that special first night, for which I was thankful.

Another year went by, another summer rolled up. My sisters and I were allowed to choose which camp we wanted to attend. I decided on Calvin Crest, a weeklong coed outfit run by the Protestant church. It wasn't much different than my usual choice of Hummel Park, managed by the Omaha City Parks and Rec—except it was a proper overnight camp, and we'd gather around the campfire for a pastoral service every evening, where we'd get to sing songs with acoustic guitar accompaniment like "Day by Day" and "Michael, Row the Boat Ashore." I liked the way it connected my body with my heart.

At the end of the week, they gave us a little booklet asking who we thought God hired to be his personal messenger. I opened the next page and found myself looking at my own reflection in a small mirror. My heart grew happy with the idea of it, so I decided right there to devote myself to winning the best sales kid award for number of saved souls per year. And I knew I was blessed in this department with the best salesman in the world to teach me. Dad.

From that summer forward, I vowed to be on the job 24/7. Anytime I met a friend who was sad, I made sure they knew they weren't alone. I'd just tell them Jesus loved them and he'd be their friend. Little did I know who my most important customer would be.

In Which I Make a Sales Pitch

Omaha, 1978—"You're wearing a cross," Mr. K said in a way that faintly suggested it was a fashion accessory he might himself wear.

"Yes," I said, in as encouraging a tone as I could.

"You're a Christian?" he asked.

"Yes." It was getting darker, which wasn't making it any easier to act friendly, especially since he wasn't taking that face mask off. "Are you?" The question slid so genuinely out of my mouth, it shocked even me. And then the idea struck me that I'd pretend Mr. K was just an octopus—like Dad's Mr. Octopus.

"Well"—he paused, thinking it over—"I guess I'm not if I'm doing this."

I jumped on that immediately. "God still loves you," I said, wanting him to believe this. Not many people asked about my cross, and given the circumstances it was hard not to get too enthusiastic.

This seemed to prompt him to open up. "You think so?" He apologized again for scaring me. Said he had just run away from home, which he added was in California, because he was having problems with his parents. He told me he moved to Omaha to be with his grandmother, but he just found out she was dying of cancer. "She doesn't have the money to see doctors, and I hardly have enough money to pay for gas."

I felt bad for him and started sensing this might be the reason for our situation. "You know, I'm certain God will understand you're trying to help your grandmother."

"I hope you're right," he said.

"Well, if I had some money I'd sure help you out."

"You'd do that?"

"You betcha." We were silent for a moment. I could tell he was feeling better. He then came out with his next question.

"Do you think your dad might help me out?"

I told him I knew it wouldn't hurt to ask, starting to feel like we might have struck on something that might help both our situations. "How much do you think you'd need?"

"Well, I think my grandmother will need close to ten thousand dollars for her medical bills."

"Wow," I said, feeling less safe. "I'm pretty sure he won't be able to give you that much money."

"Hmmm." He put the blinker on and made a right turn. I had felt earlier I might be able to find my way back to my school, but now I no longer had any sense of where we were. Octopus, Octopus, Octopus. He's an octopus.

"Grandparents?" he asked. "Maybe they could help?" The falling rain froze as soon as it hit the windshield. There were few drivers on the road. I told him my grandparents lived in Des Moines and Washington, D.C. That seemed to disappoint him.

"Well, how much money do you think your Dad could give me?"

"I really don't know—maybe one hundred dollars, but we won't find out until we ask. I don't know what I would do if my grandparents were dying of cancer. My aunt died of cancer. I didn't know her that well . . ." I thought a little longer. "Can I tell you something?" I said, with a sort of laugh of disbelief.

"Sure."

"You really scared me back there . . . I definitely thought you were going to hurt me."

Mr. K puzzled over this for a second, before he decided he liked this game. He kind of laughed. "Yeah, we had a narrow escape, didn't we?"

When I recounted this story years later to my psychiatrist, he told me I was a natural-born hostage negotiator and the FBI would be lucky to have me.

In Which I Witness Tragic Grief

Maine, 1971—Life can be so damn brutal. My thirty-three-year-old aunt Alice died of brain cancer, six months after receiving her diagnosis. Her three young boys not only lost their mother but were effectively orphaned after her grief-stricken dysfunctional husband refused to accept help from his in-laws to take care of them.

Though I didn't know what tragedy was at that age, I was aware my father's attention took a dramatic swing toward Katherine and Arlo, who were already carrying grief for two young sons. The loss of their daughter, with the additional cruelty of her being a young parent, was annihilating.

My grandparents had always been a welcome steady influence on my life. They looked like the couple in Grant Wood's painting—*American Gothic*, the portrait that features the serious-looking farmer with his pitchfork and the stern-looking woman next to him. Mark Twain would say they used a "minimum of sound to a maximum of sense." Listening to the tender way Dad would speak to them made my heart hurt.

Several months after Alice's death, we joined my grandparents at a cottage on Isle au Haut, a small island off the coast of Maine in the Penobscot Bay. I'd never seen an ocean at the age of seven, let alone an island; the closest I'd come to a coastline was a sandbar on the Platte River not far from Omaha.

In the way children are able to do in the wake of tragedy—my attention turned
to the adventure in front of me.

There was only one way to get to Isle au Haut from the mainland, and that
was by a mail boat, which left twice a day from Stonington. The captain of
the boat was more than happy to tell us tall tales when encouraged to do so
by my father. He warned us to be on the lookout for lobsters, as they snapped
off kids' toes, and for pirates, who liked to lurk in coves around the island.
I wasn't scared of pirates because I was acquainted with them, having mastered
the role of Captain Hook in our staged yard productions of *Peter Pan*, but I
could tell by Gayle's face that she was. I can still feel my hair dampened by
the salty ocean breeze as we puttered across the bay, watching the lobster fish-
erman throwing wooden traps from their boats into the water.

Arlo was waiting for us when we arrived at the landing dock. I remember
my father placing a gentle hand on his shoulder as the two of them walked
up the jetty toward a beat-up Jeep Wagoneer—one of the few island vehicles,
parked on the grass. When it quickly became clear we wouldn't all fit alongside the luggage, Arlo suggested he shuttle us in two trips, so after we waved
Mom and the baby off to the cabin—Dad, Genie, Gayle, and I went on a
scouting trip to the General Store. It had everything and nothing at the same
time: just enough cans of food to stock the pantry for a few days, just enough
hardware to start but not complete a job, just enough toilet paper to buy one
roll, just enough candles and matchsticks to keep the house lit for one night.

When Arlo returned, Dad dropped the tailgate on the jeep so we could sit in
the back and dangle our legs over the side. I was so happy I started tickling
Gayle as we were driving down a dusty road toward the Breeze Cottage, and
to stop me she accidentally pushed me off the back. Fortunately we were
going slow enough that I didn't break any bones, just ended up with serious
road rash covering my legs. Gayle felt horrid, but Dad didn't get angry; it
wasn't his style. Instead, he looped a rope across the back so we wouldn't fall
off, and told us no more monkey business. Arlo continued the drive through
a thick forest of cypress and beech trees, a forest so peaceful and undis-
turbed it seemed otherworldly.

When we arrived at Breeze Cottage, a white clapboard house named after the family who had owned it since the 1920s, I spotted Riches Cove and ran to it as if pulled by magic. As I scrambled over one boulder to the next, waves spraying me as they hit the rugged edge, I spotted my father hightailing it toward me, yelling at me to move back. I ran up and jumped on him even though I was soaking wet. He started with the safety lecture, but before he could finish, I ran into the house, where I could hear Genie and Gayle slamming doors.

There were two bedrooms upstairs, a sitting room and kitchen downstairs, and a large porch with rocking chairs and two church-style hard benches facing the ocean, a well, and a bunch of candles.

Mom was sitting on the front porch in one of those old rocking chairs with baby Jen on her lap, and it was the second time in my life I remember seeing her happy. It made me feel quirky, light-headed, and just plain weird.

In Which I Learn of the Existence of Ghosts

Maine, 1971—It didn't take us long to get to know the ocean rhythms of Riches Cove. Gayle and I spent hours checking out the small pools for starfish and sea urchins and crabs, giving them a poke enough to make them move, but with respect enough to let them be. Then we'd lie on our stomachs across the boulders, chipping away at barnacles and snails until the water started rolling in and we'd have to scramble back. The adrenaline of pushing it until the last minute was better than anything I'd ever experienced, as waves reached heights of nine feet before they crashed against the huge granite rocks where we were stretched out only minutes before.

One day when the tide was out, Gayle and I spotted what looked like a settlement of houses up a hill, so we scaled the bank toward them and found that it was an abandoned homestead sitting on hardpack dirt ground. There wasn't a sign of anyone, just one cosmic-size creepy feeling. Gayle grew scared and turned back, leaving me to explore on my own.

My first stop was at a shack, where I found a couple of horse-size wagon wheels, lobster traps, tons of pickle jars, and piles of old rusted tools. Then I moved to the house, noticing a number of broken windows. Those that weren't cracked were so thick with dust that you couldn't see through them. The front door wasn't locked, so I crept in. It appeared whoever called it home left in a hurry. The inside was modest, with a kitchen and two bedrooms. Each bedroom had a steel-framed double bed that was still made up with ancient-smelling blankets. Old dishes lined the shelves of the kitchen. Everything was covered in cobwebs and dust. If you had a vacuum cleaner and mop you could move right in, but I was moving right out because it was difficult to guess how long it had been since a human had last seen the place.

When I returned home and asked Mom who lived there, she said the house belonged to a family who died of tuberculosis in the 1920s, including their two children, and I should stay out of there. Even though the owners had died, it was still private property.

I told her I didn't see any bodies.

She laughed like I was being funny and said the family was buried up the road near the section of wood we liked to play in. I recalled the cemetery she was talking about, surrounded by a low-lying, black cast-iron gate with about fifteen graves. There were no angels, or statues or vaults, just rounded stone tablets worn down from salty air.

When bedtime came, I begged Mom not to make me go upstairs. When she asked "what the hell had gotten into you!?" there was no way I was telling her. I was not in the mood to be entertaining.

When Dad heard all the pandemonium, he came inside and asked what was going on.

I told him I would be quite happy to sleep on the wooden bench in the kitchen, but there was no way I was going up those stairs. He asked why, and I said it was because the ghosts of those dead children were under the bed.

"What children?" he asked.

"The children up the road," I said.

"What children up the road?"

"The children who died of tuberculosis," I said.

When he asked why I thought there were children who died of tuberculosis up the road, I told him it was because Mom had told me. He looked coolly at my mother. Then he offered to go upstairs with me and help me look under the bed to prove there were no ghosts. But when one is in a state of terror, it's no time to talk science. I politely but firmly told him I was not interested in looking under the bed. Ghosts were not seen; you *felt* ghosts, and therefore this exercise would serve no purpose. He said he could see my point of view and then offered me a nickel just to check.

When I said no, thank you, I wasn't looking to earn any money at the moment, he said it was very important that I face up to my fear. He vouched for my courage, and he said we would face this together.

I had never been more scared than looking under that bed. Staring fear in that ghostly face did not resolve the terror, but it did dial it down a notch so I could get to sleep. That job offer stuck with me for a number of years.

In Which I Am Introduced to British National Health

London, 1993—Thomas's uncle strongly recommended that I see a specialist after my incident at Passover, so we found ourselves sitting in the waiting area of the neurology department at the Whittington, an old Victorian hospital in northwest London.

After an hour, Thomas inquired as to what the delay was, and we were told they were trying to squeeze me into the schedule despite being short on consultants. A few minutes later we were ushered into a scanning room of bulldozer-size neuroimaging machinery. I had never been so anxious for the arrival of a professional I didn't want to see. Neurologists for me were akin to astronauts, discovering the vast frontiers of the uncharted human mind.

Cue entrance: Man of the Universe. The doctor, our young registrar, wielding a clipboard, looking not so much distracted as purposely distracted and annoyed. I was in slight awe. I apologized for bothering him, not knowing the proper etiquette for a national health system, and thanked him for seeing me. He explained this was his lunch break.

"I'm going to need to ask you some information before we begin." As he prepared himself for the questioning, clicking his pen, I realized that he reminded me of a high school teacher who had graded me unfairly.

When he asked the standard mental health questions concerning family history and past trauma, I couldn't think of anything of interest to share. My childhood drama was one I'd never buy a ticket to see, let alone recount. Sharing my mother's mental health history felt, hmmm, unsafe. What did it have to do with me? In short, I had the healthy pride of a twenty-eight-year-old at the top of her game.

When we got to the end of the list, and he asked my profession, I told him I was currently an aerobics instructor—the only job in which my American accent seemed to give me an advantage. When this didn't lighten the mood, I added that I worked for ten years in Washington, D.C., for politicians and on a presidential campaign. He made it clear that he found this information immaterial by putting the pen back in his pocket and asking rather brusquely, "Why are you seeing me today?"

I had to dig for the courage to tell him, which only seemed to annoy him further. So I just went for it. I told him I was experiencing sudden paralysis, after which I would collapse. No amount of inner coaching seemed to help. I appeared to others to be unconscious while being horrifyingly aware I wasn't.

"Why is it *horrifying*?"

His question threw me. "Well, it's awful to concern people around me. It looks like I've fallen unconscious though I'm not, yet I have no way of communicating. After a few minutes, when I feel control coming back, my limbs twitch, my jaw clenches, and if I fight it, the convulsing gets worse. Afterward I am utterly exhausted."

He asked me if I had any idea as to why this was happening. I did not. He asked if I was under a lot of stress. I replied on the contrary. I had just rid myself of an ocean between me and the man I loved after a long-distance romance of five years. Given the junior doctor's flat reaction, this was an overshare.

He then asked me to explain what it was I felt before these episodes. I shared emotional detachment, a sense of distance, and maybe fear.

"Fear often accompanies anxiety," he explained.

And with that, we entered the old chicken or the egg conundrum: he suggesting that the cause of the problem was stress of which the seizures were symptomatic, me believing the seizures were in fact the source of my stress and anxiety. He clearly wanted the interview over as soon as possible; I needed assurance he wasn't suggesting this was all in my mind and wanted to preserve a small resemblance of dignity. To help bring the matter to a head, our young doctor asked Thomas to demonstrate what the seizures looked like.

"I'd have to get on the floor," my fiancé said.

Our young doctor nodded his head in support. So Thomas, in lieu of the ridiculousness of the request, laid on the floor and hammed it up for him. I laughed, mainly to protect myself from humiliation.

"I don't think an MRI will be necessary," the intern said, scribbling more notes. "I believe your bride-to-be is experiencing pseudo-seizures and it will do her no good to go on medication."

Oh, I thought. The term *pseudo* preceding anything could not bode well. And the bride-to-be comment didn't sound good either.

Thomas took control of the conversation. "Based on this short interview, you're confident in making that solid conclusion?" The tone in which he asked the question was so angrily dead of emotion I was suddenly scared of a brawl.

"What would you like me to do?" the doctor asked.

Try not being an asshole, I thought.

"Say something that would suggest you're taking her health seriously, not to mention her safety." Thomas said. "She bikes everywhere."

"They'll likely stop on their own, but just in case, I will order more tests . . . I have to go now as I'm behind schedule. Excuse me." And with that, I watched as the voice of science and reason made its exit, medical coattails fluttering behind him.

I looked at Thomas, overwhelmed at the feeling of what was, for the first time in my life, someone stepping in to emotionally help me. His defense of me here, his uncle stepping up to help me after Passover: it made me anxious that this was new family behavior.

In Which I Fall in Love

California, 1987—Though Thomas and I were laissez-faire when it came to issues of faith, God did come up early in our relationship. We met at an unusual crossroad.

I was twenty-three and working on a U.S. senator's campaign, while also trying to finish my self-financed undergraduate degree at George Washington University in D.C., when I hit my first serious bout of depression. That's when I walked by a leaflet advertising a cross-country bicycle ride to raise money for a charity and decided the only way I was going to recover was by taking some serious time off. The adventure would get me out of D.C. in its worst swampy months and would provide the opportunity to immerse myself in the spectacular outdoor beauty of the United States while cycling seventy miles a day, and there would be thirty other cyclists to save me from the inner me—the nightmare guest who wouldn't leave.

I arrived at office headquarters in Palo Alto after an eight-hour cross-country flight from hell, sleepwalking from the effects of two all-nighters prior to my departure. Spotting a couch, and thinking I'd "check out the eyelids," a fine phrase of my father's, I plonked down for a quick refresher.

Just as I drifted into that blissful in-between state of consciousness, I heard a rhetorical question. Could I help with a job? I opened my eyes to see a student sporting a well-weathered tank top, then noted the rest of his attire—blue turquoise cycling shorts and green high-top sneakers, and a positively hunky sunbaked athletic physique. Noting his British accent, I found myself reacting to him in the nature of the long-standing feud between our people. I suggested (with some sincerity) that I might be more helpful after a "quick kip."

He, in turn, suggested perhaps I might delay the nap for "the cause," and pointed to a box in the corner full of first-aid supplies, explaining a time-sensitive need to count and divide Band-Aids. After making it a point to say it was "for the cause," I took the box outside so I might at least enjoy the warm evening temperatures, and set to work with my assigned task of multiplication and division, and then just eyeballed it.

After he finished whatever it was that he had to do in the office, the kid, who was clearly younger than me by several years, asked would I mind if he kept me company while he adjusted the balance on the spokes of his wheel—a mechanical skill he introduced as "truing." Given the effort he was making at being friendly, I felt it only fair to put my initial annoyance on the back burner. This is when I learned his name was Thomas.

He was taking what they call in England a "gap year" before he started university. His charity ride had started in Bolivia, in South America, and he had been pedaling overland for eight months, from the Andes to Central America, and up to North America. You might imagine this struck me as exotic. As he and three other British cyclists were heading in the same direction cross-country, they volunteered to lead the routes for our group.

He was dreading the end of the summer because of school. I asked him where he was going and he shared that he had an offer to study at Cambridge and was meant to begin that autumn. Though he was thankful for the spot, after seeing what he had seen of the world, the last thing he could imagine was sitting in a lecture hall. What a waste of time it seemed when there was so much in the world that needed doing. I nodded in sympathy, told him I also struggled in the classroom, and gave him my brief résumé, of which he was most impressed. It turned out we were both political scientists by nature. We were soon laughing about the contrasts of our experiences growing up: his in London, mine in the midwestern prairie. But more than that, we seriously dug into meaningful questions in life. We grew excited about ideas, grew heated over philosophical arguments, debated political views in a way that only two young twentysomethings can: like it mattered. For hours. We talked right past sunset, and soon found ourselves sitting under a huge warm summer night sky, stars splattered Jackson Pollock–like overhead.

In time, we circled back to the amazing adventure he had been on. He assured me it wasn't as romantic as it might sound. He'd had eighteen tire punctures in one week, crossing the Andes, and he was desolately lonely most of the time. And in Mexico someone tried to kill him when he stopped alongside the road to take a picture. An unidentified truck swerved out of its way to hit him. His friends found him several minutes later with a gash in the back of his head. It took sixteen stitches to sew him up—and that was by a local lady with needle and thread before he was airlifted out.

I looked at his head. "My hair grows fast," he said. "The bump is still there," and he leaned over to let me feel it. Sure enough. Lumpy. That was only a couple of months ago.

As we neared punch-drunk tiredness, he asked me if I believed in the existence of God. I laughed, surprised at the intensity of the question. He said his near-death experience gave him a lot to think about—he offered by way of the question that he didn't believe in God, and though he was Jewish, it was a cultural identity, not a religious one. I shared I didn't believe in God either, though my Christian faith had been important to me in my childhood—for that, I had no regrets.

Eventually, he balanced the tightness of spokes on his wheel and asked me where my sleeping bag was. I went to fetch it and when I returned, he rolled it out opposite to his in one long line, so our pillows lay head to head. He patted mine and told me to get in, we needed to get a good night sleep. I was too tired to mind being directed and crawled in, wrapping my arms around my pillow. He reached up and took my pinky finger in his, and I found myself sleeping the best night's sleep of my life.

We spent the next five years trying to stop thinking of each other so we could move on, but we were never able to let go fully, even while we continued in relationships with other people. Finally, we gathered the courage to make the leap. And that is how this young midwesterner ended up in London.

In Which I Discover Dr. Charcot

London, 1993—After my visit to the young neurologist at the NHS, I left wildly confused and tearful. It would take a couple of hours of chewing my mind apart to become angry, for the negative effects of the appointment to set in. Once I was at home and had an opportunity to do a little research, it only made matters worse.

It turned out our junior doctor was not so original in his interview techniques. Had I been a woman at the Salpêtrière, the hospital for lunatics in Paris in the 1920s, and fallen under the study of Jean-Martin Charcot, a French neurologist, I might have found myself a star in the weekly productions he staged. In the interests of science, he'd invite those interested to view women experiencing hysterical symptoms in the way the junior consultant had asked my future husband to display symptoms on the floor.

My next discovery was Sigmund Freud's views on another famous case concerning epilepsy, in his essay "Dostoevsky and Parricide," in which he argued that the novelist's seizure disorder was merely a symptom of "his neurosis," which "must be accordingly classified as hystero-epilepsy—that is severe hysteria."

I read on with empathy as I learned that Dostoevsky, as a political prisoner, had suffered severe trauma after being made to stand in front of a firing squad with a burlap bag over his head, only to receive a reprieve from the czar at the last moment. But that was not all. His seizures stopped after he finished writing *The Brothers Karamazov*, a book drawn from his experience of living with his murderous father and the child abuse the young Fyodor endured.

Reading the information made me feel better, but it also left me with an odd sense of déjà vu. When I told Thomas the Charcot story, he immediately guessed at what I was thinking and warned me off struggling with inappropriate stereotypes. He reassured me that I was not the type of person who would stage paralysis for attention, and said it was a horrible conclusion for anyone to draw about human suffering.

At least it was complex enough that even the medical establishment was split on what exactly "pseudo" meant. And I didn't lose sight of the good news. The doctor seemed fairly confident it wasn't epilepsy or a tumor, but he'd order the necessary tests to rule them out.

In Which the Maternal Shades of My Life Take Form

Omaha, 1974—Christmas was the time of year when Mom would become house-proud. Her preparations began immediately after Thanksgiving, when the square foldout table—usually reserved for ambitious cardboard puzzles of one-thousand-piece magnitude—moved from the dining room to prime real estate in the living room. Around the first week of December, the new beaded ornament craft kits would start arriving. Each package came with a Styrofoam ball, beautiful ornate beads, and a pattern diagram to follow. Every year cool new baubles would be added to the tree.

In addition to the ornament collection and needlework stockings with Christmas scenes on them (mine featured Rudolph), Mom added a new nativity scene each year. The most elaborate one she made from newspaper papier-mâché and plaster—three wise men, Mary and Joseph and the baby, all sprayed with gold paint.

But the best part of Christmas was my grandmother Vivian's annual visit. She was a personal assistant to the congressional lobbyist of General Motors Corporation and flew in from Washington, D.C. We'd all, including Zorro, pile into our Chevy station wagon to pick her up at Omaha's Eppley Airfield.

Vivian preferred me and my sisters to call her by her first name because she didn't want strangers thinking she was that old. I was in awe of Vivian and so had no problem with granting her that wish. She'd descend from the stairs of the plane wearing her traveling outfit—a tailored yellow wool skirt and jacket with black knee-high leather boots, her hair pulled back and twisted into a nice French roll, sparkling clip-on costume jewelry earrings, and pink coral lipstick. She made wearing furs and long gloves in Omaha look casual.

If I have not convinced you that she was the most glamorous thing on earth, then she was definitely the most glamorous person to have ever arrived in our subdivision of Lee Valley. She made you want to live big, whereby Mom made you want to run. Or play possum. Whichever was the safest.

Mom called Vivian the Ice Queen. And when she did, Vivian would just sit, back straight, ankles tucked into her thin crossed legs, and smile. She was as complete in her equanimity as my mother was intent in her campaign to destroy it. But no matter what unseen mother-daughter dynamic existed, when Vivian came to visit, Mom clearly relaxed. They'd stay up late talking for hours. Vivian would spend time during the day cleaning and organizing things you wouldn't even know were a mess.

Mom's major issue with Vivian was that she had screwed her childhood by leaving my grandfather, the Major. Mom said Vivian left him because he was cheating on her, which was an act of pure selfishness. Plenty of wives were dealing with cheating husbands in the 1950s, so they took antidepressants, but Vivian wouldn't even try medication.

I have a stack of photos featuring Vivian with the Major. In one of the pictures she and the Major are making out like they're surrendering every last bit of soul. Who the eye was behind that camera I can only wonder. In another shot, my grandfather's slender build is big with manly energy, and his arm is wrapped around Vivian's waist like she's water in a paper cup.

But my favorite picture is of a different theme. In it, my grandfather is standing with four men whom he served with in the Korean War, wearing high-waist pleated pants with suspenders, and oxford shoes. Perched on his head is a trilby hat, tilted over the eyes. He's squinting with a cigarette dangling from his mouth, oozing charisma.

According to Vivian, the two of them fell madly in love in high school and married immediately after they graduated. They were so excited about building their life together that they wasted no time in trying to get pregnant. Mom arrived just after Vivian's nineteenth birthday. Six years of family happiness followed with Mom as an only child. There were small hiccups of discontent, but nothing significant until the communists walked right into South Korea and my grandfather, being of strong nature, signed up to fight. While he was there, a hand grenade was lobbed in front of his men. He didn't even think before throwing his body on top of it. Fortunately it didn't blow up, and because of this act of heroism the United States of America awarded him a Silver Star Medal. And this is why I call him, respectfully, the Major.

Vivian went on to share that the two love birds enjoyed a few more years of happiness after the Major returned from the Korean War, but when he received his orders to move to the German base of Heidelberg in 1958, Vivian politely declined to go with him. She had gone to work at the rations office while he was away and wasn't interested in becoming a housewife again.

When I asked Vivian about my grandfather's affairs, she said there had always been a number of women in his amorous collection, but she just turned a blind eye because she knew he had a weakness in this area. There was no use fighting it, she said, because it would have changed the man she loved. But this wasn't the reason she stayed behind, she assured me. She really needed her own identity and had no hard feelings when my grandfather asked for a divorce to marry his second wife.

I'm not sure Vivian was revealing all the emotions surrounding the family breakup. She always smiled when she told stories, even when they were intense. But Mom confirmed it, that Vivian and the Major remained the best of friends. Vivian was even with the Major and his second wife when he died tragically at the age of forty-four, after the army hospital gave him the wrong blood type during an appendicitis attack. Because of that, I'd never know my grandfather, and Mom remained wounded forever, not only because she was torn from him so young in life, but because death now cheated her forever of the father-daughter relationship so critical to her self-esteem.

Trying to imagine what Vivian's mindset was at the time of the divorce, I asked Mom if she thought Vivian might have been scared at the idea of moving to a foreign country. Mom's response was that if there was one thing you could be sure of, it was that Vivian wasn't scared of anything. Vivian even pulled a gun on her one time.

When I later grilled Vivian about the gun incident, she said she most certainly did not pull a gun on my mother. Yes, when they lived in California, she did keep a revolver hidden for safety purposes in her bra-and-panties drawer to protect against burglars, and once my mother did come out with it in her hand and asked, "What is this?" Vivian recalled that the moment was tense and she had to calmly ask my mother to give her the gun. And this is when it occurred to Vivian that perhaps it might be a good idea to let Mom go live with the Major.

Vivian added, without prompting, that if she was to be honest, my mother had become "slightly scary" as a teenager, and Vivian felt overwhelmed and unprepared to guide her, but she was not prepared to tell me what "slightly scary" was. I noticed when Vivian was around other people's anger, she pulled her shoulders up as high as she could, to try to hide her head and neck like a turtle.

After she shared the gun incident, I asked her if she had been sad to see Mom go. She assured me she was not happy that her daughter wanted to live in a different country, but she understood why Mom would want to be with her father. She hoped Mom would be happy, as Vivian felt this was a respectable aim in life.

When I asked Vivian if she knew the best way for Mom to achieve this happiness, she said she wasn't sure, but at the time Mom was sixteen, Vivian thought the Major might be able to give Mom something she couldn't.

It was like she was saying, "If you love someone—set them free," just like she did with the Major.

Later I asked Mom if she felt like one of those dogs who is given up for adoption because the owner didn't want it anymore.

And she said, "You don't know how lucky you are to have two parents and a roof over your head."

In Which Our Family Chapter in Lee Valley Comes to an End

Omaha, 1975—After beginning his career selling Twinkies and Ding Dongs and then graduating to sales of a different category and higher profit margin— steel light poles, the kind used to illuminate interstates—Dad was poached by a small family business, a father-son team that had designed an advanced industrial robot. They needed a particularly good salesman to break into the market because it was so cutting edge.

A family meeting was called to break the news. Dad said it wasn't going to change much, except that he would be making a lot more money, *and* we were moving—to a new neighborhood, eight miles away in the central historic part of Omaha. Mom jumped in to share they'd found a house; in fact, it was her dream house: a five-bedroom, red-brick colonial with two fireplaces. Judging by the pride of their presentation, it was clear we were meant to be excited.

Dad threw a few more bonuses in; there were some big old trees and a municipal swimming pool down the road, and he pointed out, in case we hadn't done the math, we would each have our own room. I knew a spin when I heard one. The new job was based in a charming small town called Laurens, in northwest Iowa, which was only a three-hour drive away. My sisters and I moaned in chorus, so he added that one reason he took the new job was because they said he could work from home on Thursdays and Fridays. He was tired of being away from us on the road for so long.

Mom tried to turn up the mood in the room by cheering. This was a place where she felt she belonged—our new solidly middle-class neighborhood of Elmwood Park reflected her level of sophistication and her intelligence. At last, she would be moving among a single malt Scotch–drinking crowd.

Meanwhile, that robot and I were not starting on good terms. My suburban childhood was being flushed down the drain. Seeing the reluctant buy-in, my father stepped up his sales pitch. The company was prepared to give him a sizable increase of income, in addition to a percentage of ownership. This would be our college educations. Like I really cared at age eleven. I didn't want to leave Lee Valley. Gone would be the ease with adults who had known me since I was four and the open door stop-in policy of our neighborhood. Gone would be the folks who would gather in folding chairs with my father, drinking beer in our front yard on balmy summer evenings barbecuing Oscar Mayer wieners and hamburgers on our Weber grill while we played our outdoor games. Gone would be our regular Saturday night trip to Dairy Queen for Dilly Bars or double-dipped butterscotch ice-cream cones and all my neighborhood friends. Gone would be the velvety green groomed lawns and families with American flags hanging outside their front doors. Gone would be the golden fields of corn now full of numerous schools and shopping malls and grocery stores. A generation of children had been born and raised, and the sun still set in the horizon outside my bedroom window, but I wouldn't be there to watch it.

In Which Mr. K Drives By

Omaha, 1978—As Mr. K and I were driving around with no apparent destination, he started asking about my parents, about where my dad worked.
I told him Dad used to sell Hostess Twinkies and cupcakes, but then he
moved to selling steel light poles.

"Light poles," he repeated, confused.

"You know, the ones you see on the road."

"Cool—he sells light poles?"

"Well, now he sells robots."

In the testimony Mr. K later gave to the police, he puzzled over this part of
the conversation: "She said her father had some silly job or something." I tried
to explain what industrial robots were, but he interrupted me impatiently.

"I meant, like how much does he make? Like money?"

"Oh, I'm not sure. I think maybe sixteen thousand dollars a year or something like that." I had no idea.

"So tell me, where do you live?"

"Elmwood Park."

"Is your house nice?"

"Well, I think it's nice enough, but I liked our house in Lee Valley better."

"Let's go see it."

"My old neighborhood?"

"No, where you live now." He had become focused, like we were past the get-to-know-you part of the conversation and on to tasks. I thought about coming up with a different idea because Mr. K wasn't the kind of guy you wanted to bring home, or, more accurate, he wasn't the kind of guy you wanted knowing where home was, no matter how nice he was now acting.

"Give me something you live near." He said it in a slightly pushy manner.

"Well, we're near UNO [the University of Omaha]." It came out of my mouth against every instinct I had.

We were soon passing the Elmwood Park Swimming Pool and driving up the hill to Emile Street, where our brick colonial house came into view.

"That's a nice house," he said, slowing down to get a good view.

I suddenly felt sick to my stomach. My father and sisters were sitting inside, less than fifty yards in front of me, and I was totally helpless to reach them.

Mr K. picked up on my drop in mood; his tone changed too. "We need to get some gas," he said, pulling away.

In Which I Receive Career Coaching

Omaha, 1976—Elmwood Park was located in the heart of the city, a neighborhood developed a century before with mature trees and gardens; the houses were Colonial, Georgian, and of a Tudor Revival style. The park itself was at the end of our street, heavily forested, with vast expanses of green areas for recreation—baseball diamonds, tennis courts, areas to play Frisbee, and a municipal pool with more cement deck space than the one in Lee Valley.

A lot of the men worked at banks and insurance companies, which was similar to our old neighborhood, but here they seemed to be a step or two up the management ladder. Their cars tended to be new and clean. And they didn't arrive home with their ties loose around their neck. Even stay-at-home moms (which were the only type of mom I saw at that time) seemed to operate at a higher level of management. The open-door policy that existed in Lee Valley was gone. Kids weren't allowed to run feral in the streets. A flag football game had to be organized in advance.

The yards were smaller than they were in Lee Valley, so there weren't weekly barbecues, but there were a couple of potlucks at people's homes. They featured a good trade of Midwest food, usually enhanced with branded recipes like Kraft Macaroni and Cheese, Hamburger Helper casserole, along with the classics: apple, walnut, and celery salad, a varying array of Jell-O options, and soda pop.

The UNO campus sat on the other side of the park, so Mom, more free since Jenifer had started school, decided she was going to become a lawyer. First, she had to get a degree. She qualified for a scholarship for moms going to university, and enrolled in a full-time bachelor of arts undergraduate program to study political science. It felt like there was something exciting happening in the house now.

One of the upsides of her studying was that it moved her from discussing the burdens of childcare and the unfairness of life and the constant mournful dirge that no one loved her to topics of a much more interesting nature: how government worked, the rights of citizens, and political philosophy. I became a study buddy—she trained me to quiz her.

I learned about Congress, the Constitution, the difference between the state and federal systems, and how even though the Equal Rights Amendment had been approved by Congress, it would never pass because it would never be approved at the state level. She was passionate about the inequities of our economic system and the enduring legacy of slavery, how Roosevelt and Johnson passed public policy to help these inequalities, and though we liked to think everyone in the States had equal economic opportunity, it was a myth. "This city is so segregated you wouldn't even know black people live in Omaha," Mom pointed out.

"What about Clarence?" I asked. Dad and Clarence worked together at Valmont selling light poles. Clarence saved Dad's life when Dad was attacked by a nest of wasps and went into anaphylactic shock at Clarence's house during one of his barbecues.

"Clarence isn't really black," she said. I had no idea what she was talking about. "He has a college education and lives in a white neighborhood. You're going to have classmates next year who don't have the privileges you do."

She was referring to the policy of school busing, which was about to begin in Omaha. The U.S. Supreme Court had just ruled that Omaha public schools had "governing proof of unconstitutional desegregation." Though the entire South had instituted the changes required in the landmark ruling of *Brown v. Board of Education* in 1954, Omaha had staved off changes by arguing it wasn't practicing racial discrimination in its apportionment of resources. As a seventh grader in 1976, I was part of the first group of students who would take the bus to a school other than the one in my home district. In my case, instead of attending Norris Junior High, I would catch the bus to Lewis and Clark, which in effect only swapped one white neighborhood school for another.

But I had no negative feelings toward the policy. It was the kind of social justice we spoke about at church, the kind Jesus himself would advocate. I was still checking in with him daily. And after watching *Roots*, the television series based on Alex Haley's bestselling book, with the rest of the nation, I gained an emotional and historical understanding that explained the real reasons for what we were doing—busing was an attempt to correct inequities that existed between school districts, one of the long-standing effects of the economic plunder of those enslaved, and this, in my heart anyway, seemed a positive thing to happen.

As part of my continuing education, Mom also gave me a copy of *Watership Down*, a book about a colony of rabbits who are oppressed by brutal laws. The story just about crushed me. When I asked her why she had given me a scary book, she said my Pollyanna view of people was dangerous. When I asked her what Pollyanna meant, she said the world was full of bad people and just because I didn't want to believe it, didn't make it untrue. I told her we might have differences in our views about the good in people. Then she laughed like I had just proved how naive I was.

I have a clipping of an *Omaha World Herald* article featuring a photo of my mother with my three sisters and me sitting together. The article addressed the growing phenomenon of women returning to school after having children, and featured my mother as a role model for the second-generation wave of feminists.

"I've proved, girls, it's never too late to make your dreams come true," she said, speaking to us as the journalist took notes. "You can become anything you want to be."

During one of our late-night study sessions she asked me what I wanted to be when I grew up. I said a doctor. She inquired further. What type of doctor? A brain surgeon, I responded proudly, thinking that sounded very grand. She said, "No, you have to be more ambitious." At this point it had become clear we were playing a game of "I am thinking of something that starts with the letter . . ." but she wasn't giving me a chance to ask for any clues. So I just started making wild guesses.

"The first lady astronaut!" I said, thinking that sounded ambitious.

"Nope," she said, her ice cubes clinking against her glass as she sipped more Scotch and took a drag on her cigarette.

"A lawyer!" I said, confident I had nailed it that time.

"Getting warm," she said, encouragingly.

"A congresswoman!" I couldn't wait for this game to be over.

"Higher," she said, her voice raising the stakes.

"The first lady president of the United States?"

"Bingo," she cried. "What do you want to be?"

"The first lady president of the United States!" I repeated.

"I knew you were my daughter," she said, her eyes reddening with sentimentality. When she was drinking, she'd always reassure me our relationship was special. It's when she wasn't drinking that she was dangerous. One more slurp of the Scotch and she added, "Just make sure you don't get pregnant."

In Which I Further Deteriorate

London, 1993—Not long after seeing the young neurologist, I underwent blood tests, an MRI, and an EEG. And as he suggested, the tests came back negative for anomalies. Instead of that making me feel better, however, I felt worse. If this problem was in my mind, then didn't that mean I was unconsciously making some grab at attention? That the episodes were serving some kind of positive emotional purpose? The logic of it felt ludicrous, not to mention toxic.

I couldn't help but recognize that these fits of paralysis had similarities to the lucid dream state of night terrors. Instead of being trapped in a dream—terrified and awake, yet clinically asleep—the situation was reversed. I appeared to be unconscious, asleep, even though I was awake and fully aware of my surroundings.

I resolved that I would find a more helpful explanation for the seizures, other than they were originating from some unsettled internal conflict. After all, there was so much about the brain that neurologists had yet to understand. I'd become my own scientist, just as I had when studying my dreams. I would observe and note the episodes. I began to keep track of when and how often the seizures would occur. I documented the warning signals—for example, the changes in sensory perception. I became better at relaxing when I sensed one coming, refused to let a five-minute bout of paralysis cripple me longer than was necessary, stopped fighting my helplessness when I collapsed, and this reduced the spasms. I pushed through the extreme fatigue that would follow, not letting a seizure destroy my entire day, though sometimes I'd have no choice but to sleep for hours afterward. In summary, I took a pragmatic approach. If I couldn't stop them, I could at least become better at managing them.

And then there was the positive inventory. This wasn't a brain tumor or grand mal seizures. I was self-employed, so I didn't have to worry about losing a job. I remained physically fit and healthy. I carried huge anxieties that living in a foreign country would leave me feeling dependent, but Thomas, who had no interest in playing the role of savior, supported me in a way that kept the relationship balanced.

We were leading a rich social life in London, and six months later we moved to Oxford. I taught English literature at a tutorial college for a while before we joined forces at the radical nonprofit production company he and a few other activists started, called Undercurrents. As a result, our home was often filled with overnight guests. East Oxford dinner parties became a regular way of life. It was now 1996, we were three years into our marriage, and the honeymoon phase wasn't waning.

But neither were the seizures. In fact, they were increasing. I tried to block the anger I felt toward my body. I continued to bicycle, continued to teach aerobic classes. In fact, I added training for the London Marathon to the list just to prove I wouldn't be defeated.

But the same stubborn pride that kept me going was also going to keep me searching for answers that weren't solving the problem. The seizures were getting closer in frequency, as often as twice a week. I tried homeopathy, cranial osteopathy, herbal medicine. I even took a job at Neal's Yard Remedies so I could learn more. But it wasn't good for business when customers saw me selling remedies to treat their ailments and suddenly there I was, dropping seemingly unconscious on the floor. Okay, that only happened once, but it was enough.

I was becoming so desperate for an emotional break I enrolled in courses at an anxiety clinic. I journaled to see if I could find any repeating pattern—and managed to connect a good deal of the triggers to overexertion and lack of sleep. But it was like using a feather duster to stamp out a swarm of wasps. Mostly, it was completely ineffective. My short-term memory and speech were affected at this point. I'd accidentally reverse syllables and come out with entertaining spoonerisms I wasn't trying to construct. For example, I once described someone as *emancipated* instead of *emaciated*, used the word *amnesia* instead of *anathema*, confused *chimera* with *chiminea*, mentioned in passing I was *reading depression on literature*; and even once embarrassed myself by proclaiming I'd *hit my head on the nail.*

And then the depression set in. But I had always treated depression philosophically, a problem of the soul, not of the body. The two episodes I had in Washington introduced me to varied strategies. The first bout hit when I was twenty-two. I tried psychoanalysis with earnest beginner students (it was the best I could afford), but it only seemed to make the depression worse. I then turned to bibliotherapy—reading philosophers and literature on the soul— and supplemented my new awareness with pastoral counseling that helped steer me to working with the homeless, people with problems much bigger than my own, a wonderful distractive technique. That in turn led me to sign up for Bike-Aid, the cross-country charity bike ride where I finally found the black cloud lift and fell in love.

Four years after the onset of my first severe bout of melancholy, at the age of twenty-seven, I found myself battling it again and sought out the help of the Jungian therapist Sheldon Kopp, who had written the popular book *If You Meet the Buddha on the Road, Kill Him!*

Shelly, as he preferred to be called, raised the question of long-term romantic relationships. I told him I enjoyed plenty of romantic relationships. He asked if any had been serious. I shared there had been a wide range of both length and depth, but my heart had never quite recovered from a summer romance that turned into a long-distance love affair, before the obstacles of life tore us apart. Sheldon suggested that I might have fears of intimacy. I told him no, it was simple. There was only one man I'd ever love, and that was Thomas.

Sheldon attempted to clarify my situation. "I thought you said the relationship ended three years ago?" I clarified that no, my heart had been broken three years ago, but recently Thomas had asked me, in rather desperate romantic fashion, if I would marry him. Sheldon asked me what I feared in getting married. I said, with all seriousness, me. And that answer guided questions for the next three months. Somehow Shelly managed to convince me I was not uniquely unsuitable for marriage, and I gathered the courage needed to take the leap. It was the best money I'd ever spent.

Since saying yes to Thomas I had grown and overcome my fears of being in a relationship. I had made the right decision. Having arrived at the age of thirty-two I was truly deeply happy. So why now was my unconscious unleashing this challenge, punishing me for it? That's what it felt like in my lowest moment. My pride was beat to a pulp. I could barely form a sentence properly.

I finally revisited the idea of trying an anti-seizure medication, recommended three years before by Thomas's uncle. I was scared of how it might change me. Weight gain was one of the side effects, drowsiness another. Thomas pointed out that these were minor concerns if it would stop the seizures. Still, I couldn't view having to take medication as anything but defeat over my spirit.

Exhausted at the drag I felt I had become, I went to my local GP and asked for help. We discussed medication. She and I agreed that even though there had been no scientific tests confirming the cause of my collapses, the effect of the medication would serve as a baseline test of its own. She reassured me against my fear that I was taking the pills instead of facing my problems. On the contrary, she said, trying the medication was smart management.

Before beginning the course of indefinite emotional dampening, I carefully researched the drug and its long-term side effects. I read that in addition to being prescribed for epileptics, it was also recommended as a mood stabilizer for those experiencing psychotic disorders. I wondered if that meant I was now somehow in the same class as Mom.

Within three weeks of starting the medication, the seizures stopped. Just like that. The question of whether they were psychosomatic became simply irrelevant.

In Which Charles Graduates to Being a Violent Criminal

Omaha, 1977—Some people get addicted to drugs or alcohol, some to food, some to self-help, but Charles was obsessed with cars—the driving of the cars—and it was going to get him in trouble.

Okay, it wasn't just about the driving, because his parents gave him access to the family car. They even gave him an allowance for gas money. But Charles liked the power and rush that came with driving other people's vehicles. It was like stepping into someone else's skin for a short while; he could be incognito. In any case, he didn't steal—he borrowed. And only from those who invited it by leaving a motor running. They knew they were taking the risk, and he was just fulfilling the contract for them.

It also made him instantly popular. No one seemed to ask where he got a car if he asked them to cruise. One night, when he was out by himself, he noticed that he had a police car on his tail, which made him nervous enough that he pulled into the Target store at 350 North Saddle Creek Road. He watched with relief when the police car drove past, but it was clear he was going to have to ditch the car. That's when he saw a woman exiting the store.

He watched as she took her keys out, then made his move. As soon as she started the engine, he opened her car door, pointed a .22 rifle at her head, and commanded that she get out. Not in an overly aggressive manner. The woman started pleading and crying that she had kids, began frantically pulling the contents of her wallet out, telling him to take it, begging him not to hurt her. Again, he told her to just *get out of the damn car.*

So finally—she got out, and he got in, and that was the end of their relationship. Except it wasn't. She went straight to the police station and identified him from a photo they had of him from a previous arrest.

He could have saved himself a lot of hassle if he had only worn one of those balaclavas.

In Which Mom and Dad Invite Me on a Road Trip

Omaha, 1977—Mom and Dad announced they were going to Laurens, Iowa, for the weekend. They were leaving on a Friday morning, which happened to be the last day of my seventh-grade school year.

I tried to hide my excitement as my mind starting going rampant with juvenile ideas and plans, but Mom read my thoughts. "I don't know where you are staying yet," she said, "but it's not going to be at home." She told me she was putting Genie in charge of Gayle and Jenifer, and she wouldn't have me undermining Genie's authority.

And then she added further insult by calling the parent of a friend of mine at school and arranging a sleepover for the two of us. Our families attended the same church. I suppose Mom thought that that meant less risk of juvenile activity. She couldn't have been further from the truth. There was little difference in partying behavior between my friends at church and my friends at school. And I happened to know that my friend Susan benefited from parental burnout, trailblazed by her two older siblings. Short of committing a legal crime, she had no rules at home to break. But the real excitement for me—Susan was practiced in arranging clandestine meetings with boys.

I'd made it through the first year of junior high without partaking in any of the rebellious activities, mainly because I was scared to death of getting caught. My place on the varsity track team also kept me straight. But I was often teased about being a prude by my girlfriends—I had never been kissed. I was eager to rectify that.

Susan and I wasted no time in making plans. We coordinated a meetup with a group of friends at Peony Park, the amusement playground with a huge public pool and imported sand that created a beach. There would be *boys*, particularly Greg Osborn, whom I had been exchanging notes with for over a month. And Susan's sister would get us the beer.

The morning my parents were meant to leave, I was putting my carefully selected freshly laundered clothes in the dryer when I heard Dad call to me from upstairs. There was nothing in his tone to suggest I was in trouble, but my heart thumped with guilt and fear that our plans had been foiled.

When I arrived at the top of the stairs, he asked me if I had made any plans that I would need to cancel if I went to Laurens with them.

I confidently said no, but also let him know there was no way I wanted to go to Laurens.

"Well, we've decided we'd like your company."

"I'd rather die," I told him.

"Well, that's rather melodramatic."

"Well, I mean it."

"Well, I mean it too. I am not giving you a choice. You're coming with us."

I took a few steps up the stairs and turned around, putting my hand on the bannister. "No, I am not." I had never said anything like this to my father before. A two-year-old couldn't have done better.

His face dropped with hurt, and then anger. "You are going to come with us even if I have to carry you over my shoulder into the car."

"I have to call Susan and tell her I won't be coming."

"Your mother talked to Susan's mother. You don't have to worry about that."

The journey to Laurens took three hours. We drove west across the Missouri River to Council Bluffs, then slowly began making our way through a landscape that was as flat and as lifeless as the map I was looking at. The atmosphere in the car was odd. My parents didn't talk about why I was there and my sisters weren't. We just carried on like they actually wanted my company, so I relaxed into it and started enjoying myself.

We eventually arrived in Laurens. The welcome sign said POPULATION 1,600. My parents dropped me off at the only hotel, which had eight rooms. It didn't even have a vending machine. After getting bored watching television, I decided to walk over to Main Street. It was a stark, barren, empty, soulless strip of cement. I'd never seen such a desolate place. A grain elevator with three silos loomed on the skyline to the left, a water tower with the word LAURENS painted on it in big black letters shadowed the right, and a railway track ran in between. Main Street was two lanes wide. There was a bowling alley, a women's clothing store with six mannequins in the window who wore half the inventory, a pharmacy presumably named after its owner, George, a barbershop, a general hardware store, and three churches. As I counted the number of retail establishments, I saw a car with four teenagers pass by me and was relieved when I saw them disappear over the railroad track. Is there an act more humiliating at the age of thirteen than to be seen walking by oneself in front of other adolescents?

I watched as they made a U-turn and headed back down the street, slowing to check me out as they drove by. They made another U-turn and paraded past me again, this time with a friendly wave, like we were passing on a sidewalk. I felt like I was watching something in a National Geographic documentary. Had anyone told me I would be desperate to be inducted into this social club a year later, or I'd be lapping the town for track practice warm-up, I'd have said no way in hell. David Lynch later used this stretch of town in a movie he made about an old guy who rides a tractor mower across the state to see his dying estranged brother.

The next day on our return trip to Omaha, Dad asked me if I wanted to lean up toward the front seat so the three of us could have a talk.

"Well, why not?" I said, in my friendly neighborly voice.

"So Debora, can you tell us why you are here today?" Mom asked. The formal use of my first name was preserved for those times I was in trouble.

"I'm not sure."

I was sure though. I had been waiting for it to come as soon as my father had said they had talked to Susan's parents. I had become wiser in the ways of eluding detection, and there was no way I was going to fall for this invitation to show my hand, just in case I was wrong.

"Would you like to think about that harder?" Mom questioned.

I did, but the focus of my attention was on how I might swiftly and deftly influence my father to take my side. I wasn't accustomed to having him around for disciplinarian sessions, since he had always been on the road. In fact, I realized that he had probably orchestrated the three-day delay in conversation. It was utterly uncharacteristic of Mom.

"Well, why don't I try to help you," my mother said. "You're smoking cigarettes, aren't you?"

"No," I said in disbelief. Actually, I was, but again, she couldn't expect me to rat myself out. What kind of self-respect is that?

"Would you like to share what your plans were when we left? Is it true that you intended to go drinking with your friends at Peony Park?"

"Oh, well," I said bravely. "You have me."

"See, I told you, Jim."

Dad appeared to be concentrating on his driving. I couldn't help but feel slightly paranoid. I hadn't a clue how they had found out and couldn't exactly ask.

Once we returned home, my mother's campaign to save my deteriorating character included grounding me for a week, then continued with more lectures and rants of shame after Dad left. But it didn't stop me from acting with my impulsive unthinking adolescent brain, and I decided that the best way to captain my own ship was to carry on with experimentation.

A few weeks later a couple of friends and I were down at the neighborhood pool in Elmwood Park. Someone said they had a joint and suggested that we walk over to the grotto in the woods, a hundred yards from our beach towels. I was aware of the risk I was taking if Mom found out, especially since I had just been freed of house arrest. But I was much more concerned with having fun and not being a prude, especially after having had our party plans at Peony Park scuppered. After a few puffs I didn't feel anything and grew deeply disappointed. But as I was walking, I suddenly felt the weight of the universe lifting, and I skipped home under a clear blue sky.

In Which I Am Scared Straight

Omaha, 1977—Two weeks later, I was kicking a ball in the street with a couple of friends. My mother called me into the house, unusually calm, like she had a friendly favor to ask.

"I have a phone call to make, and I'd like you to be here while I make it." I had no idea who she was calling. I casually leaned against the counter.

"Yes, she is here," my mother said as if she were continuing a previous conversation, turning her back slightly toward me so that she could concentrate, then a pause as if she were being asked a question. "My daughter is smoking marijuana. I would like to have her arrested."

I realized my error immediately: I had told my younger sister Gayle, thinking it was important to share these sorts of experiences in life. And she told Mom out of eleven-year-old concern.

My mother continued, "No. She's not high at this moment, but she did get high." She drew in on her cigarette. "A joint." Another pause.

I didn't know whether to remain or run. This was my mother. "Two weeks ago, at Elmwood Park," she continued. My sister—definitely. Mom looked

out the window, wrapped the telephone cord around her finger, tucked the
phone under her ear and shoulder so she could take another drag of her
burning cigarette. "I see," she said, exhaling—glancing in my direction for a
split second. "What if I brought her down to the station? Is there an officer
who speaks to young criminals?"

She put down the phone, stubbed out her cigarette, and said, "You're coming
with me." Once we got into the car, she refused to talk until we pulled into
the parking lot of the local police station, with cruisers parked outside. "You're
lucky I'm doing this," she said, swinging the car door open. We entered the
building and went to reception. Mom spoke to the desk officer. I watched as
he looked at me, then looked at her, then looked at me. And with a hint of
impatience in his voice, said he would see if he could get the sergeant. His
annoyance increased my embarrassment.

Eventually the sergeant came out and suggested that my mother wait in her
chair as he showed me into his office and shut the door. He then motioned
for me to take a seat. The smile on his face and his relaxed manner disarmed
me enough to move from feeling terrified to uneasy. He looked like the volunteer coach of my baseball team.

"So why are you here today?" he asked. It was more like a "Can I help you?"
question.

"My mother wants you to arrest me." I felt the blood rushing to my cheeks.

"Yes, I've heard. I hear you have been smoking marijuana," he said, almost
impressed.

"Yes." I lowered my head. "But I didn't inhale."

"That statement wouldn't help you in a court of law, you know. But truth-
fully"—he tilted his head toward her through the window, raised his eyebrows
signaling an unspoken comradery—"your mother's behavior is a little odd."

I looked at him, unsure of the appropriate response. Maybe this was an interrogation technique.

"It's a little intense, a mother trying to get her kid arrested. You also seem like a smart kid, and you don't really strike me as the criminal type."

I nodded in agreement, a glint of hope he might be serious. He asked me if I enjoyed school—what kind of grades I had. I told him I had proudly made honor roll that term. I was on the student council and I had just been nominated for homecoming court. It didn't feel like something to brag about, but he asked. I also added that I was on the track team.

"How about out of school?" he asked. I told him I went to youth group once a week, and church choir once a week, and Bible class and service on Sunday. And I used to be in 4-H Club, but I was too busy now.

"Uh hum," he said, pausing, thinking. "Listen, I'm sure your mother is doing the best she can, but if I am totally honest, I don't think it's necessary that she brought you down here, and quite frankly, it has me a little concerned."

He had a few more questions about our relationship, then asked about other adults in my life, a support system. He went on to explain the concept of a scapegoat and boldly suggested that perhaps my mother's tough love approach might not be helpful, and then kind of looked like he felt sorry for me. I was so overwhelmed with his support I didn't know what to say. It made me feel anxious yet affirmed, the way a horrid truth does when it feels right. He gave me a warm sympathetic smile, knowing the comment had landed where he wanted it to, told me to not take drugs, especially at my age because it could stunt my brain growth. He then gave me a card and told me to call if I ever felt like I needed anything.

Mom was reading a Sidney Sheldon novel when we came out.

"Well, Mrs. Cackler"—the officer walked me forward and patted my back as if he were handing me over—"I think I can say with all honesty, you don't have to worry about your daughter. She has a sensible head on her shoulders."

It was clear by the look on her face it was not the verdict Mom expected, and she looked at me like she wanted to cuff me, like I was to blame. As we left, I turned around to give the officer a good-bye-thank-you look, and in return he gave me a no-problem-take-care-of-yourself smile.

That handsome police officer is definitely going on the shelf of those who kept me straight.

In Which Charles Visits a Judge

Omaha, 1977—Six months from the day he was arrested for putting a .22 rifle in a woman's face and thrown into the Douglas County Jail, Charles Goodwin appeared in front of Judge Murphy for his official sentence. Charles would get credit for time served, but he wouldn't get any consideration for what he endured as a sixteen-year-old being held in the adult holding tank, when a white racist indulged his violent sadism by raping him.

Judge Murphy was the grandfatherly type—benevolent, caring, patient. He genuinely wanted to know how to help this young man. He asked Charles why he had this problem of stealing automobiles when his parents gave him access to the family car and an allowance. And then the judge shuffled back a piece of paper or two, and corrected himself—Charles's *stepfather* and his mother.

Charles corrected him and told him Paul Goodwin wasn't his stepdad. And the following conversation went something like this:

Judge Murphy said, "Well, it says here on the record that you were adopted."

"Well, that isn't right. My dad probably just said it as a figure of speech." It wasn't easy telling a judge that he's wrong.

"You're not helping yourself here, son," Judge Murphy said.

Charles had no idea what he was talking about, and the judge knew it by looking at his face. He looked over at Dorothy Goodwin for clarification.

"Can you please confirm for the court, Mrs. Goodwin, who Charles's natural parents are?"

"My husband is his adoptive father, but I am his natural mother."

And while the biggest betrayal of his life was sinking in, the judge went forward with sentencing Charles to five more months at the Kearney Youth Development Center, even after witnessing what had just gone down. There was a real poetry to it, the state taking custody of him at the moment he found out his real father was a mystery man. That judge played it like he cared, but the sentence made it clear he didn't.

Five months later, on November 12, 1978, Charles Goodwin was released from the Kearney Youth Development Center. After a quick stop at home, the first thing he did was take a bus downtown to the courthouse to see Judge Murphy with a revolver in his pocket.

When Charles entered the elevator, Judge Murphy just happened to be inside. The judge recognized Charles and asked him with all sincerity how he was doing, as though he were glad to see him back on the streets. That was when Charles lost his nerve.

Instead, he told the judge it was nice to be home and he was looking forward to going back to school. So he rode the elevator up with the judge and then rode it back down again. It was more like a ride on a fairground than the mano a mano he had planned.

In Which I Am Rescued

Omaha, 1977—After hearing about our scared-straight trip to the police precinct, Dad decided to take charge of my rehab in his own way.

"So," he said, one Saturday morning as he poured the eggs into the skillet over diced-up Spam, "I want to sell you an idea. I need an assistant for a ten-day business trip to New York." A pocket of pork lard popped. I wondered if I heard him right.

"I want to try the Taurus out in factories. I can't pay you, but we'd have fun. Here"—he handed me the spatula—"can you give this a stir?"

He returned a few moments later with a map, with the stops we were going to make—Des Moines, Dubuque and Davenport, Peoria, Chicago, South Bend, Indianapolis, Cincinnati, Pittsburgh, Johnstown, Philadelphia, Scranton, Syracuse, Rockville, and NYC. Then he showed me the call sheets he had made for the companies where he had made appointments. I was impressed at the genius of his organizational system and was excited about the job.

And that's when Mom walked in the kitchen. "I suppose she thinks this is your idea?" She looked at my father and then at me. "I thought if your father took you with him, it would assure you won't land in prison at the age of thir-teen, which everyone knows is where you're headed, young lady."

I wasn't sure who this collective "everyone" being cited was, but I caught a look from Dad, a silent plea to not provoke her further, before he assumed his normal deferred posture. It suddenly occurred to me how new it was for him to be around when I was in trouble. I dropped my head for his sake, slumped my shoulders, oozed glumness and shame the best I could. It sealed the deal.

A few days later, Dad drove up to the house in a red-and-white Ford transit van pulling a small flatbed trailer, a turquoise blue hydraulic arm attached. The Taurus robot was cutting-edge technology in 1977. It was a back-saving device that enabled its operator to grasp heavy items by use of a remote control, allowing them to tilt or rotate pieces by 360 degrees, before setting them into place. I quickly developed affection for it as if it were a pet. I don't know if there was any formal connection, but I knew Dad's zodiac birth sign was the Taurus—the sign of the bull, which may have had zero relevance except for the fact that Dad clearly believed they were fated by the stars to be aligned.

We set off early on a Monday, taking Interstate 80, crossed the Mormon Bridge, and headed out of Omaha. Objects slid by: farmstead silos, barns and grain elevators, water towers with town names painted on their bulbous sides, rest stops, trucker's cafés, and exits with fast food—Kentucky Fried Chicken, Wendy's, Arby's. As we passed other cars, they reacted with a "what the hell is that?" look as if we might be pulling a large circus animal.

I couldn't help but feel a little like Laura Ingalls Wilder with Pa, as I thought of the technological progress we had made since pioneers drove Conestoga wagons through that high prairie grass. After the first hour of growing rest-less, I began my on-the-job training.

Dad told me if I checked under my seat I'd find a manufacturer's book that contained the locations of companies who produced steel products such as John Deere tractors, construction beams, and engine parts. My job was to identify any company that might fall in our route between his scheduled stops.

He then gave me a spiral notebook that featured teenage-dream hunk Harrison Ford, from the movie *Star Wars*. My job was to staple our receipts to the pages so that the tax man could see we weren't using the money to go to Tahiti, maintain a log of the miles we covered each day to show the government that we had used a car instead of a horse, and keep a journal, so that I could keep track of the deposits my father and I made to our joint memory account.

My induction over, Dad let me dither with the radio frequencies. We were so far in the boonies that I'd get a station dialed in just in time to lose it again. After the second hour, I complained.

"Dad, this scenery is so boring it's hypnotizing me." I couldn't imagine surviving ten days of this.

He grew enthusiastic. "That's a sign the trance is settling in—it's a good thing. A road trip is a state of mind, not a destination. My best ideas come when I'm looking out across those plains or up at the sky. I also find chewing gum helps pass the time." He reached into a brown paper lunch bag with a huge stash of Bazooka Joe bubble gum and tossed me a piece. "You have to read me the fortune."

"Dad! You must have one hundred pieces in there."

"Nah, fifty."

I unwrapped the waxy cartoon paper and shoved the rock between my molars, chomped down on it a few times, waited for the saliva to take hold. "You need the jaws of a cow to chew this stuff, Dad." I churned the gum a few more times while I read the fortune.

"It says, 'If your Mom says no, there's always your Dad.'"

"No, it doesn't say that."

"Yes, it does. Take a look."

"I can't because I'm driving, but stick it in here," and he opened his clean ashtray. "I always like to review them at the end of a trip. Let's open another one. See what we get."

I dug in, pulled one out, peeled back the wrapper with care so I wouldn't rip the cartoon, read it to myself, then groaned at its dryness. "Bazooka Joe says, 'Don't let anyone burst your bubble.'"

"That's perfect. Blow me a bubble. Let's see what you're made of." He watched the road with patience as I attempted to position the gum with the help of my tongue against the inside of my teeth. Once I gained a handle on the wad and gave it my best, I pliffed a small bubble, which then snapped.

"You can't rush it. The trick is chewing it so the consistency is even. And don't cross your eyes like that when you're blowing. You'll get a headache."

Eventually I blew what I thought to be a brilliant bubble about the size of a dime.

"Not bad," he exclaimed. "I see you have inherent talent." He made it clear it was important that I not mistake this coaching for an exercise in frivolity. I think he could still sense how deflated I had been and that I was in the throes of a serious adolescent crisis of identity. He wasn't going to let me drift without a fight, though. There would be no permission from him to adopt a loser mentality. The real lesson was never to set the bar of expectations low. I had perfected the double and was practicing the triple bubble.

After my jaw grew stiff from chewing, we were near enough to Des Moines to dial in FM radio, and Dad introduced me to National Public Radio. Finally, I spotted the exit exchange on I-35, the turn signal did its blinking, and we started navigating the wide boulevard of Grand Avenue into the city, the Taurus on its trailer bumping behind us, traffic lights punctuating our stops.

In Which Dad Hosts His Next Chautauqua

Interstate 80, 1977—We stopped in Des Moines for a quick visit to Katherine and Arlo's, after which we rolled east on Interstate 80. Before long we were nearing the Quad Cities on the Mississippi River, which brought up conversations about Huck Finn and Jim making their escape on a raft two hours south of where we'd be crossing. This launched a conversation about antiheroes—"Those people were naughty," Dad explained, "but you understand their reasons for breaking the rules."

It turned out that he was, in fact, prepping me for an introduction to his own crew of real-life antiheroes—truck drivers. I assumed that when we pulled into the next gas station, we were filling up, but it turned into something more than that. Dad didn't immediately go to the pump after he turned the engine off. Instead, after he jumped out of the van he started fiddling under the back seat like a man with a serious mission. When I asked him what he was looking for, he told me to hold on, then pulled out a black box that looked like it contained explosives, came around the driver's side, hopped in, and slipped it into an empty mount below the ashtray stuffed with Bazooka Joe comics.

"I didn't know if I should show you this, but I think I can trust you to understand the difference between right and wrong. And if we don't use it, this trip is going to take twice as long." And with that he presented me with a citizens band radio. I waited with my questions while he attached a handheld speaker by a black curly telephone-looking cord and screwed the two in tight, plugged the power into the ashtray lighter, turned the radio on, then fiddled with the dial. Static. "We'll find buddies when we hit the road. And if we're lucky we'll join a few of the boys and form a convoy."

He then switched off the CB radio and told me he'd explain in a minute, but meanwhile I wasn't to touch the power button—*ever*—when he wasn't with me. He made me look at him and cross my heart. And with that, he went around the car and opened the fuel tank lid and stuck the nozzle in. I sat there staring at the black metal contraption. And then almost like he picked up my thoughts through the airwaves, he knocked on the window, motioning for me to roll it down.

"I realize that wasn't a fair thing to ask," he said, standing there as the fuel hose got on with the job and numbers turned over on the pump. "I'm sorry, but a young girl can't just get on that radio—as long as truckers know who's on there, they're polite enough, but I'll need to introduce you first." And then he went to finish the pumping job.

This was new, this calling me a girl. His attitude as a father with four daughters had always been to let the world be our teacher, and at home there was no sign of gendered conditioning. He taught me to use a hammer at the age of six; a handsaw at age ten, when he let me help build our playhouse; and more recently he trusted me with the power saw when we built his office and family room in the basement. Not by myself, but still. I'd been mowing the lawn for years. He's the one who persuaded me to go for my paper delivery route—even though I didn't think I had a chance against the boys.

My gripe was interrupted when I saw him coming out of the convenience store. His arms were so full of snacks and soda pop that he used his butt to push the door open, before striding over con moto to the car with a roguish grin. He motioned for me to open my door so he could drop a week's supply of Hostess Pies and Coca-Cola on my lap. "If you want to look like me, you have to eat like me," he sang, before two-stepping it around the front of the vehicle and hopping back into the driver's seat. "Shall we blow this joint?"

Once we were back at coasting speed, Dad launched into the next Chautauqua. Before the CB radio could become the portal it was to a vast underground, there was background I needed to understand, really understand, if I was to grasp the challenges of his modern-day hero. Everything from food to oil depended on the underpaid and overworked truck driver. This led to a historical cross-comparison of job descriptions between cowboys and truck drivers, an introduction to the Teamsters Union, and the weaving in of American-made steel, which Dad always found a way to mention, for it was important I never forget that pillar of patriotism.

Impatient to turn the radio on, I tried to be polite by suggesting we were taking the long way round to the point of the story, but Dad said it was necessary. If I didn't understand how truck drivers made their money, I wouldn't appreciate the cultural institution he was about to induct me into or the economic genius of the contraption we were about to use.

He introduced me to the basics of CB banter. I'd have to have my own nickname—a handle. His was Blue Bull (for the Taurus, of course), and he suggested I might like Scout, as I had been reading him excerpts from *To Kill a Mockingbird*. "Breaker breaker one-nine," Dad started. "This here is the Blue Bull. Anyone out there—me and my daughter Scout are looking for a long-haul train today."

It took all of about thirty seconds before we heard from Bubba Ducky, who was "taking a load of spanking new cars to Columbus." And with that, the party began. Dad was an expert at teasing stories out of the guys about their families, joking about their rigs, finding out what they were hauling and from where, and using the fake southern accent that most of them used for some reason. There was nothing more exciting than watching a driver we'd been talking to for a good hour materialize behind us. They'd cruise by, pulling the string on one of those huge horns, and I'd excitedly jump up and down while waving. Once we had a convoy of eight trucks going, but the most common size of a train was three or four. Sometimes a driver would catch up with us just to see the robot on the back of Dad's van.

When I inquired about whether I could be a truck driver, Dad apologized and said it just wasn't a safe job for women, and when I said there's no reason a woman couldn't drive a truck, he said I was right, except it wasn't safe and he wasn't discussing it any further.

As we neared Philadelphia on our fourth night, Dad suggested we go see a movie. He really wanted to see *Rocky*. I voted for something more exciting, something other than a two-men-punching-each-other drama, but Dad looked so disappointed I didn't feel like I could let him down. Once we sat down with our popcorn and those huge letters R-O-C-K-Y started rolling accompanied by the sound of trumpets, Dad gave me a look, like he knew I could feel it too. They don't warn you about movies like this. The opening music score itself about knocked us out of our seats.

Rocky doesn't win the fight, but he does take Apollo Creed down, and makes the full eight rounds—beating impossible odds. But even more important, we see him win in love as Adrian beats her way through the roaring crowd in the end and throws her arms around him, his face smashed to a bloody pulp, and they embrace in joy as the music melts your heart.

Best of all were the training sequences that Dad and I were bonding over in our mutual adoration. Rocky rises before the sun, laces up his high-top sneakers, puts his gray sweats and hood on, downs a few raw eggs, and steps into a dark winter morning sky. The fear on his face is as visible as the frost on his breath. You now get it—this guy isn't a loser: he's massively depressed.

I couldn't figure it out. How was it that this huge big guy, Sylvester Stallone, could make me, a thirteen-year-old girl, feel like him? Like Rocky Balboa. Dad and I ended up giving the movie a standing ovation and threw our arms around each other at the end. Whatever kind of team we were before that movie—it was nothing compared to what we were after. Before leaving Philadelphia, we took the Rocky run up the stairs of the Philadelphia Art

Museum, bought ourselves a fresh pretzel, and then got serious about seeing New York City, only a couple of hours away.

It was dark by the time I caught my first glimpse of the Statue of Liberty, from a distance over the Hudson, the Manhattan skyline glittering in the dark like a huge Christmas village. I just about hyperventilated with excitement, reacting in the way you might expect a kid who had grown up on the edge of a cornfield to react—electrified at the fabulous spectacle in front of me.

I could tell my enthusiasm was contagious, and I started laughing so hard I became light-headed. As we entered the Holland Tunnel and then emerged in downtown proper, I bounced up and down in my seat asking Dad where we were going first. Then impressed him by firing off the list of neighborhoods I had learned by heart after ten years of watching the televised Macy's Thanksgiving Day Parade.

As we approached Times Square, Dad started singing, "These little town blues, are fading away . . . ," before he stopped short, told me to cover my eyes, and when I asked him why, he said there were just some things a young woman didn't need to see, which of course was an excuse to open my eyes and get a glimpse of what he was trying to prevent me from seeing.

"How come you didn't want me looking?"

"Well, I suppose maybe thirteen years is old enough to understand, those are ladies of the evening."

"You mean prostitutes? I know what prostitutes are, Dad." Actually, I had no idea what prostitutes were, as much as the moral reaction the word provoked. From the quick glimpse I managed, these ladies looked more like stars out of Broadway.

It was the crown jewel of the trip, New York City. Dad put the hammer down as we headed back west, shaving hours off our travel time, since all the factory sales calls had been made. We planned one last stop at the world's biggest truck stop in Walcott, Iowa. The view was impressive as we pulled in, the parking lot a massive village of semitrucks. I took my time eating my last stack of buttermilk pancakes before we hit the road back to Omaha, and felt like a mopey little monster the rest of the way home.

As we pulled up in front of our house and climbed out of the car, my father leaned over and put his arm around my shoulder. Gave me a tight squeeze. "I'm so lucky to be your dad." Then he ruffled my hair.

I stored that one. Deep.

In Which We Meet a Gas Attendant

Omaha, 1978—Mr. K pulled into the gas station at Fiftieth and Dodge, about five minutes away from my house. I noticed the lights on the forecourt were on, and evening was beginning to fall. There were two full-service pumps.

"Hey," Mr. K said, like he wanted my attention and was reading my thoughts. I looked over and noticed his hand in his coat around an object. "This is a gun. Don't do anything stupid." The gun might have made me fearful if I hadn't already been terrified of being stabbed. He told me to look straight out the window, and if he saw my head turn, "Then you know what." He said it with a particular angry glare through his ski mask, like you'd tell a badly behaved dog on a lead to sit. I went numb. Nodded like we were on the same team.

In what was the slowest minute of my life, the attendant emerged from his perch behind the register and pushed his way out the door. I watched my potential rescuer *so* carefully, hoping he might give a sign that he had registered the danger of my situation. Instead, he came around the front of the van to the driver's side, approached Mr. K with an almost earnest cheerfulness, rubbed his hands and blew into his fingers as he waited for the window to go down. When Mr. K requested two dollars' worth, he said "sure" like "hey, no problem—happy to help," all folksy. As if the sight in front of him was normal, a guy in a balaclava sitting next to a young terrified girl.

Mr. K rolled the window up. Turned the radio back on. My heart thumped so hard I thought I was going to cry. I eyed the door. How real was the gun? I looked over at the attendant, thought again about screaming but felt choked. I understood then. The attendant wasn't indifferent. He was afraid. I watched desperately as he knocked on the van window, signaling he'd finished filling the tank with two dollars of gas. The window went down. Cash was handed over. "Happy Thanksgiving," the attendant said, then waved us off with a little hand gesture. He might just as well have dropped a trap cellar door on me.

"Now," Mr. K said, turning the corner, "we've got a phone call to make."

In Which I Contemplate Rebellion

Omaha, 1977—Dad returned to his normal routine after we got back from our road trip. I pined for him like a pup. His promise of being around disappeared as quickly as he did—instead of three days a week in Iowa he was spending closer to five. He'd leave on Sunday night and wouldn't get back until late Friday. And to make matters worse, we had to put Zorro down due to old age.

I dealt with my grief by retreating into my room on the third floor, whose location was prime real estate under the conditions. Mom could never make unannounced visits—I could always hear her coming up the stairs. She told me it would take time to heal the trust I had broken over the summer, so we hadn't resumed our late-night study sessions. It was her second year of classes at UNO, and she had taken to drinking Coca-Cola as part of her new lifestyle, making it clear that the sugar-sweetened caffeine boost was not for us kids to drink. One day, however, I saw a nice cold glass sitting on the table in the living room with ice cubes and, being an independent thinker, or a thief, couldn't resist helping myself to a few gulps.

Ten minutes later, I heard her calling me from the base of the stairs. She asked if there was any chance I had helped myself to some of her Coke? Of course, I said no. Then she asked me to come down the stairs and look her in the eye, and then tell her again I didn't drink her Coke, which I did with no problem at all, and she said, "I believe you because out of all my girls, you are the one who I know doesn't lie." I think she was alluding to my Christianity, and I was sure it wasn't a compliment.

I went back up to the third floor and shut my bedroom door, feeling anxious, not because I just lied, but because everything about her was off. She was in one of those moods—I could see it in her cold eyes.

About half an hour later, I heard her raised voice through my floorboards. I realized she was in Jenifer's room, and it didn't sound good. Creeping down the stairs, I saw my two younger sisters through the half open bedroom door and froze. Mom's belt was meeting flesh. I heard her say she'd be back in fifteen minutes and the liar better speak up. She didn't acknowledge my presence when she finally walked by me, went into her bedroom, and shut her door.

I went into my sisters' room. Their cheeks were wet with tears, but they weren't crying. Gayle was ten years old, Jenifer six. I looked at the back of their legs—Mom had flayed the skin. I went to the bathroom and threw up. Then I reached into the medicine cabinet and grabbed some hydrogen peroxide to blot the blood and fetched ice for their welts. None of us spoke. We waited for my mother to come back, but she didn't. She stayed in her room for the rest of the evening. After my sisters fell asleep, I lay awake all night. I was so ashamed at being a coward—which might explain what happened next at school.

In Which I Try My Hand at Boxing

Omaha, 1977—There was a gang of five bullies who particularly enjoyed dominating the rest of us in physical education class. We divided along racial lines, as was normal. That day's exercise entailed running up and down the length of the gym, which was two full-sized basketball courts. We had to touch the floor outside the taped line at one end, then sprint to the other side and do the same.

One of my meeker friends, Julie, had difficulties coordinating the speed it took to touch the floor before turning back. I was just finishing a sprint when I saw Bessie, who held the esteemed position of chief bully, trip Julie, who fell, her face hitting the floor. As she stood and picked up her broken spectacles, blood dripped down her cheek. She was being remarkably brave, but she was in tears as she left for the infirmary. The next day she arrived at school with four stitches in her cheek.

The following week, we were told to practice volleyball serves by forming into circles and having someone stand in the center and serve the ball. As usual, the teachers then disappeared to wherever it was that they disappeared to. Bessie appointed herself as captain. She served the ball. We all took turns bumping it back, our forearms pressed together, wrists up in volleyball batting position. Things were going well until Bessie reached Mary Hobber, a girl heavier than most, with short, frizzy red hair and large round cheeks. Bessie smashed the ball at her face with a speed that even the most skilled of us would have had trouble returning, and Mary, clearly terrified, ducked. Bessie served the ball once more, harder, and again, Mary failed to make the return. This occurred several times, Bessie increasing the force with which she was throwing the ball. Giving up, Mary shielded her face, and we all stood in our fourteen-girl circle, ashamed at our cowardliness, frozen by fear to change it. I looked around for a teacher, but they were still absent. There wasn't an adult in sight. So I blurted it out. "Haven't you had enough fun?"

The gym went quiet. Bessie turned around and scanned our faces. "Did someone just say something?"

"Yes," I said, too far in now to back out. "Don't you think you've had enough fun?" One of Bessie's friends, a small, skinny girl, slapped her knees in laughter. Bessie looked at her, then at me, then at her, and seemed to decide that yeah, it was kind of funny, so she smirked, and then threw the ball at the next person. When she came around to me, she was of friendlier demeanor. She served, I returned, and she moved on. The whistle blew, and we saw the teacher, Mrs. Flores, enter the gym to tell us that class was over.

"Okay, put the balls away, girls, and follow me."

I noticed Bessie talking quietly to a group of her friends, and I grew nervous as she sauntered in my direction. We filed out of the gym and piled into the hall, where we waited for Mrs. Flores to unlock the door. Suddenly, Bessie's hands were around my neck, and I was pushed against the wall. While I was grasping at her hands, Mrs. Flores blew her whistle and yelled "break it up, girls" without so much as turning around. Bessie released me with a look that assured me we weren't done. At that point, my friends cleared the way so I could push up front. I didn't make it three steps before I felt the gang on my back, kicking my legs and punching my head, as I was slammed against the locker doors. Bessie swung at my stomach before moving to my head and then aimed at my face. My survival instinct kicked in, and I hit back. I thought it would be clear to anyone I was acting in self-defense. But Mrs. Flores didn't see it that way. She rounded the corner in time to see me land a kick that sent Bessie flying backward. We were sent to the vice principal's office.

As we walked down the hall, Bessie asked, with the anxiety of a younger sister, what I thought they would do with us.

"I don't think it will be so bad," I said.

"Are you going to snitch on me?"

"Nope," I said. It became a bonding moment, this walk. Vice Principal Andes came out of his office looking like that detective in *The Mod Squad*, his Afro beautifully shaped, wearing a loud flower-printed silk shirt under his jacket and a styling pair of bell-bottoms. He had to be the coolest-looking VP ever. He looked at us, alternating between my swollen eye and Bessie's bloody lip.

"Who wants to go first?"

Both of us shrugged shoulders. He flipped a coin. Bessie lost. She was in for about ten minutes and then came out pouting. We seemed to have lost a small bit of the camaraderie established in the hallway, but there was no sign of the bully I had seen in the gym. Mr. Andes told her to stay put while he spoke with me. Bessie plopped down in the chair I had been sitting in and folded her arms. I followed the VP into the office as he shut the door behind me and offered me the chair in front of his desk.

"So, Debbie Cackler," he said, folding his hands on his lap and rocking back in his chair, smiling and then smoothing his mustache out. "Looks like you took a couple of punches." We both laughed like it was something he respected. Like I had survived in the ring. "So tell me what happened," he asked, leaning back in his chair.

After I finished telling him the story, he said he was going to have to suspend us both, because even if I didn't think I did anything wrong, I had—by challenging her in front of everyone. I had another choice. I should have gone to the teacher. When I pointed out our gym coach wasn't around, a normal state of affairs it seemed, he said he was really sorry, this is just the way it had to be. When I defended myself again by saying I didn't attack her, he said the gym teacher saw something else. I said that something else would have been self-defense. I respect that, he told me. But I still have to suspend you. Coming from Mr. Andes, though, I couldn't take it personally.

After Bessie and I were kicked out of school for a week, a curfew was issued. Students were warned against loitering on school grounds or at the nearby shopping mall after hours.

This was because of a racially divided gang fight the year before, which started after two boys squared up in the hallway. A fight had been organized for later at a parking lot at Crossroads, the nearby shopping mall. By the time police arrived, one student had been hit by a crowbar and ended up in intensive care, and a knife had been brandished.

When Mom came to pick me up and saw my face, she asked me what happened. I told her. She asked me if I hit the girl back. I said I kicked back to get her off me. She said I would have had her permission to beat the crap out of the girl, and then forgot about the incident the minute we walked in the door.

In Which Dad and I Have a Man-to-Man Chat

Oxford, 1997—Dad, after hearing that I was having a difficult time with the seizures and was adjusting to medication, called to ask if he could come visit us in Oxford. It would just be him. Mom wasn't quite up to a trip yet, and then he added, oddly, that they had agreed in couples counseling that it would be okay. I took it as his way of notifying me things were changing.

When he arrived in Oxford, he was more buoyant and happier than I had ever seen him, like someone who had climbed out of a basement bunker after living there for decades. He told me he was looking forward to a five-day fitness camp and wanted me to bring it on. We had put in a lot of running hours together in my high school years, when we would hit the high school gym at six A.M. before anyone else would arrive, and put the *Rocky* theme on the boom box while running the bleachers.

Before we got out the door, Dad realized that he had no running shoes, so I took him down to the local sports store. After I had regaled him with how I had used a heart-rate monitor to pace myself during the London Marathon the year before, he purchased one too so I could train him to do the same. After a good aerobic warm-up, we started out from our house in East Oxford, ran down Cowley Road, across Magdalene Bridge, and circled over to Christ Church Meadows, an expansive formal park that sits at the back of a row of the older colleges, bordered also by the River Cherwell. Dad noted that the spires looked like they were trying to outpoke each other into the sky. His mixture of admiration and awe for the architecture renewed my own excitement over the buildings and their beauty, and it was like we were instantly back to that elevated place he could take me, where the real world felt like stage sets we were running through.

We jogged over to see Thomas at the field where he was playing Frisbee, before heading down the towpath along the River Isis, rowers in their boats speeding past, coxswains yelling orders, blowing whistles in prep for a regatta. That's where I told him that after four years of marriage, I was intentionally and delightfully pregnant.

"Really?!" He beamed and threw his arm around my shoulder. "I have to tell you, kid, you two had me convinced you were serious with that Couples Against Kids Club. Is it still safe when you're thirty-three?" I assured him everything was okay.

That night we took him down to Mario's—a small Italian restaurant in East Oxford—owned by an ebullient elderly flirt who was often generous with his Sambuca and loved nothing more than a good party. He and Dad became instant pals, and I couldn't help but react with pride when Mario pulled up a chair to join us at the table.

Dad told him that Thomas was his son-in-law and he was to be a new grandfather, and Mario called for another round of drinks for all remaining customers. I wanted to point out that I was his daughter, and pregnant, too, but with all the male bonding that was going on, it would have seemed like poor sportsmanship.

After the merriment died down and Mario returned to work, the conversation moved on to child-rearing. The three of us, without knowing it, were negotiating the terms of how we would interact now that the next generation was on its way. Dad was eager to share what he had been hearing from Dr. Laura, a conservative radio host commentator, about kids and respect. I was about to ask him when he had started listening to conservative radio, but was stopped when he made an offhanded comment about Genie, my elder

he had just popped the tab on a shaken

sister, cutting herself off from the family, like he couldn't fathom what had gotten into her. "Really?" I balked.

The last time I saw Genie, she was home from college for Christmas. We were in her bedroom, and she was shaking a book at me written by Alice Miller, a preeminent expert on child abuse, called *For Your Own Good*, demanding that I stop normalizing Mom's child-rearing techniques. As she was throwing a book argument at me, I offered a relativist's perspective—Mom was doing her best. The book literally hit me in the nose from across the room.

All three of my sisters and I were in full alignment when it came to our painful memories of Mom, but our strategies in dealing with her damage were different. Our sisterhood bond, made especially strong by the trauma we survived, helped the four of us navigate our differences, but in the end it wasn't enough. Genie's estrangement took time, and when she cut herself off from the entire family, Gayle, Jen, and I couldn't help but feel we had done something seriously wrong. Our grief for her was raw. So for Dad to pass this off so lightly was unusually insensitive.

While I was thinking these thoughts, Thomas jumped in. Maybe comfortable after all that male bonding and drinking, he came straight out and asked my father if he was aware of how differently my mother ran the house when he was traveling. It was as if he had just popped the tab on a shaken can of beer. I couldn't help but be slightly awed by the guts of it, but still, the loaded awkwardness following the question was excruciating.

Dad went quiet. I watched his face as he mulled the question over in his mind. There has to be a kind of permission granted from a parent before agreeing to a job review by an adult child, let alone her husband. In addition, he had always made clear throughout my life that he genuinely believed there was no benefit in exploring the past, that it implied shame and weakness of character. Yet there was something different about this moment. This day. He looked at me, giving me the silent approval to go on, encouraging me to say what was on my mind. But having the emotional courage to break a taboo of a lifetime isn't something one does in an instant.

I ventured delicately. Tested the water. I reminded him of the harm he himself saved us from, the winter when she had locked us in the garage. He nodded, giving me permission to continue. I assured him there were many more incidents that I could dredge up, if needed. "But do you really need me to provide examples, Dad? I'm not talking about her psychotic attacks—like the knife attack, or even that day in the garage. I'm talking about the day-to-day fear of living with her—her rages, the things she would say behind our backs, the shaming, her 'tough love,' the drama, her drinking. She was and sometimes still is completely different when you aren't around, which was 80 percent of the time."

"Yeah, I know. She was young and ill-equipped to be a mother. I should have never left her alone that often."

"Dad, that's no excuse for the behavior I'm talking about, or for who she became. She's never been interested in growing or changing. Why should she, when you insist she's the victim?"

After a long pause, Thomas asked Dad if he ever thought of removing us from her custody, leaving her, protecting us.

"I honestly still have a problem imagining it was as bad as you are saying. I'm not denying it, I'm just saying I never saw it."

I looked at Thomas, pleading for him not to say more.

I could see Dad thinking it through. "We were both young. Of course I thought about leaving her. Everyone does at some point in a marriage. But if I had, I wouldn't have had a chance of getting custody of you kids. You remember that movie *Kramer vs. Kramer*?"

He was looking at me now. "This was the 1970s. Even if I found a sympathetic judge, I couldn't take care of four small daughters and work. And I would still have had to support her. You don't just get rid of a wife. And I saw the damage your grandparents' divorce did to her, even permanent damage. I didn't want you girls suffering a broken home."

As I listened to him talk, it sounded like he was rehashing a legal opinion and wondered if he had actually paid for it. It was beginning to sound like he was admitting he knew there was a serious problem.

He changed tack and began pointing out things I might not have considered, like how much better we were served by him earning a decent income. How we had a bigger house, a nicer neighborhood, well-resourced schools, great teachers, and family vacations. I had to imagine running that logic through the emotional filter of him being an adopted kid for me to appreciate his point.

"Dad, my concern isn't who she was then, it's who she is now." How was I supposed to trust her when, instinctually, I found myself recoiling when I was around her? Dad had no idea. Worse than the past pain of our hurtful relationship, Mom and I had no relationship to hurt. She had found reason to reject me, time and time again. I would have taken it personally if she hadn't done the same with my sisters. But Dad was shutting the conversation down, falling back to the new party line after her six weeks in hospital, that she had changed substantially since then.

He wrapped up our conversation by saying he'd made a vow. And at the end of the day, he had a duty to take care of his wife. He was thankful for the cud chewing and couldn't wait to see what Day 2 at fitness camp had in store.

As we finished the evening, it was clear Thomas wasn't nearly as impressed with Dad's response as I had been. But I was so happy to be with Dad, I was desperate to get to the other side of that conversation.

In Which I Learn Respect

Omaha, 1977—It was a Sunday, the morning I heard my mother call my name. I thought if I hurried I might be able to help her before the mood escalated to red alert. As I opened her bedroom door, I inhaled lingering cigarette smoke.

"Am I right in thinking that laundry is your responsibility this week?"

This was, of course, a rhetorical question.

"Yes—sorry. I did it, but forgot to bring it upstairs."

"Isn't that a part of the job? Folding the clothes and bringing them upstairs?"

I let her words bounce off me and stared at the ceiling fan. In other words, it would be fair to say that on one level, I provoked her.

"You know out of the four of you girls, you are the only one that seems to think your life is more important than anyone else's. *Our* lives do not revolve around yours. When do you think you might find time to bring the laundry up?"

I'd like to think I made a good show of strength and said something like "Maybe next week." But I can assure you whatever my exasperated snarky juvenile response was, it wasn't that creative. It quickly became clear I had just asked for a beating, and she told me to get her favorite implement of choice for such an occasion—her belt—and then did her best to effect within me a transformation of some kind. Respect? She struck my head, she struck my neck, she struck my upper back, became more and more enraged when she could not produce a sound from me. I think I might have even heard her grunt. I suddenly realized what this was. Barbarity.

When she exhausted herself, I turned around, looked at her widely dilated pupils, her sweaty lip, and almost felt empathy for the animal in her. It was here I discovered my superheroine powers of detaching pain from emotion and emotion from the body. And it was here I finally set my mind against her, that I recognized a me that could not accept her. I asked her if I should put the belt away for her. She instructed me to leave the room.

Three weeks later she raised her hand to me for "mouthing off." I told her if she touched me, I'd slap her back, and then walked away. It was the last time she ever physically threatened me.

After that, I began feeling guilty for the loathing I carried for her, and I resented it almost more, this emotional duplicity. It was important to me to be a good person, a generous person even. I had feelings of loyalty toward her, was wired to love her. And I needed her to love me. I couldn't let go of the fantasy that if I did the right thing, tried harder, some day she would see I wasn't the manipulative, controlling, self-centered, immature, untrustworthy person she wanted me to think I was.

Simply put—I hoped I wasn't transforming into the criminal she had me down for being. Or Darth Vader.

In Which We Drop By for a Big Mac

Omaha, 1978—Mr. K picked up on my drop in mood; his tone changed too. "Let's go find a phone," he said. "I want to see what kind of man your father is," and we pulled away from the gas station. We drove ten minutes without speaking. It was pitch-black now, and traffic was picking up with drivers who hadn't left work early to beat the storm.

Mr. K turned into a McDonald's at a busy intersection on Center Street. I saw him looking at a pay phone booth, the type with a folded hinged door. We were also close enough to the street that I was able to see the faces of drivers sitting behind their steering wheels as they waited for the traffic light to turn. I couldn't believe I was in clear view, so near to so many people yet totally helpless.

"Don't try anything," Mr. K warned as he turned the motor off. And in a blur of movement he was out the door and on my side of the van, yanking me out. He put the knife to my throat again. "Now walk," he told me, pinning my arm behind me. I struggled not to lose my balance, as I looked around me in helpless horror. No one seemed to notice this masked man dragging me into the phone booth at knifepoint. We were close enough to the store window to read the prices of the Big Mac and double cheeseburger on the menu board inside.

"You okay?" he asked, concerned as if he were my babysitter, after he had shut the booth door.

My teeth were chattering. I nodded, the steam of my breath visible in the glare of the lights on the glass, streaked with tiny water rivulets. Rain was still falling half frozen, and the wind was bitter.

"Call your father and tell him that I need ten thousand dollars, and that he better give it to me." He took a glove off, reached into his pocket for change, shoved a dime into the phone, and handed me the receiver.

"Dial."

In Which I Become Captain Kisser

Omaha, 1977—When it came to the game of girls and boys, I seemed to have no problem with attention, but the freedom to pursue any kind of kissing games outside school hours was thwarted at every turn by my mother. Boys were banned from our house—and coed parties were not allowed until the age of sixteen, two rules that in retrospect seem not so unreasonable. But as a teenager living under the weight of her tyrannical moods, I was convinced with all my soul that this draconian measure to prevent adolescent trysts seemed unbearably unjust.

I cruised through the sixth and seventh years of school with plenty of exchanged notes and flirtations, and even a few public declarations of mutual adoration without consummation of the relationship by a kiss. But then Jack arrived, the first boy who made his affection clear, in a way that suggested I might be missing out if I didn't manage to find a way to be together outside school hours. He invited me to a party being thrown by a friend of his.

Perhaps it was the two years of moping and crying and moaning about all the other kids who were allowed to attend boy-girl parties, but for some reason, on this one, I managed to wear my parents down. They said I could attend the party as long as no alcohol would be present and the parents were home. It seemed a respectable enough agreement. And easy enough to break. The parents of the boy hosting the party would be home, but they couldn't care less about what was going on in the basement—and though they told my parents there would be no alcohol allowed, the boy's eighteen-year-old brother supplied plenty.

Jack and I ended up on a waterbed making out after I had three beers. I had never felt anything so delicious in my life. He covered my neck in hickeys. I went home and once again made the mistake of telling Gayle, for the same reason I told her about smoking a joint. I felt it was important as her older sister to blaze trails for her.

A few days later, I was at a friend's house when Dad made a rare appearance to pick me up. On the ride home he asked me if I had really gotten drunk at the party they had allowed me to attend. We sat in silence. I had never seen him so angry.

When I walked in the front door, Mom's eyes were full of rage. My lack of reaction no doubt infuriated her further. She announced I was grounded for a month. I was happy to confine myself to my bedroom for the rest of the evening.

I passed Gayle wincing on the stairs with an "I am so sorry" look. I knew she was clueless, incapable of keeping a secret. I told her it wasn't her fault. When I woke up on Saturday, keeping my usual teen hours, I came down to grab some lunch. Dad was leaning against the counter, Mom at the table.

"Tell your daughter I can't stand being in her presence," she said.

Dad and I looked at each other. She was serious, but it had that particular brand of over-the-top-ness that made it impossible to take seriously. Out of my mother's view, Dad raised an eyebrow, and I gave him our secret sign, then acted as if I had made a wrong turn and headed back up toward my bedroom. Halfway up the first set of stairs, the phone rang. I heard my mother tell whomever was on the other end of the phone that I no longer lived there. I tried to imagine which friend she had just embarrassed, all of mine being the polite kind.

Dad went out of town on Monday, and I went off to school, relieved to be free from the relentless noise that was traveling through my nerves and into my head. I thought for sure Mom's mood would blow over in a couple of days, but the silent shame treatment continued throughout the week.

When Saturday morning rolled around, I overheard one of the neighbors whom I regularly babysat for at the door, telling Mom she was dropping off the money she owed me and asking if I could help them that night. My mother, intent on her campaign, said I wasn't available because I was grounded for drinking. It had the effect she hoped for, as I came down the stairs, hoping to interrupt her, but the neighbor had left. Mom threw the eight dollars at me. "There's your drug money. You're not responsible enough to babysit." I picked the bills off the floor and climbed the stairs, humiliated.

That night all I could think about was my Sunday reprieve was close. I was still quite active in my church: youth group, choir, Sunday school, Sunday service. It was a serious activity for me, like a sport—I trained regularly. Some of that had to do with convenience of location; the church we had joined was right across from my junior high school parking lot, so I wasn't dependent on my parents to get me there.

But it was also because the teenage youth program at this church was unusually strong, no doubt because of its progressive outlook. We'd talk about things like feelings in our youth group retreats. The youth choir was popular due to the choir director, whose name was Mel Olson. He was in his fifties, wore saggy jeans, a beard, and high-top sneakers. Just the choir itself had one hundred teenagers, ages thirteen to eighteen, the cool kind you'd want to hang out with. Besides offering excellent vocal coaching, the director organized a singing tour.

We traveled by bus through the Badlands in South Dakota, stopping in shopping malls, then over the Grand Tetons in Wyoming, hitting a series of retirement homes, before dropping down to Utah to visit a Mormon church, and then heading back over the flat panhandle that is Nebraska, stopping at Native American reservations along the way. At night we'd camp, perform skits, and tell ghost stories around a campfire. It was actually easier to score booze and marijuana if you wanted it there than it was at school.

On Sundays, I usually caught a lift from a couple who served as youth group leaders and lived nearby. Church was the place I'd get my inner equilibrium back. My community there was bound to help me sort my feelings out, figure out what I could do to make it right. But that morning, I woke up late and missed the ride. The house was oddly quiet, which is perhaps why I over-slept. When I came downstairs, there was a note waiting, saying the family had gone to a movie. I don't think our family had ever gone to see a movie together.

I ran back up to my room and sobbed. I couldn't imagine how long the confinement was going to continue, how much more I could take. It had been near ten days now, long enough for it to start feeling like the new norm. I knew Dad was leaving the next morning, and true to form, he hadn't dared inter-fere with the management. He'd never say it, but we knew it—it wouldn't be worth the scene Mom was assured to create.

The worst of it was that I had been wrong to drink, and it was worse that I lied about it. That made her 100 percent right and me 100 percent wrong. She was right to be angry. But not for two weeks. As I began reorganizing my room for the fifth time, I found a leaflet in a pile of papers they had given us at a youth church seminar. It said, "Ever Feel Like Running Away?" It was a brochure on a halfway home for teenagers called the Walt Whitman Center. They advertised a counseling hotline and said they provided a home away from home for troubled youth.

I dialed the number and explained I felt like running away like it said on the leaflet. The woman on the line kindly explained that kids were usually placed there by the state after they had broken a law. So I explained I had broken the law, and after a brief hesitation, the counselor said yes, I could come. There was one thing, though—I would have to tell my parents where I was going in person. She asked, did I feel I could do that?

When Dad, Mom, and my three sisters returned from the movies, I was waiting with my suitcase at the bottom of the stairs. I explained to my parents that I was going to the Walt Whitman Center, that it would probably be best for all of us, and asked if they could give me a ride.

"You're running away and expecting us to drive you?" Mom smirked in disbelief. She was actually stunned, yet at the same time amused at my audacity.

I looked at Dad and told him I'd be happy to call a cab.

"Listen to that, Jim. She's happy to call a cab." Which I did.

And so I voluntarily turned myself over to state custody to be "rehabilitated" with other juveniles who were making their way through the Nebraska State penal system. I was surprised when we pulled up to find myself at a normal house in a neighborhood in easy traveling distance from my school. It was one of those Sears and Roebuck catalog houses: four large bedrooms upstairs and a warm cozy living room downstairs with a good-size kitchen.

The next morning, I caught the city bus to school and arranged for rides to and from church activities. A few friends knew of the change, but the center had made the transition effortless. Group counseling sessions were held at four-thirty P.M., and everyone in the house was required to attend. We had a couple of hard drug addicts, a dealer, a prostitute, a teen mother, a kid who robbed stores, and a car thief—all aged between thirteen and sixteen.

We were allowed to smoke, the one concession to an otherwise strict code of regulations including rules about curfews, house chores, language used, respect, fights, and any kind of sexual contact between housemates.

The general mood between staff and kids was one of mutual respect. A lot of the conversation involved the jargon of Narcotics Anonymous, a recovery program for drug addicts, and Alateen, a support program for kids affected by someone else's alcoholism. For the first time in my life, I was hearing stories that reflected my experience at home with Mom.

Though I wasn't guilty of breaking any serious laws, my problems were taken seriously. I was made to feel my choice in asking for support was wise, and not a way of denying responsibility for my behavior as my mother claimed it was. No one was laughing at me for packing my bags. And the staff became more empathetic when Mom came in for the family therapy sessions.

After five weeks, they told me that I was reaching the limit of my allowable stay. I was going to have to go back home or choose another option—foster care. I started to grow desperate. Just when I was beginning to feel what it was to have my own emotional equilibrium, free from the threat of Mom's next mood, I couldn't believe I was going to have to go back to living under the same roof as her.

I started breaking the rules. I cussed, I made out with one of the housemates, and finally I came home two hours past the five P.M. curfew. But it didn't work. They had no choice but to call my parents to come pick me up. I didn't care. My mother was thrilled when she was called. I had just proved again that I was definitely on the road to criminality, that the rules held for everyone but me. Even a court-mandated halfway home was kicking me out.

In Which I Ponder a Father-Daughter Connection

Oxford, 1997—Six months after Dad returned home from our visit in Oxford, I got a call from Mom, telling me Dad had checked himself into the psychiatric ward at the hospital for depression. I choked.

"What happened?" I asked. "Was there some kind of episode?" He had seemed so perfectly happy in Oxford.

Mom said he just woke up and asked her to take him in. And then she shared that they diagnosed him with bipolar disorder, that he wasn't going into any intensive therapy, they were just holding him until the medication had a chance to kick in.

It occurred to me, looking through my adult eyes, that this wasn't the first time Dad may have been clinically depressed. But manic? I was just recently with a friend whose illness was on the manic end of the spectrum. I'd never seen Dad approaching this hyperactive state of mind.

"Did something happen to trigger the depression?"

"No, he just said he was seriously depressed, so I told him we could take him to the hospital."

I thought back to the conversation we'd had at Mario's, but making his breakdown about our Oxford dinner conversation teetered on grossly self-centered.

"I understand the depression, Mom, but what cause did they have for the manic-depressive diagnosis?"

"Well, you know, he's been impulsively buying things."

"Like what?"

"He bought that old army jeep. Then there was the John Deere riding mower. And let's not forget the time he bought three vans"—she paused—"on the same day. Did he tell you about that? And then there's the time he went out for a walk and came home with a pregnant mare he bought from a farmer he had met in a field. And there was all that running gear he bought in Oxford. Weren't you with him when he did that?"

I suddenly wondered if Mom had been providing input to the doctors and I grew irritated. In defense of my father, it wasn't like he made all these purchases in the last couple of months—he had acquired them over two years, and there was sensible logic behind each.

The army jeep had only cost five hundred dollars and had nostalgic value, bringing back good times in the service.

The John Deere "Made in America" tractor mower—well, that had been a fantasy as long as I had known him, a sort of homage to all the guys at the John Deere factory he used to work with. He was older and spent a lot of time in the garden, always had, and mowed the lawn religiously on Sundays. So what if it was overkill for the size of his lawn?

The van? He had told me that day on the phone it had been a sloppy process, but it's not like he kept all three. He just kept changing up for a better deal, and it just so happened all on the same day. If he hadn't been successful in taking the first one back, he would have never dreamt about returning the second when his real dream vehicle drove by with a For Sale sign on it. He saved himself ten thousand dollars. He wasn't being ruled by his impulses, he just had more courage than most to correct his mistakes. At least that's how I remembered it.

And the horse? The owner didn't think he could sell her pregnant and needed her moved. Dad told me he offered to help him out with sales skills, and after running the numbers decided it would be a good investment.

"And then there was the inflatable boat," Mom said.

"What inflatable boat?"

"The one at the condo."

"What condo?!"

"Didn't he tell you about the condo?" She told me that she had found a vacation condominium near Myrtle Beach in South Carolina that was a dream property investment. She had hired a management company to rent it out when they weren't there. It had been her idea. I believed her. That Mom was smarter than Dad was obvious to everyone.

"But when has he been manic, Mom? I've never seen him manic." Well, maybe there was that one time . . .

In Which My Father and I Share Notes on Depression

Washington, D.C., 1986—In the years after I left home at eighteen (an abrupt departure, I might add, as Mom, in a dramatic scene of Shakespearean proportions, insisted Dad kick me out or she'd leave), I would occasionally call my father at his office for a little coaching, a self-help recharge. It was like we'd pull over at a highway rest stop to pause for a moment.

As I no longer had to contend with Mom's moods at home, I found Dad's skills as a life coach of great value. Three-ring-binder tape cassette courses had replaced his collection of self-help books, and he'd listen to them on his sales trips across the Rust Belt. Driving through Illinois, Michigan, Ohio, and the western part of Pennsylvania provided lots of listening hours. He had moved from the Stoics to their modern counterparts. He could have taught Dale Carnegie's Leadership and Sales Training Course without referring to a manual, was able to cite all the greats—Stephen Covey's *The 7 Habits of Highly Effective People*, Zig Ziglar's *See You at the Top*, Tony Robbins's *Awaken the Giant Within*. Our calls would bring me back to our childhood Chautauquas.

If I wasn't in the mood for self-help, he'd cheer me up with his corny humor or a little karaoke. He'd sing the background line to the Blue Swede's seventies pop song "Hooked on a Feeling"—"Ooga-Chaka-Ooga-Ooga." It developed into a game where we'd try to zap each other. Dad—"I was talking to a union guy at the Pittsburgh plant the other day, and we were discussing the talking points he'd use to recruit members. Those guys have a job cut out for them. You would have loved the conversation. You'll never guess what he said to me." "What? What'd he say?" And then he'd zap me by singing "Ooga-Chaka-Ooga-Ooga."

Though I could always count on him to veer wide around history, he'd go deep in the present with practical questions. How was I sleeping? Was I avoiding the drink? (I never did manage my alcohol well, so I made the pragmatic decision to quit when I was twenty-two.) How about exercise? It never crossed my mind that we might be sharing notes on mutual depression.

One day a package arrived. It was a Walkman with a cassette of the *Rocky* soundtrack inside. I also found a scrawled note in his handwriting, recalling our time in New York, reminding me of early morning winter runs up the wooden gym bleachers, suggesting I use the theme song, "Gonna Fly Now," to power me up the U.S. Capitol stairs. On another occasion he sent a letter that, when I opened it, spewed hundreds of those little dots cut from a hole puncher.

Then there was that time he called me. He asked how things were going. I gave him the background brief, waiting for the real reason he called. He shared that he had finally run for town mayor, and that my mother had left him— both in the same sentence. She had been "friendly about it," he said. "You know, she was never happy here in Laurens, and I didn't listen. It's my fault and I deserve it." And then he added the zinger, "If I'm honest though, it's not so bad. I'm kind of enjoying being on my own."

It wasn't said with full-hearted enthusiasm, yet I heard a mighty crack. My father had never said one thing that would suggest anything but absolute loyalty to my mother, and though he was careful to take responsibility—"I deserve it"—the "it's not so bad . . . I'm kind of enjoying being on my own" phrasing meant we might finally be free to negotiate the terms of a more honest relationship. It was clear it hadn't occurred to him that the real reason

Mom left was because she had her own behavior she didn't want brought up for public scrutiny.

He went on to tell me that Mom had moved north thirty miles to Emmetsburg, the town where her job was located. This forced him to reexamine what he was doing with his life, to make a few big decisions.

He was leaving his company, selling his shares, putting the house on the market, and the reason he called was to ask if there was anything I might want. He was holding an auction for everything Mom left behind. I thought about it, my emotions catching up. My bedroom had been dismantled long before, my lion poster disposed of, and my books were with me, so the answer was no. Finally, he shared the real kicker.

He had bought himself a brand-new Honda Gold Wing motorcycle that had room enough to strap a dog carrier on the back—for his newly adopted rescue sheepdog, Ralph. He was taking off west to California, a dream he had had since he was thirteen. He hoped I understood.

I tried to match my tone to the ease of his. I didn't want to scare him with my wild enthusiasm and respect. Sure, Dad. Did I think he was awful? No, Dad. Granted, it sounded a little unbalanced, but he was at an age when a midlife crisis provided positively levelheaded reason for blowing up one's life. I put the phone down, chanting "Go, Dad, Go."

Two months later, Dad called again. He had moved to Indianapolis following a "fateful moment in Nebraska." A fateful moment? "A moment of great epiphany," he called it.

He told me on the second night of his journey, he was camped out in a cornfield under the stars, cuddled up with Ralph. He was contemplating his trip west, where booze and wild women waited, when suddenly the sky began to cloud. He continued to contemplate the lifestyle in front of him, the lifestyle he had dreamt of since thirteen and opted out of at twenty-two for fatherhood, marriage, and the American Dream, but then—it began to rain. And rain. And then it began to storm. And it was under this cascading heaven that he was suddenly seized with the absurdity of his situation.

There he was, a forty-five-year-old man, his four daughters having grown, with a wife who had left him after begging for ten years to live in a town that had a major highway within fifty miles—drenched and cold, hugging a soggy mutt.

The next morning he woke, covered with corn pollen, to a fresh early dawn, turned south to join his cousins who were running a Bible camp for juvenile delinquents, volunteered for a month, and moved to Indianapolis to start over, a humbled man. I imagined his silhouette appearing back over the horizon on his Gold Wing—the dog in goggles behind him.

It was shortly after this that Mom moved to Indianapolis, and the two of them picked up where they left off.

In Which I Consult with the Philosophers on Mental Health

Oxford, 1997—So, yes, I had to give it to Mom—there was that one period of Dad's life when he may have been manic. Or it may have been a courageous decision to free himself from an unhappy life, followed by a fear reaction. But whatever Mom was trying to imply about him being fiscally irresponsible, Dad's monetary management was admirable.

He'd made a financial comeback, even though he was forced to sell the home where they had invested all their savings at a time when the rural Iowa economy had collapsed. The number of farm foreclosures around Laurens had been brutal, and even grain and corn transport had moved to trucks after the train stopped coming through. Within three years of setting up his own industrial sales business, he was out of debt and back in the housing market and, as I just heard, had bought a vacation retreat.

Meanwhile, my mother had retired and was enjoying three months on a private beach with a balcony view. I asked her if Dad's "manic spending spree" of two years might be a disagreement about doodads, not cause for a bipolar diagnosis. She greeted this with silence. But it was important. I had nothing but respect for her mastery at dialing up our feelings of mental instability. But rather than pick a further fight with her about Dad's medical diagnosis, I asked if I'd be able to speak to him at the hospital if I called. She provided a phone number.

Before dialing, I thought about Dad's broader picture, the larger stresses. His parents, Katherine and Arlo, were no longer able to live on their own and had recently moved from Des Moines to an assisted care unit in Indianapolis. Dad stopped in to see them before and after work. Even then, my grandmother, who was suffering from dementia, would sometimes call Dad as many as five times a day. Meanwhile, his mother-in-law, Vivian, had just undergone chemotherapy treatment for cancer, and he had remodeled two bedrooms into comfortable in-law quarters for her after she had to leave her apartment in Washington, D.C.

Mom hardly left the house. She did the bookkeeping for the business from home and spent endless hours playing solitaire. I knew Dad's greatest sense of joy came from playing the role of second father to his grandson, who was living with Gayle in a house across the street. And to add to his responsibilities, his business was growing. He had eight full-time staff whom he managed.

If I was worried about him before I called, I was devastated when I spoke to him. He didn't sound present. In fact, he hardly appeared to understand what I was saying. He shared that he was taking sodium valproate, the same drug I was on, but double the dose, and said he was sleeping a lot. He thought that he'd be going home soon. It was like talking to a sad robot.

I hung up the phone feeling thoroughly down, and spent the next week painstakingly crafting an eight-page, single-spaced anti-psychiatry rant, pleading with him not to let them convince him his strengths—his instincts, his creativity, his *joi de vivre*—were weaknesses. I shared with him everything I had learned about the mind-body connection, about diagnosis, when and why the *Diagnostic and Statistical Manual of Mental Disorders* was helpful, and why the insurance companies needed it. I provided a list of reading material of my top fifteen thinkers on the subject. Threw a few R. D. Laing books in there, even a little Nietzsche. I wanted to heal him, fix him, fight for him—for us. Mostly, I told him I loved him and he wasn't weak. He just needed time and sleep. And I still couldn't help but think the answer was so simple—if he would just leave my mother.

But the agreements two people work out in a lifelong marriage aren't always apparent to those of us who watch from the outside. Maybe it was time I began to support their decision to remain together. After all, their marriage had survived continual dramatic episodes that played their way out through hospital depressive wards, couple's therapy sessions, pharmaceutical drug regimes, and other practices that aided the late twentieth-century institution of marriage.

As I dropped the letter into the mail, it suddenly occurred to me I'd spent so many years being scared of turning into my mother—that there might be another reason, other than our soul-felt connection, that I was my father's daughter.

In Which I Make the Most Important Sales Call of My Life

Omaha, 1978—I listened to the different tones as I pushed the telephone buttons, registering that Mr. K's pupils were hugely dilated. It rang. Dad picked up with his usual work greeting, "Jim Cackler," and any last bubble of denial I had was pierced.

"Hi Dad, it's Deb." I felt the huge soul-wracking sob of my heart breaking.

"Hey, where are you? Are you at a friend's house?"

My heart was hammering in my ears. "I've been kidnapped, Dad." I wanted to spare him as much pain as I could while throwing a reassuring look at Mr. K, who had the nervous energy of a kid who had drunk twenty coffees. "The man needs ten thousand dollars." It came out unexpectedly light, like I was asking for a chocolate bar. The sudden change in Mr. K's pupils made it clear it wasn't the gravitas of delivery he expected.

"Where are you?" Dad said, on the edge of getting impatient. "I've been worried—I've been on the phone, calling everyone I could think of."

I continued, trying to keep confident, raising my eyebrows and holding eye contact with Mr. K—like I was a trainee looking for an approving nod.

"No, Dad, I need you to understand I am standing in a phone booth with a man who has a knife at my throat and . . ."

"Tell him this is no fucking joke!" Mr. K contributed.

Dad's silence made it clear he had overheard, but it was too late. I sucked back tears. "Dad, I know this is difficult to believe." I began to tremble. "If you want to see me again, you are going to have to get this guy some money."

Mr. K grabbed the phone, the muscles of his brow flexed in fury, and I immediately shrank, expecting a blow, my shoulders up to my ears as he yelled into the receiver.

"LISTEN ASSHOLE, THIS IS REAL. THIS IS SERIOUS. IF YOU WANT TO SEE YOUR DAUGHTER ALIVE, YOU BETTER GET ME SOME GODDAMN MONEY." He slammed the receiver on top of the box as a display of he-man force.

It was clear he now had Dad's full attention, and as Mr. K spelled out his instructions, I began to understand I was immaterial to this transaction, really—that it was my father this man was most interested in—that I was of no importance other than simply serving as an asset, the leverage to ensure the deal took place.

He instructed Dad to bring the money to the Center Shopping Center parking garage, ground-floor level, in thirty minutes. He added that if my father called the cops, he would track him down and kill him, too. At this threat, my heart nearly broke with fear. He slammed the phone down. "Now we're going to see what kind of asshole your father is."

Calling Dad an "asshole" felt like a physical punch, and it raised my protective instinct. I wasn't able to feel ferocious long. When we returned to the van, he told me to get on the floor behind the driver's seat. When I asked why, he told me to shut the fuck up. He put a burlap bag over my head and tied my hands. As he resumed driving, I told myself we would be at the shopping mall soon and that Dad would have the money and then Mr. K would let me go and I could go home and it would be over. But as we continued to move, I noticed the lights were getting dimmer, that traffic was becoming thinner. It shouldn't have been that way. We should have been moving toward lights, or at least staying on illuminated roads. But it was getting darker, and it was getting quieter. I heard the van's motor underneath me as its gears shifted, and we started slowing down, and then I felt the bumpiness of a gravel road. We were no longer on cement, and I wanted to throw up. The van stopped. It was quiet, no sound of traffic and no light, even from a distance.

"Where are we?" I asked.

He didn't answer. He came around and slid open the van door, took the bag off my head, untied my hands, told me to get up and sit in the passenger seat.

"Turn your back against the door," he ordered.

I did as he said.

I could see the whites of his eyes as he stared at me through the holes of the ski mask, heard his breathing. He seemed to be enjoying the fear he provoked. I looked down, too terrified to look at his face. We were next to a brick building that was illuminated by bright lights somewhere in the distance. I noticed graffiti on the wall. I fought back tears. I wondered why we were there and told myself we were waiting to give Dad time. But then he instructed me to take my jacket off.

In Which I Ponder a Rural Idyll

Omaha, 1978—Several months into what was meant to be my third and final year at Lewis and Clark Junior High, the ninth grade, Dad called a family meeting. He declared he was missing us all, and he was tired of being without his girls. I almost felt sorry for him. Then he joked that it would be safer to raise four teenage daughters in the middle of nowhere, as there would be less temptation to get into trouble. And in the same jokey, chatty tone, he announced that we were all moving to Laurens, Iowa, in January.

"What the hell?!" I cried.

"Debbie-Doogan, don't cuss."

"You can't be serious. January what? 1979? You can't be talking about this January. That's four months away."

"Yup."

"Are you kidding?" I got up and started pleading. "I've been there, remember? It's in the middle of the biggest hole in the state of Iowa, and you know I'm not exaggerating. Are you trying to end my life? The nearest movie theater is forty miles away."

I looked at the rest of "Dad's girls" for some support. No one was saying a thing. The only noise was the tick-tock of the grandfather clock.

I looked at Mom. What was she going to do about law school? She had just been accepted to Creighton University in Omaha. Even though it was her achievement, it was about me, too. Helping her study, even with her drinking, was the one way I had found we could be together. I felt empowered by her example. I had picked up her passion for politics in the same way I picked up her love for Jesus the night she brought him home. And she was giving it up. There was no sign she felt disappointed at all.

Gayle and Jenifer were just picking up on Dad's feigned excitement. They had no idea what they were being deprived of yet. Genie wasn't saying a word.

"January?!" I cried in further disbelief. "Can't we at least finish the school year out?"

"I'm sorry. The decision has been made."

"I've got human rights, you know."

Mom chipped in then. "If you have another family that will take you, then go for it."

In Which I Enjoy My Last Day of Childhood

Omaha, 1978—The morning of November 22, 1978, I boarded the school bus at seven-thirty A.M. on Leavenworth Street, no differently than I did every other morning. As I climbed in, holding my Hinky Dinky grocery bag, our driver, Bev, a woman in her sixties, asked me where my hat and gloves were. "What do you want to do, die of pneumonia? And zip up that coat." But I couldn't because my zipper was broken. Although the National Weather Service had warned about a storm with record-breaking temperatures on its way that morning, it wasn't even freezing yet.

Bev was just one of those people who always had an opinion to offer. But the only thing I cared about that morning as Bev recited her daily platitude was whether I had everything I needed. It was Picture Day, a seriously important day, with no shortage of reasons. Imagine, for instance, that this photo might be needed for television. If I was to become the first woman president of the United States, or a serial killer, they would need a picture to project on the blue screen behind the news presenter.

There was a high probability that this would be the only photo of me taken at the age of fourteen. Though my parents had a Kodak Polaroid camera, they rarely took pictures because they never thought to buy film or flashbulbs.

So now you might understand what was at risk this day, and why, while Bev the bus driver was warning us about the perils of prairie living, I was counting everything I had in that bag on my lap, which included the outfit I had planned all week, my curling iron, and a comb.

Later, I stood in my English classroom with my thirty other classmates, reciting the Pledge of Allegiance. Before we began class, our teacher reminded us it was the fifteenth anniversary of John F. Kennedy's death. And even though I had no reason for it to feel personal, I felt a sense of grief. I looked out the window and noticed the sky had turned so dark that the streetlights were flickering on and off. I looked up at the teacher, who was writing notes for that day's lesson on the blackboard, the chalk clicking against green slate as my classmates worked on the assigned essay. Every hour or so, a voice would boom over the intercom like some Orwellian Big Brother, directing all those whose last name started with *G* to *J* or *P* to *T* to the gymnasium to have their school picture taken. Since I was a *C*, my turn came early.

I was relieved, as I wanted to get it over with and was concerned about my feathered hair. I stopped in the bathroom for a quick fix with my curling iron. I stuck the plug in, grabbed my bangs, rolled them under, pushed the steam button, then brushed them out to the side with the big-toothed handle comb. Then I snuck on a little mascara that I borrowed from one of the girls doing the same thing I was. Arranged the fashionable cowl-neck I was wearing under my dark green sweater, pulled the tights I was wearing under my light green gauchos up from inside my high-cut brown leather boots—it was a sort of cowgirl look. I glanced at myself in the mirror and wondered what my family and friends would see. I thought about the picture being in the yearbook, when my classmates signed the back with platitudes like "May the sun always shine on your face and the wind blow on your back" and "May you find happiness wherever you go."

Feeling awkward and overly self-conscious, I left the bathroom and headed toward the gymnasium. There, I found my place in the picture line, filed through, took my spot on the wooden crate with the blue backdrop, and, after the man tilted my chin up to the perfect angle, smiled.

"Hold it, look into the camera now, that's it, SMILE." Flash explosion. It was done. Looks and age on that day captured forever in time.

After my picture was taken, I headed back to class for what was the longest day of my school career. It was impossible to focus, as it was also the last day before our four-day Thanksgiving break. When the bell finally did ring, I walked back to drop my things in my locker. Wednesdays were the day I got to meet my favorite teacher, Kent Friesen, for the weekly math tutoring session, but he wasn't there, which was unusual for him. I found a bag of popcorn on his desk instead and a note lying next to it. He apologized and said he had been asked to fill in for a referee who couldn't get to the wrestling match, then left a funny scribbled face with its tongue stuck out. I drooped on a stool, ate the popcorn, and licked the salt off my fingers while thinking ahead to my next move. Choir practice didn't begin until four P.M., so I decided to check out the wrestling match taking place in the school gym.

On the way down the hall, I saw Ken Sorenson, skinny with a brown shag haircut, freckles, and bell-bottom pants. He told me he was going to the Crossroads Shopping Mall to buy tickets for the upcoming Kiss concert. Going to the mall sounded better than going to the wrestling match. I asked if he would mind if I went with him.

"Sure, no problem," he said enthusiastically.

Ken zipped up his gray down winter jacket, pulled his wool hat over his ears, put on thick leather gloves, punched his fist into his hand, and swung his arms as if to say, let's go. And then I caught a glimpse outside. It wasn't snowing; instead, it was doing a weird rain/sleet/flurry combination, and there were signs of ice. I had no hat, no gloves, and a coat that still would not zip, so I began to think twice about the plan. The glass doors opened and the wind hit. It was cold enough to freeze a flying bird.

But I thought myself indestructible at this age, as one does. I shoved my hands into the pockets of my thin coat, brought my shoulders up to my ears. The parking lot was like an ice-skating rink, so we walked like Frankenstein's monster. Once we reached the top of the hill, I sat and slid down the slope. Even the blades of grass were covered in ice. Ken flew ahead of me, laughing and flailing his arms in every direction. We finally reached bottom, waited for the traffic light, crossed the street, and arrived at J. C. Penney, where they sold tickets. It felt unbelievably good to be warm again.

Ken pulled the cash from his pocket when we reached the ticket counter and carefully counted out single bills. He turned and grinned at me, the grin of a fan's victory. He was heading home, so we said our good-byes. After I wandered around the mall for another twenty minutes, it was time to go back for choir practice.

I walked through the ladies department in J. C. Penney with stacks of sweaters and neat piles of pants, caught the escalator. I remember the smell of leather and perfume. The automatic doors opened, and I was hit with a warm blast from a grate underneath the door, then wind and sleet. I could see the church—all I had to do was make it up that hill.

In Which I Meet a Dark Night

Omaha, 1978—After Mr. K was done with me, he gave me my shirt and gauchos back, tied my hands, covered my head with the burlap bag again, and pushed me into the space behind the driver's seat. Lying there on the metal floor, I began to tremble, my teeth began to chatter, though it wasn't from the cold. The keys clinked against each other as he placed them into the ignition, turned the alternator, revved the engine. Backed out over crunching gravel. The van turned. I could see lights again. We were in traffic.

I reached into that place where prayer would take me, but felt none of the comfort I would feel when clasping my cross; the personal nature of my relationship with God—any feeling of spiritual connection—was gone. Several moments later I felt myself falling into a trancelike sleep. I felt soothed by a warm comforting light and then came a flood of images—of the many people who loved me throughout my life, of a community going as far back in my childhood as I could remember, a web of connection that held me. My body lost all feeling of weight, and I felt light enough to float. I had no idea how long I spent in this state, but after some time the spell was broken by a horrid smell. The air was suddenly thick with the unmistakable stench of stockyards, the Omaha stockyards. We weren't nearing the Center Shopping Center where we were meant to meet my father; we were in the wrong part of town. The van slowed, turned, stopped. I could just make out the glow of a streetlamp in the distance through the burlap. Mr. K rolled the van door open.

"Please, don't leave me here." I said it calmly, with warmth, with confidence that I would reach that part of him that would save us both. It conveyed nothing of my growing panic. I picked up a lull in his thoughts.

"Sit up." He said it in a softer tone, as if he were relieved, glad even, to hear me speak.

"I can't—because of the way you've tied my hands." I struggled to demonstrate. "Please." I couldn't help it then. I began to cry, to sob, "Please, please don't kill me."

Another silence. And then again, another shift in mood. "It's okay," he said, growing awkward with his expression of care as he moved toward me. "I'll come back for you." He touched my shoulder, told me to reach up with my bound hands, then helped me up—the perfect gentleman.

But I was certain that the minute I stepped out of the van, it would be the end of my life. I'd learn later the temperature had dropped to twenty degrees, and the wind chill was even colder. If he didn't intend to murder me by force, the cold would do it. He put my coat over my shoulders and helped me step out of the van onto the ice. The stink from the cattle yards was so fierce I fought to control my gagging reflex. I was shaking so badly from the combined shock and cold, I didn't know how long my legs would hold out, and I still couldn't see. I felt gravel under my feet as he pulled me down a long narrow corridor, a distance of what felt to be about one hundred yards. We stopped. He positioned me up against something solid.

"Don't move. I'll be back in fifteen minutes." I nodded. I could make out his silhouette through the burlap bag, looking, thinking. I anticipated the final finishing move. But it didn't come. Instead, he turned, and I listened as his footsteps faded away.

A few minutes passed. My trance broke. A new kind of terror filled the silence. I tried not to panic, but the pressure of the freezing temperature felt as if it were driving into my chest. The moisture in my eyes and nose stung. The smell of manure was so pungent I could taste it. If I moved, the jacket hanging off my shoulders was going to fall. My body began to shake. I stood tall, slowly, the first movement I had dared since he left, listened for footsteps, for any kind of clue of him. I saw what looked like a wall, screened through the fibers of the burlap bag. I guessed it was a couple of feet in front of me. I could make out some kind of corridor. I heard the gears of a truck shift faintly. How close was I to a road?

As I stood there, I began to calculate my odds—the choice to live wasn't entirely mine, the choice to die not so straightforward either, though it became increasingly apparent inertia had its own outcome. If I moved, how far could I get?

I prayed. "Lord, please help me." Nothing came back, the worsening silence growing more horrific. "Please God," I began again, reaching a little deeper, "Is anyone out there?!!" At last, I heard the rattling sound of a semi-truck, but not even close. "SOMEONE PLEASE HELP ME!" It rumbled away.

I revisited the reason I was waiting, then the task of leaving. This raised the painful truth as reality sank in. My standing there, praying, screaming, waiting for a grand rescue wasn't going to help. It wasn't as if Dad could suddenly appear miraculously, trudging his legs through snow as he worked his way up the hill like he did that day in Lee Valley. I was utterly alone. So hopeless that even the increasing odds that Mr. K had, in fact, left didn't make things easier. God wasn't going to intervene—not to save me, not to comfort me, or with intuitive guidance.

I grew wildly confused as my own stupidity began to sink in. I thought back on how earnest I had been in my efforts to save this man, how convinced I was that cash would solve his problem. I even told him God was certain to forgive him for abducting me. The irony that I had been taken from my church parking lot, because of my dogged determinedness to make choir practice, made it worse. My rage erupted. I screamed into the night air—WHY? And was greeted by nothing but the starkness of my broken voice. I began to kick behind me in fury and helplessness until pain surged up my leg, shocking me into reality. And then I let out a huge, heart-wrenching, body-wracked wail, screaming out the Lord's name one last time so deep from within my

soul that something in me cracked. It was over, as if a metaphysical empti-
ness swallowed the whole of my spirit.

At this moment of complete physical depletion, Dad's image surfaced,
flooding me with that love only he could make me feel. I pictured Mr. K's
anger in the phone booth and remembered his threat to kill my father if he
called the police, grew angry again at the audacity of the man to call my father
an asshole—I had no idea what Dad would do, but if Mr. K wasn't here, there
was a good chance he had gone to meet him. I became overwhelmed by fear
for Dad—I had to do something to protect him. Again I felt Dad's love for
me, undeniable, solid, a rope hold out of this nightmare.

I began to move, pushing against desperation and fear that I had wasted
too much time. That Mr. K might already be at the Center Shopping Center.
It occurred to me to rub the burlap bag off my head by scraping my forehead
against the wall. Soon I had the bottom of the bag above my eyes, and I
could see. I was next to a railcar, not a wall, between a train and a loading
dock. A streetlamp shone at the end of the corridor, about three railcars
away. I inched forward, leaning my shoulder against the train for balance;
the ice beneath my feet was patchy, not solid. Eventually I could see a trailer
office about fifty yards away, and a woman. She was locking the front door.

I checked both ways to see if the van was anywhere in sight, took a deep
breath, and swallowed what felt to be the whole of my childhood before I
stepped into exposed space.

In Which I Enter Stage Left

Omaha, 1978—The woman walked to a car in the parking lot, and I started making my way toward her. She looked up, graciously put pieces together before I had the words out of my mouth, and helped me into her trailer office. I remember her calling the police, then loosening my hands enough that I could take the phone.

I told the officer on the other end of the line that I was fourteen and I had been kidnapped. A man had forced me to call my father and ask for a ransom and was now on his way to meet him. He said he was going to kill Dad if he didn't have the money and that he would be coming back for me, and told me if I moved he'd kill me, too.

The police operator asked how long it had been since he'd left. I said I didn't know—maybe twenty minutes. He asked for my location, and all I could say was I was close to the stockyards. The woman who rescued me picked up the phone in another room, said she could take it from there. After putting the receiver down, I remained staked out in the chair, looking for the swish of lights that might signal Mr. K's arrival.

I could tell then, I was different. I didn't feel a thing.

The night air soon filled with the glow of flashing red bulbs. The officers quickly came through the door, and I again explained the situation with my father. The officer in charge was kind, in his mid-thirties, gentle, not awkward, confident, but clearly concerned for my pain as he had to ask further questions. I assured him I felt strong, okay, the only thing I cared about was my father's safety. He told me Dad was safe, that he contacted the police right after my phone call. The whole department had been working overtime in their search for me.

I found out later that the kidnapping had been broadcast on the television news, that 85 percent of children who are abducted by strangers in violent sex crimes are killed within five hours, and that I had crested the curve.

The officer in charge shared encouragingly that I'd see Dad soon, but first we had to wait for another patrol car to arrive. In case the man driving the van came back. Did I think I could do that? Yes. Could I tell them what happened? I didn't hesitate; I started at the point I headed to choir practice, told them I was walking through my church parking lot, the pain of God's abandonment the only thing that slowed me as I provided details of my captivity, skipping over the physical attack, which resulted in a pain I could not comprehend at the age of fourteen. One need only look at me to understand the nature of the assault. The officer sensitively told me I could stop if I needed to, affirmed how brave I was being, but the state of trauma I was in allowed me to continue as if I were talking about a normal day at school. When we finished, he expressed a deep respect at how well I had done. Asked if I was okay to ride with him and the other officer in the squad car to the hospital, where my parents would meet me. Did I think I could do that, and I nodded and said yes, thankful for his kind voice. It felt as if something big and exciting was about to happen. They assisted me to the police car, and as we drove away, I looked out the window at all the lights and the humans and the cars in the darkness. It had been three hours since I was at school.

When we reached the hospital, several staff members were waiting for me at the sliding glass doors and took me directly into a private room, protecting me from the view of strangers. A kind nurse stayed with me, told me my parents were on the way. I begged her to tell me where the bathroom was. She looked at me as if her heart were going to break and asked me if I could hold on a little while longer. I asked for a glass of water, but again, she explained it would be better if I could wait. I still remember the pain on her face. And then a minute later there was a knock on the door. It was Mom. Her face was white. She looked scared, young even. Clearly hesitant to approach me.

My heart sank. "Where's Dad?"

"He isn't here yet. And I wanted to check to make sure you wanted to see him."

I struggled to understand what she was saying. Looked over at the nurse to see if she might help.

"Because, honey, I thought you might be scared of men." She paused.

There was a knock on the door, and the nurse stuck her head out. "Your father's here," she said, smiling. "Shall I show him in?"

A few seconds later Dad stepped in the room. The joy I expected to see wasn't there. I grew self-conscious, wondering how I must look sitting there on the medical table. I hoped not like the half-slaughtered calf saved from the stockyard I felt. Dad's face was serious. Almost businesslike. After a delayed response, he came over and wrapped his arms around me. I found myself not only wilting in spirit but swallowing his silence, adopting his same numbed state, mirroring his emotional cues: the alternative, recognition that he was not able to parent me at the greatest moment of need in my life, was too painful to contemplate.

Mom did us a favor by interrupting our sad sack of a reunion. She told Dad the doctor was waiting, and she needed a minute with me. I watched as what was left of my heart walked out the door. Dad. That was Dad. And that was the worst hug of my life.

Mom asked if I was certain I wanted to see the doctor, assured me I could just go home, that I didn't owe an explanation to anyone. Again, I didn't understand. The nurse knocked on the door. I told Mom I would be okay. She left, the doctor came in. The invasiveness and blinding pain of the procedures were made worse by how badly I needed to use the bathroom, but the tenderness of a nurse who held my hand throughout gave me strength.

When I returned to the lobby after we were done, I noticed several police officers talking with my parents. The one who seemed most senior in rank approached me, smiled gravely. Did I feel able to be strong a little while longer, he asked. They needed to find this man, and I was in the best position to help. I answered yes with such confidence that he looked surprised. He then asked if I'd be comfortable going with two of the officers, if I could help them retrace the route in their car. The questions they needed to ask could be difficult to answer. We could stop at any point if I found it too much. And Dad could follow behind us in a squad car. I agreed, so numb it required no effort.

When we went to leave, I glanced back at Dad staring into the distance and watched as a police officer gently touched him on the arm to indicate it was time to go.

I climbed in the back of the four-door sedan, behind the steel cage. They asked if I was hungry, and a bag of french fries appeared. A chocolate milkshake followed. We were at the McDonald's where Mr. K had called my father. The salt of the fries tasted delicious. The heaviness of the chocolate milkshake soothed my stomach. I was in a police car, and I was warm and safe with the taste of salt on my tongue, and I liked the police officers I was with, and I thought of nothing but sharing as much information as I had. As I began to talk, I was amazed at the amount of detail I could recall, not just the spot where he had picked me up and the direction we drove, but traffic intersections, street signs, trees we had passed. I was able to direct them this way and that, with a confidence of something practiced one thousand times.

The officers asked, as we were pulling out of the site, if I had ever ridden in a police car before. I told them no. They asked if I would like them to turn the lights on, the siren on. I said yes. We pulled into the road like we were on a chase. The whir of the siren overtook my senses, the winter darkness filled with a pulsing red glow, on-off, on-off, on-off. When the siren stopped, it was work time again. We were at my junior high school, Lewis and Clark. A couple of light poles illuminated the parking lot, swirls of snow dusted the ice, and sporadic wind gusts shook the car. My church was right in front of me, but when I looked at it, it was void of any feeling of familiarity.

Soon after, we were back in my neighborhood, driving down the street toward our house. The police officers turned and told me again how brave I was being, what an amazing job I was doing. It felt good to help. We were all sad to say good-bye, as a real sense of comradery had been formed in that short time.

Looking back, I feel sorry for that kid coming home. And for the dad at the police station giving his own statement. We'd have our moment. I knew it, but I didn't know when. I'd tell him then. His love for me saved my life.

In Which Charles Goes for a Burger

Omaha, 1978—After Charles left the girl, he drove the two miles to the Center Shopping multilevel parking garage to meet her father. As he pulled into the complex he saw no sign of anyone standing by the doors holding a suitcase, but as he cruised by the second level he spotted a couple of middle-aged guys positioned aimlessly inside the entryway. Would the father have had time to go to the police? He continued up the ramp to the third level. After he parked the van and headed toward the stairs, a security guard approached him.

"Hey, do you own that green van?" the guard asked. Seeing Charles wasn't quick to respond, he offered, "The lights are on."

Charles recovered quickly, said no, he was just waiting for a lift from a friend for a ride home. Then he asked the security guard if he could give him a dime so he could call his friend who was supposed to be picking him up. He was proud of that move. And while the guard stood there acting like he was doing his job, scanning the garage, Charles dialed a random number. A woman answered. He faked a conversation with her, telling her he couldn't wait that long, he'd walk. And that's when he spied a convergence of police cars pulling in on the ground floor. When he turned around, he saw that the security guard had walked off. Charles took a flight of stairs down. He wasn't getting a good feeling. Given what went down with the girl, he was in a lot more trouble now.

When he reached the second floor, he could see that the two men were still hovering around the inside of the doors of the shopping center. He needed a new plan. It was too risky to go back to the van. He could walk over to the bus stop. Damn, it was cold, though. Too cold to be standing around outside, so instead he made his way up the hill to the Veteran's Medical Center, entered the glass doors, and took shelter in the front lobby while he warmed up. Ten minutes later, three guys entered. They looked like plainclothes police to him. He watched them as they passed and went upstairs, so he went downstairs to the canteen. As he stood there thinking about how he might get some food without any money, he noticed the officers had come into the cafeteria. Something wasn't right. They were definitely searching for someone. They looked right at him though and then kept scanning the room. He was relieved when they left. He was so hungry he couldn't think, so he walked up to McDonald's on Fortieth and Dodge where his friend Valerie worked. He knew she'd give him a burger. After finishing his meal, he walked home. The van, the girl: history.

Preacher Paul was sitting in front of the television when Charles walked in. "Look at what some crazy guy did to a poor young girl," the Reverend said. "Thank God she's alive." Hearing his dad talk about him in the third person like that—it freaked him out.

In Which Reality Hits

Omaha, 1978—My eyes opened. It was four A.M. My heart was racing. I was short of breath. I couldn't shake the feeling of there being a thin layer between my mind and the room. I blinked, hard. It didn't help. I couldn't feel my body. Time was out of sync. I realized I was in Genie's bedroom, in her bed, and she was trying to comfort me.

I don't remember speaking as much as I remember being horrified at the nightmare I was recounting and the dawning realization it was all real. I'm not sure how or when, or after what passage of time, but eventually we fell asleep.

Later that morning, the six of us got into the station wagon to drive to my grandparents in Des Moines for Thanksgiving, as was the plan. We sat in silence the full three hours. The sense of family cohesiveness we had on our road trip to Florida disappeared long ago, and it wasn't going to magically resurrect itself now. The roads were covered with melting slush. My grandmother greeted me at the door with a long hug, which said all the words we'd never exchange. I had a tear on my face when Arlo said grace at the Thanksgiving meal. I could only stare at the pearl onions in cream sauce. I looked at the purple bruised marks on my wrists and wondered how long it would take for them to go away.

Later that evening, Arlo moved the mattresses from the basement into the living room so my sisters and I could sleep upstairs. The house went dark. Quiet. I lay wide awake, listening as the clock in the living room struck each quarter of an hour. At one point Gayle whispered, "Are you okay?" and I replied, "Ahum." She asked if I could tell her what had happened. Feeling protective after sensing I had traumatized Genie the night before, I told her she didn't ever want to know.

The day after Thanksgiving, Mom asked if I wanted to go shopping at the Merle Hay Mall to buy a new coat. It was Black Friday sales day. And then I remembered, of course! I needed a new coat. My old one with the broken zipper had been kept as evidence. Mom steered me to the outdoor section, pulled out a feather-down jacket, and suggested I deserved a white one. I couldn't equate losing my virginity with the pain that night—I was blind-folded and had had no experience to give me even an idea of what had happened to my body. But Mom smiled. I looked at the white puffy coat. Why not make her feel good? And then she held up a cute teddy bear. I'd never been into stuffed animals—I'd always preferred my comfort objects in abstract form—Jesus, Mr. Octopus. And then I remembered they had both been rendered meaningless by Mr. K. I took the bear.

Arlo had purchased tickets for me and my sisters to attend the Ice Follies. I knew seats were expensive and hard to get, so when I was asked if I still wanted to go, I said sure.

We were dropped off, the four of us—Genie, age sixteen, Gayle, twelve, Jenifer, eight, and me in my new astro-psychic form—at the front entry to the sixteen-thousand-seat venue and off we went, circumambulating the arena's concrete halls until we found the tunnel leading us to our seats. I felt trapped between two surreal worlds, a state that became so much a part of me that within a week I no longer responded to the fear or anxiety it triggered. But on that day, less than forty-eight hours after being left alongside that railcar where I chose life over death, I was stuck in that dark auditorium, laser lights sweeping and swishing across thousands of faces in rows, paralyzed in the chokehold of terror. As dancers skated in with their sequined costumes, I responded to the pageantry of lights—the ones that flooded me with helplessness as I stood in the phone booth with Mr. K: the red, yellow, and green of changing traffic lights, the headlight beams, the luminous faces of drivers aglow from dashboard lights, the customers in the blaze of lights at McDonald's. Other than my face being damp with tears, I had no idea what I was feeling—but I do remember what I was thinking. I was thinking I didn't understand a goddamned thing about humans, and desperately wished Arlo had purchased tickets to the circus instead. Watching trained animals would have been more comforting.

In Which Charles Smells Turkey

Omaha, 1978—Charles slept the death of angels that night. The next morning he woke up to the smell of roast turkey. He rolled over and checked the time. It was ten A.M. And then he remembered the events from the day before.

He got up and wandered out to the kitchen, but after finding no one in the house sat on the couch and flipped on the television. He was looking forward to the Macy's parade. He liked watching those Rockettes. And then he saw the newspaper lying on the coffee table in front of him, began immediately leafing through the pages. There was a story on page 5, he could have easily missed it: POLICE SEEK RAPE SUSPECT. Wow. So the girl was alive. That was lucky. He hoped. He read the police were conducting an extensive search. He wondered what an extensive search entailed. The article said a security guard had spotted "a suspicious looking man" on the second level of the Center Shopping Center parking garage at six P.M. They had him as twenty years old—that was good. It meant no one would be checking juvenile records, and they wouldn't check for a high school student. At least she never saw his face. Now he had to hope she didn't remember his name— what the hell had he been thinking by telling her his name.

They had the amount of money wrong, too. They said it was a couple of thousand dollars. Why the hell would he go through all that trouble for a couple of thousand dollars? And they also made it sound like their little session happened somewhere near the shopping center. That was weird. These journalists should get their facts right.

In Which I Learn God Is Dead

Omaha, 1978—On Saturday we left my grandparents' home in Des Moines to return home. The senior minister from the First United Methodist Church, Dr. Holston, called that afternoon to ask if I would like to meet after church. I had attended services for almost three years but never had reason to talk to him personally; my direct relationship was with our junior minister, Rebecca. The request felt appropriate, though, like the announcement of a funeral.

Mom said she couldn't handle the social demands of a public appearance, and Dad wouldn't be able to make it. I told her I understood and offered to call Floyd and Bonnie Morehead, volunteers who helped coordinate group logistics for our youth choir. I had grown close to them on the summer tour our youth choir took out west and knew they'd come pick me up. I completely forgot it was Thanksgiving Sunday and had no emotion when I thought back to the effort I'd made to get to Wednesday's practice. I told Mom I'd be back by one P.M., and walked out the door as if all were normal.

Floyd and Bonnie picked me up. I felt so relieved to be with them. They told me they were honored that I had chosen to go to church with them and that I was the bravest kid they had ever met. It felt like we were celebrating that I was alive. When we arrived at the choir chapel, I saw the tear-strewn faces of my closest friends as they hugged me. Twenty minutes later, as our youth choir filed into the main chapel from the side door, I remember thinking as I looked out at the church congregation that Thanksgiving Sunday was as packed as I thought it would be. Subsumed by shock, I got through the service without a further thought.

After the service, Floyd and Bonnie accompanied me to the Reverend's office, still as delightful in their warmhearted cheer as they had been when they picked me up. They weren't afraid of my need to lighten the mood with a laugh, walked the balance of care and compassion perfectly. Once the Reverend arrived and we all exchanged greetings, it was clear that I was comfortable, so Bonnie discreetly pointed to the chairs outside his office where they would wait.

Dr. Holston, a former college football player who stood about six feet tall, carried his potentially imposing presence quietly. His style at the pulpit wasn't overtly emotional—he was more the philosopher type, so I was hoping for a bookish conversation. He offered me a chair in front of his huge dark-oak desk while he hung his white robe on the hanger on the back of the office door. I kept myself busy by looking around the room at his bookshelves, the pictures of his family, his wife, two sons. I reached up to fiddle with my cross and felt a pang. It was no longer around my neck. I didn't know when I had lost it. He seemed to be delaying. I sensed he had none of the confidence I usually felt in his presence. He sat down, paused.

If I had gone first, I would have told him that my heart was broken. That I was grieving the loss of both God and Jesus as if they were human. But he saved me when he took the lead. He reminded me of the story of Job. I listened as he assured me what had happened was not my fault—that sometimes people can feel, after bad things happen, that they must have done something to deserve it. But this was no test from God. This was a horrifying thing to happen. And God would help me through this difficult time. I nodded. He offered me a book. I looked at the cover—*When Bad Things Happen to Good People*. I thanked him. Coming from a man of his position, it felt meaningful. We shook hands.

Sadly, I walked out knowing that no matter how well intentioned the meeting had been, I would never go to church again. I couldn't go on pretending. I was done with God.

I was fifteen minutes late arriving home. Mom was standing at the door, furious. It would seem I had been grossly insensitive by worrying her. Her volume was unsettling, too much for my senses. I went straight up the stairs to put distance between us. A moment later, she was at my bedroom door.

"You aren't the only one who has gone through a horrendous experience," she yelled. "The rest of this family went through something, too." She insisted that I look at her. "You can choose to hole yourself up in this bedroom and cut yourself off from the world, or you can stop feeling sorry for yourself and start living."

I went to school the next day. Monday. Day 5.

In Which I Wonder Where Dad Is

Omaha, 1978—Other than seeing the shadow of his image, I have few memories of my father from over the next month. He was there, but more not there, a hint of Dad.

I never got to say that I was alive because of him. The opportunity just never seemed to surface.

Nor did we talk about my experience near the stockyards, or my narrowly escaped murder.

Maybe he didn't ask because he was afraid I would break.

Or that he would.

In Which Charles Reviews the News Headlines

Omaha, 1978—Two days had passed. Charles checked in with his probation officer. Yep. All good. No problems. Then he worked his shift at Godfather's Pizza.

When he got home, he read the *Omaha World Herald* on the kitchen table. His mother was impressed with his sudden interest in current affairs. Red China's power struggle after Mao Tse-tung's death and Jim Jones and the Jonestown Massacre were top-fold stories. He flipped the paper up to open to the inside pages, and that's when he saw it. On the bottom fold.

AGONY OF RAPE VICTIM'S FATHER: NO ONE HELPED

The layout of the article was slightly different from the others—it had all these subtitles. It took up almost a quarter of the page. "Put yourself in the shoes of the father whose 14-year-old daughter was kidnapped and raped." Apparently, the parents were "shocked, horrified and hurt, but not embittered."

It then went on to roll through his crime and list all the places that people might have intervened. Turned out there was a woman watching them when they'd been in the phone booth outside McDonald's. She said she wasn't sure what was happening so she didn't get involved. He wondered where the hell she had been standing. And then there was the guy at the service station. He told the police that he thought the van driver was going to rob him and was just relieved when the van left. And then the police spokesman told the reporter they wondered why no one who was driving by the phone booth did anything. It would have been an odd picture—a man in a ski mask with his arm wrapped around the neck of a young girl, even if they hadn't seen the knife. Well, honestly, Charles was stumped, surprised even, when he thought back on it.

They now were reporting him at five foot eleven, two inches away from his five foot nine, and they mentioned his sideburns. And the school PTA announced they'd raised one thousand dollars toward a reward fund. The paper described the girl as "popular, good looking and active at her church and junior high." Well, it didn't surprise him she was popular.

He went back to the article. The reporter said that the reason the girl didn't struggle to escape at the gas station was due to "a mixture of fear and belief that her best chance for safety was to cooperate." Well, she was some good fake because he never noticed her being scared of him. Until the phone call to her dad; he showed both of them who was in charge then!

The father was quoted as saying she's "fighting this thing." Apparently, the girl was now back at school and went to church on Sunday, then sledding with school friends. Good for her.

But it was on the front page—*wow*.

In Which I Carry On

Omaha, 1978—If home was my hell, then school was my respite. Learning how to walk to the school bus again was my first conscious step in risk-taking. Once I was at school, my favorite science teacher, Kent Friesen, took me aside and gave me the championship coaching speech of my life. He told me I was the bravest kid he had ever met and I was his hero. He also said he never felt so bad about missing someone—referring to Wednesday when he was called away to coach for the wrestling tournament and left me that note on his desk. Said when he found the empty bag of popcorn on Monday, he felt sick, he was so sad.

It hadn't take long for friends at school to put the pieces together. After my abduction was broadcast on the news, classmates began calling each other to see who was missing, and a couple of them had called my house. I couldn't help but notice my presence had the power to induce a level of emotion in others I was unaccustomed to experiencing.

Someone's mother organized a lunch for some of my schoolmates over the weekend. A high school teacher who had been raped by a student came in to discuss the experience and its long-term effects on her. And because Mr. K was still out there, they gave students mace spray for protection. It quickly became clear that I had an extended support team.

Further support came from unexpected corners. Bessie, my old sparring partner, walked up to me in our girls' gym class and asked loudly if I was the girl who had been raped. The gym went silent. "Yeah," I told her, though I might have described the experience differently. But as I knew everyone was thinking about it, it was nice to have it out there in the open. The room suddenly filled with looks of empathy, including something resembling emotion from Bessie. "Oh." She shrugged. And we all went back to bouncing our basketballs.

Six days after the abduction, I was in the kitchen eating breakfast when I saw the newspaper on the counter with the headline REWARD $3000 FOR RAPE INFORMATION. In addition to the PTA's money, there was $1,500 from the Independent Insurance Agents of Omaha, $300 from the Omaha Chartered Property Casualty Underwriters, and more from the Lewis and Clark Parent Teacher Association.

Later when I asked my mother about it, she said not to worry about it, and then told me she and Dad had agreed on a closing date with the buyers for our house. We would be leaving Omaha in four weeks. The plans to move to Iowa had been made that summer, and my parents saw the "incident" as motivation to hold course.

Feeling desperate and overwhelmed at the thought of losing all the friends and adults who were holding me together, I remembered the conversation with the nurse at the hospital who encouraged me to call the Rape Crisis Hotline. I hated the idea of talking to a stranger over the phone, but overcame my reluctance. Within minutes of talking to the volunteer, I felt some stress lift. She affirmed the courageous step I had taken in calling and, after we chatted for fifteen minutes, she encouraged me to ask Mom for help finding a counselor.

Mom was happy to support me in this endeavor, but she was surprised when, finally, I chose a male pastoral counselor named Robin. Our second meeting was a family session at our house, though it quickly devolved into a showdown between Mom and Genie. Since the night of my abduction, Genie had retreated further into her own world. When Mom insisted that Genie join us in the living room, and then continued to push her to share her feelings, Genie exploded and let Robin know that he had no idea what happened that night, suggesting there was a side to the story he hadn't heard. I copped Dad's numb position on that one, couldn't bear the idea of asking her what this awful truth was. And that was the last family session.

I attended three more sessions with Robin before we left Omaha. He made a heroic effort to try to salvage my faith, even encouraged me to take a more intellectual approach by asking if I'd like to coauthor an article with him. If I didn't mind, he'd be happy to do a first draft. We agreed on the major points.

One of the most difficult issues I faced was waking up to my religious naivete. Having spent years enjoying the comfort of a personal relationship with God, I was hugely disappointed to discover the persona I had created had all been in my imagination. Those moments I spent hoping to be miraculously saved nearly cost me my life.

But that was not all. I felt anger at the fact I had been abducted in my church parking lot after braving a storm of biblical proportions to make it to choir practice.

Most troubling of all were the conversations with Mr. K. How could someone claim to love God yet commit such an evil act? I felt foolish about assuring him of God's all-encompassing love. Finally, the significance of my cross necklace disappearing seemed too poetic, too metaphoric in meaning.

But when the counselor asked my parents, with my permission, if it would be okay to publish, Mom made it clear he had grossly overstepped a boundary.

It was a damn good draft though.

In Which Charles Grows Busy with His Social Life

Omaha, 1978—Three days passed. Charles was bored, bored, bored. And then Mark and Dean surprised him by stopping in to welcome him home. He hadn't seen them in the two weeks he'd been out of the Kearney Youth Development Center. They both wanted to do something to celebrate, mark the rite of passage, as they say, so he suggested they drive over to Godfather's Pizza and take advantage of his employee discount. After lunch, they drove Mark's car to the arcade at Westroads and played Skee-Ball. It was as if the year he'd been away hadn't happened at all.

They dropped by the next day and took him to services at the Center Baptist Church, just like old times. Afterward, they headed back to Godfather's to join a few more kids. Charles felt like he was hosting a new social club, he was that popular.

Later, they drove over to Mark's house and hung out in his room. Mark played the guitar and sang a few of his own songs that he had worked on over the past year. He wanted to become a musician someday. Charles liked that about him.

On Monday and Tuesday, Charles went to school and then worked his shift at the restaurant. Life was good. Nothing to report. On Wednesday, Charles pulled up to Mark's in a tan '78 Buick with cool spoke wheels. He told Mark it was his sister's car. Mark didn't seem to worry where he got it. As they cruised around, Charles asked Mark if he'd heard about the story of that fourteen-year-old girl and how the police were trying to catch the guy. Evidently the kidnapper had taken her over to Norris, their junior high school. "Want to go check it out?" "Check what out?" Mark asked. "Let's drive on over to Norris," Charles said.

As the school came into view, Charles started feeling his adrenaline pump. He got the urge to tell Mark. It was too exciting to keep to himself. "You want to see where that girl was raped?" Mark said okay—but without too much fervor, Charles noticed.

They drove around to the football stadium and pulled up behind the baseball diamond pit. Charles thought he'd test the waters a bit. "The papers don't say so but I know this is where the guy took that girl." Mark didn't seem too interested. They sat in the car in silence for a few moments. Mark suggested they go to the Center Shopping Center to play a few games. Charles wasn't going near the Center Shopping Center. "Let's go to Westroads instead," he suggested, feeling after the enormity of sharing his secret that he and Mark were now even closer, like brothers.

Driving toward Westroads, Charles asked Mark if they could stop at the used car lot next to the Rosebowl on Saddlecreek Road. There was a Corvette he wanted to look at. When he pulled up, Mark said he would wait in the car. "Sure," why not, Charles thought. It would give him more range in the conversation to work the sales guy.

Charles went in, asked the salesman if he could take the Corvette out for a test drive. "Sure," said the salesman, "if you have a license and a credit card." Charles felt for his back pocket. "Ah, no, I must have forgot it. My friend out there can vouch for me, though. And that's my car. I can give you the keys."

The guy looked out at the Buick. Saw a kid in the passenger's seat looking bored.

"Sorry, I can't let you go without a license and credit card."

"I understand. You have to a job to do," Charles said, being friendly. "Do you mind showing me the car anyway? Maybe starting her up so I can see how she runs?"

The guy grabbed the keys, and they walked toward the vehicle. As they crossed the lot, Charles glanced over and noticed Mark hunting around in the Buick's glove compartment. Very unlike Mark. He never cared before if a vehicle was hot. He'd find the papers, figure out it wasn't Charles's sister's car, but that's not what worried him. What worried him was the ski mask in the glove compartment. It was an item listed in the description of him in the newspapers.

He said thanks to the guy, but sorry, just remembered, gotta get back for something, and he headed toward the Buick. Got in. Mark was shutting the glove compartment. They both acted as if the moment had no significance. Charles pulled out fast, laying rubber down on the road, the tail of the car swerved. He laughed, looked over at Mark's face to see if he was impressed, and Mark laughed too, said, "You're a madman." Charles started to relax again.

He knew that Mark would be honest with him if he was bothered. He was that kind of friend. Didn't have the nerve to be a Judas. Wasn't the betraying kind.

A couple of days went by, and Charles started enjoying his new routine. On Friday, December 1, eight days after the crime, he picked Mark up after school in the Buick. They discussed going to pick Dean up at church, but Mark said he wouldn't be available for another hour, and suggested they head over to his house to fill the time.

Charles pulled the Buick into Mark's driveway. Instead of getting out, Mark turned on the radio, and they started talking about the song. Then Charles noticed Mark glance out the window, followed what he was looking at. Noticed the guy next door run out the door to the car in his driveway. Something was going down.

Charles watched as the neighbor backed his car out into the street and suddenly understood, as the car pulled up behind him, that he had just been trapped. He looked at Mark. Then he heard the police sirens.

In Which Eyes Prove to Be the Mirror of the Soul

Omaha, 1978—I looked at my mother, who was looking at me with something clearly important to convey. They had a suspect at the police station. I didn't have to go. Why wouldn't I go? I felt like I was traveling in some weird virtual travel machine with the sound turned down. Of course I would go. I wanted to be helpful.

My parents and I arrived at the police station just as the potential suspects were being marched down the hall to the lineup room. One of the officers yelled at them to stop so our paths didn't cross. My parents rushed me into the identifying room like we were trying to avoid a collision at a train junction.

We watched through a mirrored window as the men were brought in for the lineup. I knew him as soon as I saw his eyes, fourth from the left. I said that's him. I could sense the four adults in the room with me stiffen. And it was only because of their looks that I understood, perhaps there should be an emotional response from me? But the boy in the lineup. That wasn't Mr. K. Mr. K had on a mask. No, that teenager was a stranger in a crowd—just someone whose eyes I would never mistake. The officer asked me if I was sure. I said yes. He asked me again, looking at my parents, who were looking at me. I said yes again. I heard him tell my parents that the boy was the same one the previous witness had identified.

Everyone relaxed, the reduction of tension lightening the atmosphere. I wondered who the previous witness might be. I then heard, but pretended not to hear, as is polite when it's clear you are not a part of the conversation, that it was a security guard at the pickup spot where Mr. K turned up to meet Dad. So! Mr. K had gone to meet my father. My brain recorded that fact in the file, and it disappeared into the stacks seconds later.

After we had finished at the police station, we drove home and pulled into our driveway. Dad turned off the motor. In the ten days since the kidnapping, his soul seemed to have sunk further.

Mom asked if we should talk a few moments before we went inside. I said sure. She offered her pack of cigarettes to me. I thought it was a test of some kind, this strange twist in permission, but she told me just to take it and enjoy. So I did. And I remember what a cool thing I thought it was to smoke that Benson & Hedges menthol cigarette in the car.

"We need to check in," she said. "How do you feel about that?"

I thought she was referring to the cigarette. She was talking about the lineup. "Fine," I said.

"It would be okay if you were scared, you know." She assured me I had picked the right man. I said I knew it was the right man. I wasn't intentionally shutting her out. I was enjoying the smoke rings I was puffing, though.

"Now that he's caught, the problem is the state of Nebraska's," she said, "so let's put it behind us." If there was any emotional reaction from Dad I didn't see it, and so you might say I adopted the same dissociative flat emotional response.

So there. So not.

In Which Charles Ponders the Meaning of Friendship

Omaha, 1978—Charles was sitting in his Douglas County jail cell when he received the interview request from the *Omaha World Herald*. He had two more months to go before his trial and not a chance of getting out on bail, which had been set at one hundred thousand dollars.

The journalist was upfront, mentioned that he was a member of the First United Methodist Church where the girl and her family attended services, but assured him there would be no conflict of interest. He wanted to write a "soft piece." Charles didn't mind. It's not like he had anything better to do with his time. It turned into a pleasant afternoon, and the reporter promised he'd send Charles a copy of the article.

It was a story about a friendship. The journalist painted a nice picture: of Mark and Charles going out for pizza together, playing pinball machines, hanging out at each other's houses, said that Mark had even bought a television for Charles to watch while he was in his prison cell. The article mentioned Charles's pride in Mark's musical abilities, and quoted Charles when he said he felt that Mark was the closest friend he'd ever known, that he was like a brother, that Charles felt no ill will toward him. "He didn't have to explain anything," Charles was quoted as saying about Mark. "It wasn't like he was turning me in. He really was trying to help."

The journalist even told the story about the time Mark got into a fight with a guy who made a racial slur about Charles, shared that Charles had pulled Mark off the guy. For Charles, it was no big thing—but Mark, not used to hearing a racist so comfortable in using such language, had been offended.

The article finished by saying that if Mark received the three-thousand-dollar reward, he might give it to the victim or use it to help pay for his college education. Charles thought the article cast him in a positive light and hoped that the judge would read it before sentencing.

But if the judge had read the article, it wasn't helpful. On April 1979, Charles and Judge Murphy were meeting once again. He pleaded guilty to kidnapping and first-degree assault. His defense lawyer had told him that confessing was his only hope for a lighter sentence, given the irrefutable evidence he'd left: the call to the girl's father, the van with evidence of blood, the number of police he involved, witnesses, the hospital report—not to mention the original statement he gave to the police. Charles could tell, as Judge Murphy worked himself up to deliver his closing speech, that things weren't going to go well.

"The family is the bedrock of our society. Kidnapping is an attack on the very existence of love between parents and children," the judge started. He would like to have the "luxury" of passing a sentence that would be in Goodwin's interests, but he had "a duty to protect the people of this community and to ensure that their children are not kidnapped and raped again."

And with that, Charles, not yet eighteen, was sentenced as an adult to two six-to-ten-year terms for kidnapping and first-degree sexual assault in the Nebraska Penal Complex.

In Which We Cross the Pond

Oxford, 2001—When our children were two and three years old, my husband and I found ourselves with a coinciding break between jobs—the television station we jointly managed had just run out of money, so we decided to revisit the list of pros and cons of raising a young family in England versus the United States.

If we were to move, the disruption would be minimal. We thought a couple of years of downsized living while the kids were small would be terrific. America had the advantages of plenty of sunshine and a national park system with huge benefits for outdoor enthusiasts. After a good deal of research to identify the perfect community, we decided on Shepherdstown, West Virginia, an idyllic, small historic town, sixty miles outside Washington, D.C. It was close enough to the city that Thomas would have a chance to establish himself as a journalist if that's what he wanted to do, and I could go back to work in D.C., the city that had been my professional home for ten years. And we'd have the natural beauty of West Virginia at our doorstep to enjoy as a family. It looked perfect.

Despite all the dysfunction and pain of the past, when I told my parents we'd made the decision to move back to America, they responded with such enthusiasm, even Mom, that I couldn't help but get caught up in their joy.

We had a few practice visits from my parents in England that had been pleasant and easy. Mom, who didn't help with the babies, had managed to make herself so absent in her presence that I never had to worry, and Dad was as great with his grandkids as he had been with us.

It felt good—Mom's excitement at my return—like she had discovered some need for me, some pride in me for the first time in my life. I felt a vestige of hope that maybe we still had a chance, maybe she would heal the open wound I still had, the hole in me I was desperate for her to fill. She'd see who I was, a daughter who needed her love, and we could start making up for lost time. It might be this new chapter could work, that the storm had passed. That now that they had retired from being parents and were now grandparents, we could become an all-American family.

Dad suggested that we fly into Indianapolis so he could gift us with an old Jeep Cherokee he was no longer using, and I said yes, thanking him. So on June 11, 2001, we closed the door of our cozy cottage in England for the last time and twelve hours later landed at Indianapolis International Airport.

Thomas and I couldn't help but smile at each other when we heard Neil Diamond's song "America" so loud we assumed it was being piped through the airport speakers. Once we arrived at the gate, it turned out it was playing just for us. My family was there in force, dressed up in professionally rented costumes: Dad as Uncle Sam, Mom regal as Lady Liberty with a torch, Vivian as Pocahontas in a leather dress and moccasins with a feather headband, my eight-year-old nephew Taylor, dressed as a football player, and Gayle in charge of a huge boom box sitting next to them, conducting tech support. A performance that would have them hauled off by security these days, but before 9/11, was damn good public entertainment.

We drove to their neighborhood, first making a stop at Dairy Queen. Dad was so natural with the kids, so straight in with the play, so happy in being a grandfather that I couldn't help but feel nostalgic.

We stayed with Gayle and Taylor, who lived across the street from my parents. It was in large part due to Gayle that I had overcome my fear of being a parent. She was six years ahead of me in the journey, a swap from her younger sister role. She clearly loved being a mother and adored her son. And it wasn't as if her road had been smooth. After graduating from the University of Iowa, she had moved to Los Angeles and obtained her dream job in no time, working at Universal Studios. She couldn't have been happier, until she dated a man twenty years her senior who totally misrepresented himself. Fast-forward two years later, and she moved back home with Mom and Dad, with her one-year-old son, saddled with forty thousand dollars of debt her ex-husband had spent in her name.

A couple of months after she moved in, Mom tried to kick her out of the house in one of her rages. Gayle found a women's shelter that would take her and her toddler. Dad intervened and implored her not to leave.

After living with Mom and Dad for more than two years, she had saved enough money to buy her own home. When Dad realized she and his grandson were not only leaving but moving several miles away, he went to Des Moines and summoned up an early inheritance from Katherine and Arlo to help Gayle with a down payment to buy a house right across the street.

Gayle was in great shape now. She was making a decent income in Dad's business selling industrial manufacturing products. I admired the setup they all had—it seemed to work. My nephew had not only Dad across the street but Vivian too. And Mom in her new form seemed to be in check.

Mom and Dad were both incredibly generous in supplying us with basic household goods, and after enjoying a few days in Indianapolis, we set off in the jeep to West Virginia.

In Which Charles Conducts a Moral Inventory

Lincoln, 1980—In his second year inside, Charles was assigned a new prison counselor. He knew this guy would have only limited information on his case.

Charles told the counselor that he wasn't guilty of the crime he was serving jail time for, that his girlfriend's father trumped up the charges of rape because he was racist, and that Charles was advised to accept the plea bargain by his public defender.

Worse than that, after Charles was arrested, his girlfriend's father moved her to Iowa so no one would ever know about them. Charles didn't even have a forwarding address for her, nothing, no way to contact her. He was feeling suicidal, he missed her so much. He knew she'd be as desperate to hear from him, and he had no way to write her.

When Charles finished, he could tell the guy felt so bad for him that he figured it was safe to ask him to get the girl's address in Iowa. The guy said it was the least he could do. His story was almost as tragic as Romeo and Juliet.

Charles found nice stationery at the prison commissary—sky blue with white doves on it. In his letter, he told the girl that he had found a new relationship with Jesus and he knew she'd like to hear that.

And then he added for good measure that she should "avoid the fast lane and not smoke cigarettes because it was bad for her health."

In Which I Take off the Shades

Shepherdstown, 2001—I can't say our transition to West Virginia was smooth. It took us a couple of months to find a house in town. During that time we rented a cabin in Monongahela National Park in the southern part of the state. We had put money in savings after we sold the house in England and were still technically on vacation, but I started feeling anxiety about how much time I could go without work before it would be difficult to get back into the job market. By the end of summer a property came up in Shepherdstown, a fixer-upper, and we jumped on it.

One afternoon the children and I were out in the yard planting a vegetable garden. The two of them usually got along incredibly well, but that day they were winding each other up. I threatened to separate them with more impatience than my usual tone. My son's face dropped and his eyes teared up. Our moods were nearly always aligned, and the clear pain of it for him made me feel so bad I apologized instantly. He was fine; it wasn't the trauma I imagined it. We moved on to the next activity.

But I felt like the most horrid parent on earth, and as I reflected on what had just gone wrong, a punch rushed at me out of nowhere as I was hit with the childhood memory of Gayle in the garage that winter day Mom had locked us out. This wasn't repressed memory. My sisters and I often shared Mom's "best moments"; in fact, Jenifer and I would joke about which of Mom's melo-dramas were the most outrageous, which of her tantrums were the worst.

But this was different. It wasn't my own experience that was coming up, it was seeing the hurt on my son's face that triggered the memory of seeing the pain on my sister's face—it was my parent self looking at four-year-old Gayle. And the pain that had just swept over me was anguish at the sudden realiza-tion that Mom's physical violence didn't erupt from uncontrolled outbursts but from the way she seemed to enjoy her calculated sense of control, her need to assert her dominance. And as quick as the rush of thoughts happened, I shut them down.

Whatever that line of thought was, it wasn't going to do me or anyone else any good to think about. I was in a much better position to be more compas-sionate as a parent than she was. And we were safely beyond those years. For me to continue to judge her, to renew a sense of her guilt, wasn't going to be helpful.

In fact, Mom and Dad had just made a visit to Shepherdstown, and though trying to emotionally connect with Mom for any of us was like trying to fix a broken cup with an empty glue stick, she was trying hard. And there was no doubt she was taking joy in being a grandmother. She genuinely enjoyed buying the kids things—crayons, Legos, she even needlepointed blankets with their names on them. She would read the occasional book, but for the most part she was comfortable waiting for them to come to her and didn't take it personally that they didn't. She kept Dad company as he played with them, as he bathed them, as he read them stories. She was doing what she needed to do to ensure we were all able to exist together.

I reminded myself how good it felt, after all these years, to have a sense of being a family. It made me wonder about my twenties, which hadn't been easy with her. But perhaps I had confused Mom's rejection of me with my rejec-tion of her? And as quickly as that good feeling came, for the several minutes it lasted, I was filled with anger again. *Let it go, let it go, let it go,* I said to myself, as I cleaned up the garden tools and watched the kids playing with the hose.

But how does any adult get to the point they are that violently out of control? And then the next memory surfaced. The time Mom beat Gayle and Jen after I drank the Coca-Cola. Gayle told me years later about her experience that day. That Mom had taken an hour to stage that trial. While I had been upstairs, Mom called Gayle into Jenifer's into room, and when neither admitted to drinking the Coke, she sent them to their separate bedrooms for a half hour before calling them again. And then opened their legs with a belt. Gayle said that the worst of it for her was Mom insisting she not miss her piano lesson immediately after, and having to endure the pain while sitting on the bench. Lucky for me, both Gayle and Jen forgave me, as we understood none of us had a chance of steering anything at home.

I felt gross, recalling all this, like I was poisoning myself with anger. Of course my mother didn't delight in hurting us. I couldn't read her mind. I didn't know what it was like to be in her inner world. But as quickly as I felt the empathy for her condition as a young mother, my emotions swung back. Why was it that we had never had an honest conversation about these incidents? The nearest I had ever come to raising the issue was with Dad when he came to Oxford on his own, a few months before his breakdown.

That's not the total truth. I did try to have a conversation one night with Mom when I had come home for Christmas from college. She asked me to fix her a White Russian cocktail. After her second, I asked her to tell me what it had been like for her as a young mother, carefully framing the question in a feminist context—mentioning the social forces I knew she was up against. I broached a few of the memories sensitively. To my surprise, she appeared interested in exploring this subject.

I told her the question had been triggered by a conversation with a new friend at college, who suggested that Mom's child-rearing techniques sounded harsh, and perhaps if she shared with me what she was feeling at the time, then maybe I could stop thinking about it for good.

She said she never wanted to be a mother. (This was not a new insight—though I always wondered why she had four children.) She said she wondered herself on occasion if she had been too tough on us, whether she was guilty of some kind of broken devotion, then realized maybe she had been, but it was only because she loved us and was scared about how we might develop. This was quickly followed by her saying that she did the best she could, and if you looked at how we had turned out, she had obviously done good enough. She wasn't perfect. When I tried to continue the discussion, she shut me down by asking for another White Russian.

The truth was, I felt guilty just for thinking Mom's behavior was cruel and barbaric. What good was judgment going to do at this stage? Why couldn't I just let it go? I so wanted this new family togetherness we had all informally fallen into. But revisiting the truth of the past would definitely ruin this unspoken truce. The few times we had gotten close to broaching the truth of the abusive dynamic, Mom was a master at turning the questions around on me—so what if she did? What was I going to do about it now? I was an adult. I wasn't a kid anymore.

I'd better get it clear. If what was in her was also in me, then who was I to think the two of us were different in nature? If all conditions of our parenting had been the same, if she had all the advantages I had before becoming a parent, did I really think she would have acted in the same manner? What if being vigilant over my own thinking, my own actions, was not enough?

Suddenly, the fear that I might be capable of the same kind of violence against my children knocked any confidence I had in my parenting out from under me. If I could not be certain that I was incapable of hurting my children, then I resolved to kill myself rather than wake up one day to discover I had. And I was most serious. I understood what it was to stand next to death, and I was not scared of it. I couldn't bear the idea of my children being hurt in the same way my mother had hurt us, even worse—hurt by me. This was a rational moral conclusion.

I'd like to say my ability to steer my own thoughts began to improve, but it didn't. I had resolved the question of what to do with myself. But the harder I worked to assert my will in forgiving my mother a past she couldn't fix, the faster my thinking became, which inflamed my anger only further. The window between waking and falling asleep grew even more difficult. I began to hear her voice in a lucid way, criticizing any emotion I had. I knew this weird macabre mental game was my own creation, and these episodes were followed with shame and anger for not getting these feelings under control.

Why was I doing this? We weren't even living together. The more I struggled with my conscience, the larger her present energy grew. I began to imagine her voice ridiculing me throughout the day. The more I floundered in my ability to gain equilibrium, the more I heard her mock me. And just when I thought this inner drama would erupt into reality, cut any tie to the present I had, destroy the enormous gift I had been given of *my* family, my husband and two children, just when I thought I was actually going to go mad with the pain, I couldn't bear it anymore, her voice would change to one of saccharine sentimental phoniness. The woman she was now. And I'd feel like the most pathetic human being on earth.

I sank. The challenge of getting out of bed in the mornings was just the start. The oppressiveness of my critical inner voice made the morning almost intolerable. By afternoon, my mind would tire, the inner voice would recede, and my day would feel more normal. Seeing people, which usually served as a source of energy, now left me feeling painfully inadequate. I'd find myself in an almost catatonic state of self-absorption, making me a bore even to myself.

My time with my children was my only reprieve. I would make a mental note of our moments throughout the day together, those magically charged interactions, so I could write them down in the evening. But I noticed I was beginning to feel increasingly anxious about writing the memories down, like it was bad luck. I kept thinking about one of them being hurt, had sudden anxiety that something terrible was going to happen to them. That there was nothing I could do to keep them safe. I became anxious about how my thoughts might even affect them. Every moment I spent with them felt so joyous it hurt. They'd smile at me, do something lovely, and my eyes would tear. Oh my god. How could anyone ever hurt a child? And then I would make sure I dialed down the intensity of my survivor gratitude, as I was convinced it was going to suffocate them.

It was about this time Dad called and asked how things were going. I told him, honestly, I was having a difficult time. That I was down and I was struggling to fight against it. He suggested it might be because I hadn't gone back to work yet, that as much as I enjoyed being with the kids, it might not be enough. I told him that didn't feel right. If anything, I was enjoying being with the kids even more now that I wasn't having to work, and was feeling anxious about leaving them.

He asked how the work was going on the house. I looked around me. It was a construction site. We hadn't counted on having to replace the wiring and the plumbing, so the walls on the first floor had been totally gutted. He asked how much of the house we were able to use, and after I told him we had plastic taped to the doors of each room to stop dust from moving around, he suggested that maybe I should borrow their RV for a couple of months. I was thankful for the suggestion. It gave me hope that there might be an immediate plausible cause for why I was so down.

After speaking with Thomas, I called back and said I'd drive up to Indianapolis with the kids and swap the jeep for the RV. Despite my dread of seeing Mom.

In Which Charles Meets a Hot Chick

Lincoln, 1986—No one had ever believed Charles was guilty of the charges brought against him. Not even his parents. And the regular visits by the Reverend and Charles's mom certainly helped reinforce his reputation for being kind and polite now that he was at the Lincoln Community Release Center. The staff hardly ever hassled him. He came and went from his classes at the university and his job at the student gym almost as if he were a civilian.

He was proud of what he had accomplished in eight years. He'd entered the Nebraska State Penitentiary as an eighteen-year-old, without a high school degree and with few friends. Now, not only had he gotten his GED certificate, but he had earned a psychology degree from the University of Nebraska at Lincoln—and was debt-free. In addition to that, he had taken advantage of many of the programs offered, especially the cognitive behavioral therapy courses.

In fact, he felt confident in saying that a number of fine people believed in his moral character. For example, two weeks ago he met a hot college intern working in the prison. Her name was Kim and she had beautiful long red hair, green eyes, and, man, she must be five foot ten. And what a sense of humor. He loved making her laugh. The first night she was assigned to roll count of the inmates, he volunteered to walk her through the facility. In fact, he flat-out told her she shouldn't be doing that alone as it wasn't safe. And since then, he'd wait for her to show up at work.

Last time he saw her, they chatted for a half hour, just shooting the breeze. Kim asked what a nice guy like him was doing in prison. He said the charges against him were cooked up. The girl's father didn't like him, said that he had raped her. She was white. The truth was the girl and he were dating. Charles got the reaction he was hoping for. Kim responded like most prison justice warriors—with shock and sympathy.

The next week, she asked him in the cafeteria if she could use him as a case study for her final essay. She had to pick a model prisoner who had little chance at repeat offending. He was more than happy to help her with that, especially if he could use it in his upcoming parole hearing. He had served eight years out of a ten-year sentence, and he was hoping that they would let him out for good behavior.

Kim brought the papers around the next day for his signature. She needed permission to look at his prison record. Yeah, he had no problem with that. He happily signed, and they agreed to a meeting schedule. He was looking forward to their private interviews. The first would be the following day. But Kim never showed up.

A week later, Charles heard that Mike the senior supervisor wanted to see him. There would be a few others present: Charles's caseworker and counselor. That intern Kim would be there too.

In Which Dad and I Convene Another Chautauqua

Indianapolis, 2001—When the kids and I pulled into my parents' driveway that evening, Dad was taking spins around the yard to show off his John Deere tractor mower. After giving his grandkids a ride, and then letting me do a few circles myself, Dad asked me if I wanted to accompany him on a walk with Indiana Jones, his big blond Labrador.

I was pleased to get him to myself for a short time. Maybe all those hours on the road had made me bold, but after a few moments I just straight-out asked Dad if we could discuss the time he spent at the hospital for depression. He went down a gear in terms of mood, but said he'd be happy to talk to me about it. Said it hadn't done a whole lot of good other than get him some much-needed sleep while he adjusted to medication. And then he added that he wished he hadn't let Mom persuade him into going.

I tried not to react. Dad continued, said he came off the pills six weeks later. He didn't like the side effects, and the cost of medication robbed his bank account. His co-payment only covered 20 percent.

I suggested another way to look at it. That getting help might have financially protected him. While we stopped so Indiana Jones could do his business, Dad added that the six weeks of therapy he went into afterward forced him to think about issues he'd never been comfortable with, like the impact of his adoption, something he wasn't willing to think about before he lost Katherine and Arlo roughly three years ago.

He paused, then asked if he might tell me something else.

"Of course," I said.

"I've never talked about it, but I broke my neck when I was eleven years old."

I raised my eyebrows, signaling for him to go on. I could see that he was collecting the right words.

"It was clumsiness. I fell backward off a fence. I was in the hospital for a week, in traction so I wouldn't move my neck. I won't go into detail"—he paused— "but I thought it may be helpful for you to know. There was a nurse who did things to me no adult should ever do to a child."

I stopped. We looked at each other. "I don't want you to say anything," he added. It was an instruction, not a request. "I just wanted you to know."

"Okay. But Dad," I said, my heart catching up with the sadness of what he'd just told me, "I am so sorry."

"Thanks," he said. "But it's not necessary. It's over—it was a long time ago." He wasn't telling me, but he was. His childhood had been shattered by a sexual crime, and he had kept it to himself for sixty-three years. It's one of those things that just happen in life, so we aren't discussing it, he seemed to be saying.

We walked quietly for a few moments, as the consequence of what he revealed sank in. We had never talked about what happened to me the night of the kidnapping. He never asked. I never offered. And we had been renewing the contract every year since. Quite happily for me, I might add. Not talking about the trauma had its strong benefits.

Dad stopped to exchange pleasantries with a neighbor, who was walking a cocker spaniel, which gave me more time to think about what I had just heard.

I couldn't help but wonder, since I had become a parent, what it must have been like for Dad that night, wondering if I was coming back dead or alive. The fact that he had been sexually assaulted himself might explain his emotional absence at the hospital, that horrible hug.

Thinking about it made me want to ask him the most inane questions about that night, like did the police give him real cash? Where did he wait—inside the shopping center or in the multilevel open-air parking lot? My thoughts were interrupted when a water sprinkler system went off next to the sidewalk, and I jumped out of startled shock, which clearly entertained Dad and his neighbor as they said their good-byes.

Dad motioned me toward his backyard. "Let me show you my new flagpole," he said. It was a full forty feet tall, with spotlights installed underneath. He put his arm around me as we both looked up proudly as the stars and stripes snapped in the wind.

"There's another thing I need to say." I knew this tone of voice. It had that edge that signaled he was going to try to convince me of something I was going to disagree with. "I've made it too easy for you to think too highly of me, especially in relation to your mother."

I wanted to stop him there. Dad hadn't a clue, when it came to the honest history between Mom and me. After we moved to Laurens, her physical violence stopped but her oppression didn't. Her drinking moved to a whole different level. I couldn't count the number of times I had been forced to pour her drinks, join her as she spent hours talking into the night, get her out of bed in the mornings for work when she was hungover, deal with the embarrassment of hearing from my classmates about the stories she was telling while drinking at the town bar, clean her up after she'd been sick. And it didn't stop her personal attacks on me. But the worst was having to witness her relationships with a few men outside their marriage. And they were repugnant. And I don't know why we never told Dad, except for Mom's threats that he'd hate us, not her.

And so, I could almost predict where this conversation we were having was going to go. I heard him say it before—that it was his fault she was so miserable. His fault she tried to kill him. That if he had been a better husband, she would have been able to be a better mother. And I could tell he really thought he could convince me of it. And then sure enough . . .

"I was having an affair with someone the last year we lived in Omaha. She was in Laurens. You may remember your mom was drinking a lot and I wasn't around."

I definitely hadn't expected that one and wanted to say bravo. And then the conversation took yet another unexpected turn. Dad mentioned he joined a men-only Christian group called Promise Keepers, a fellowship started by Bill McCartney, who was the coach for the University of Colorado football team.

"What, you get together like Boy Scouts?" I asked him, as we walked into the kitchen.

"No. We meet in large gatherings and have speakers that address the brotherhood."

I asked him how many met, as I opened myself a can of A&W Root Beer. He said the last one he had attended was at the civic auditorium in Indianapolis, and there had been ten thousand men. They'd get together to talk about their shared family values, their roles as husbands and fathers. Looking at my face, he assured me this was a good thing, said he could already tell I was overthinking it.

I told him I was interested. Really. I had heard about these men's groups in London started by the poet Robert Bly, where they'd get together to beat on drums and pass around a talking stick. I asked him if Promise Keepers was like that.

"Well, yeah," he said. "You're getting closer. Except my group knows a woman's place is at home. We're fighting those Feminazis for men's rights." Then he chortled.

"That's incredibly offensive, Dad, not funny."

"Oh, I'm just teasing you. You want a fried egg sandwich?"

"Well, it's not funny, equating feminists to Nazis is not funny. And it makes me sad when you act like we're a different species."

He apologized as though he meant it, as if he were troubled by what made him say it. But it was the first of a series of jokes that I noticed increasingly being slipped into conversations—dumb blonde jokes, and more offensive racist cracks, even though he lived in what had become a predominantly black neighborhood and was granddad to every kid on the block.

He'd tell me I was being too sensitive. I couldn't help but think this had something to do with the fact that all his self-help cassettes had disappeared—the Dale Carnegie Library that used to sit in the back seat was no longer there. Norman Vincent Peale and his positive thinking, gone, replaced by talk radio shows in all the hours he spent on the road with his sales calls. He denied these folks had political agendas. He said they were closer to comic motivational speakers, would exaggerate things, but they didn't mean anything they really said. And it occurred to me that in the same way he had picked up the coaching techniques of his self-help tapes, he was internalizing the humor of Rush Limbaugh.

And then he suggested maybe I'd like to take my mother out for lunch, which we both knew I'd like to do about as much as having my front tooth pulled out, even at the age of thirty-seven. But I agreed to do it in the interest of our newfound family equilibrium.

In Which I Take Mom Out for a Heart-to-Heart

Indianapolis, 2001—Mom wanted to go for lunch at Applebee's. So many new chain restaurants had sprung up in America during my ten years away, I could hardly keep track. Once we were seated, I asked for waffles with a side of bacon. Mom ordered a Cobb salad. Several minutes later, the waitress set a glass of wine down in front of my mother. Just a little lunchtime Chardonnay to complement the meal.

"Don't worry," she said, noticing my look. "I haven't had any problem managing my alcohol since you kids left home." She picked up her glass and took a sip to reassure me there would be no discussion, then glided right into conversation.

"So your father mentioned you're having a difficult time." She took a bite of breadstick, giving me a chance to open up, though it wasn't a question. I couldn't remember a time I had ever felt safe enough to willingly share my inner world with my mother, and it left me uneasy. Why would Dad tell her? When I appeared more interested in her passing the butter, she filled in the space. "Of course, I've had some experience in that realm," she joked, as if we had something to bond over. "Parenting isn't so easy, is it?"

When I told her I'd been more tired than usual, she dove straight into the details of her unfortunate altercation with my father. I tried to stop her but didn't stand a chance. She was well out of the gate.

I don't know what I was thinking when I brought up the next topic—perhaps if she could so openly discuss going after Dad with a knife with such light-hearted verve, I might be able to counsel her into acknowledging it as part of a chain of behavior. Maybe even claiming some culpability.

I put my fork down. I explained that I was having curious memories, not really memories, more hints, never clear. In other words, coward that I was, I supplicated myself in front of her as best I possibly could, suggesting it might be my own mixed-up mind, but was there any chance she might have experienced similar outbursts of rage when we were growing up? I didn't use those words exactly, but there was no mistaking what I was raising. I picked my fork back up and shoveled in a huge bite of waffle, signaling it was her turn.

"If I was tough on you girls," she said, "it was only because I was scared for you. Certainly not out of malice. Your sister Gayle, now I might owe her an apology."

I raised my eyebrows and chewed.

"You remember that time you came home from school and told me about that girl who said she had been molested by her father?" Of course I remembered it—how could I forget? "Well, I called the school and reported him. And then your sister went and told his daughter the next day. It scared me to death. I thought for sure he was going to show up at our doorstep. I definitely let her have it that time. In fact, someone called the social worker on me. I think it was that girl's father." She picked up her glass and took a sip. "Can you believe that?"

"Wow, Mom," I said carefully.

And then I saw it, the instant flash of a look, enough to signal I'd given too much away, that the minute she wanted to become my oppressor, she could, that she was making an effort and I best not upset that.

"If you want to talk about history, why don't you just say you want to talk about history," she said fiercely.

It was a warning, against having the conversation with my father. That she didn't want me shaking up the newfound family equilibrium.

"Mom, I'm not angry. I'm just trying to understand." What was I thinking? That she'd use this as an opportunity to bring us closer, heal our relationship a little, even? Admit she enjoyed beating us as kids, but she understood now how she had been wrong. What hurt the most—I still wanted that mother hole she had left in me to be filled by her and was looking for any small thing she might give me.

Feeling far worse about myself than before I arrived, I checked my watch and suggested we'd better head back. The kids would be waiting, and I had a long drive ahead. I caught the waitress's attention and let Mom know the mother-daughter meal was on me.

In Which Charles Gets a Promotion

Lincoln, 1986—Early in the morning, Charles was escorted into a small meeting room at the Release Center. Kim was sitting in a chair next to Mike. Even though Charles expected to see her, it threw him. He still had a crush on her and it unnerved him.

His caseworker and counselor were standing behind Mike and Kim, and for some reason there was a security guard stationed by the door. No one was looking too friendly. And the room was a little crowded with six folks. But that didn't stop Charles from displaying his own cordial manners. He asked them how they all were doing, as he took his seat. Mike then started the conversation.

"I understand, Charles, that you've been working with Kim? And that you gave her permission to go into your folder?"

"Yes, she wanted to do a report." Charles flashed Mike one of those smiles that usually squares trust between two people, then added, "I thought I'd be helpful." But Mike clearly wasn't interested in establishing a rapport.

"You know, Charles, the reason we're meeting today is because Kim found a very odd, loose hand-written note in your file. It had the name and address of her best friend at school—the victim of your crime. Can you tell us why this girl's name is in your folder, Charles?"

Charles glanced at his caseworker and counselor, but neither responded. "I'm not sure." He could see that this conversation wasn't going in a good direction. But there's no way Kim was the girl's best friend; that would be too weird, like, statistically impossible.

"Did you ask someone to obtain the address for you, Charles?"

"Well, my previous counselor told me he'd get it for me because I was worried about her."

"You were worried about your victim, Charles? So you thought you'd write to her?"

"It's complicated." Charles looked at Kim, who seemed angry.

"It's not complicated. This is the victim's address. Why don't we give you a chance to tell us about the violent crime that put you in here, Charles."

He looked at them all. "I don't understand."

Mike stopped to look at Kim, who was no longer disguising her fury. "Maybe I can help you," Kim said. "You know that story you told me, the one you've been telling everyone else in here for years? That the charges against you are cooked up? That you were dating my girlfriend and it was her father who brought the charges against you? Well, it's gross. I know every detail of your crime, including the fact that you forced my friend to call her father while you had a knife at her throat. And that my friend talked to you about God."

Charles felt jolted, like someone had just punched the air out of him. He put his head down on his arms and began to sob, overwhelmed with shame. He couldn't control himself. He never felt more humiliated, or terrified. What were the chances? How the hell was he supposed to lift his head?

"I'm going to ask you again," said Mike. "Would you like to tell us what happened that day?"

Charles nodded. "Yes, please just give me a minute."

"I can't imagine this is easy," added Mike.

"No, sir, it's not." He couldn't bring himself to even look at Kim.

The group waited another couple of minutes while he collected himself. And then Kim began. She recounted what he had been wearing that day. She knew he had been arrested eleven days after the crime; she remembered because everyone, parents and students, were living in terror, waiting for him to victimize someone again. Then she talked about a sledding party they had for the girl a week later, and said that none of them could believe how strong she was being. And finally there was the party, when the girl had been hauled away in an ambulance after she almost killed herself with alcohol poisoning. Kim paused and then said, "In fact, you're the monster I've always been afraid of, the reason I decided to study criminal psychology."

Charles sat stunned.

He had worked so damn hard to put it all behind him. The crime was almost eight years ago. He wasn't the same person. He was almost twenty-five years old now. He'd done loads of personal work since then. "All I can say is I am so thankful that this is finally out in the open. So I can stop lying about it." He continued, "You might imagine, as hard as it is for you to be meeting the monster, it isn't easier being the monster."

He took some deep breaths. He needed to bring them around, to make sense of it for them. Why he had done all those terrible things.

It had all begun after he and his friends were bused to Norris Junior High School. He'd never known anything about racism until then. Soon after, four white kids attacked him—for no reason other than he was black. One of the bullies even went at him with a baseball bat. It made him so mad. Shortly after that he was arrested for carjacking. While he waited for his trial, they kept him in a holding cell at the Douglas County Jail, age fifteen, where he became the target for another racist attack. This time a guy choked him until he went unconscious. When he woke, he discovered his teeth were loose and had to hold them in place with his tongue. He finally saw a prison dentist, four months later, and the guy told him his jaw had been broken.

Then, a few days after he'd been let out of Kearney, he drove over to one of the kids' houses to get revenge, but a cop car pulled in. So he headed over to see if he could pick up his cousin Crystal at school. And that's when he saw the girl, in the church parking lot. Charles looked at Kim and said, "She was just in the wrong place at the wrong time. And I was stupid and angry."

After things spiraled so out of control, he was going to kill the girl and then kill himself. He drove her to the railway line near the stockyards. But by then, the two of them had spent so much time talking about God, that he couldn't bring himself to do it. She actually felt like a friend. So he just left her there.

His first six months in prison he felt so awful about what he'd done that he was suicidal. And that's why he had asked his counselor to get the girl's address. To see if she was okay. To apologize.

He looked at them all.

"You might be scared of me, but now I'm scared of you because you know me."

Well, he meant it to sound like shame.

Six months later, he was paroled.

In Which I Ponder a Disorder of Nerves

Shepherdstown, 2001—Though picking up the RV had been a great idea, the trip to my parents' home triggered something. My depression grew worse. Much worse. One evening as I lay on the couch, my pillow over my head, groaning about being me, Thomas brought up the fact that I was no longer working out. In the fifteen years he had known me, my fitness had been a critical part of my mental health. He was right. I couldn't bear to think about doing anything. And that was it, the floodgates opened. I told him I had no idea what was happening to me and why I couldn't pull myself together. I knew what it was like to be depressed, but this was different, and it felt overwhelming.

It had kicked off at the time of 9/11. I hadn't been able to rid myself of the feeling that Thomas and the kids were going to be taken from me, in some tragic happenstance. But my biggest fear wasn't that an outside threat was about to land. I couldn't bear being inside my own head. I was starting to fear all I had ahead of me was a lifetime of fighting these mental cycles. And it was becoming all-consuming, scary. At what point did we have to seriously talk about options?

"Options?" Thomas asked.

"Like checking me in somewhere. What if I hurt someone? Jesus, what if I lose control and hurt the kids? . . . Like Mom. If it was the 1920s, you would have had me committed to an asylum a long time ago."

"Well, aren't you lucky it's not the 1920s, then," Thomas said, wrapping his arms around me and pulling me close. Teasing me usually pulled me out of myself, but this time it triggered a further dip of insecurity. I said with all seriousness that I would understand if Thomas wanted to leave me.

"You're just depressed, it will pass." He suggested we could get more help in, so I could catch up on sleep. He'd take the morning shift with the kids instead of the afternoon. He jostled me with a smile, then saw the tears well up in my eyes.

"Hey, I'm serious," he said. He pointed out that though my inner world was really scary for me, the reality for him and the kids was very different. If I hadn't told him what was going on in my mind, he wouldn't have been able to tell. It's not how I appeared when I was with them. They'd be lost without me, devastated if I wasn't with them. I was an amazing mother he reassured me. We just needed to find a good doctor, a good therapist. I took a deep breath. Laid my head on his chest. And then, oddly, like he knew something I didn't, he suggested we dial down the frequency of contact with my parents for a while.

After all the work I had done in learning to manage the seizures, and then the medication, it was disappointing to find myself needing to ask for help again. Especially after the happiness I experienced since having my children, in becoming a mother. I thought my love for them would protect me from anything, would give me superpowers over anything that might come between us that would threaten their welfare, even depression—especially depression. I had never been comfortable sharing my inner world without it causing extreme anxiety. Half the time, I didn't know what I was feeling, let alone have the ability to articulate it. I reminded myself the best decision of my life—the decision to get married—had been made because of a positive therapeutic relationship. Unfortunately, Sheldon passed away in 1999. His skepticism of psychiatry in general, and his humor in particular, were perfect for me at that time. But the existential approach to treatment might have been too generalized, and I couldn't help but wonder if it also helped further sublimate the emotional load I had been carrying.

I made a couple of stop-and-start attempts at working with someone local, practitioners who had different techniques. I found them experienced and fluent at their art, but on both occasions, I found their approaches too vague to allow my internal censor to relax. I was beginning to wonder if perhaps I wasn't interested in being helped, that I was sabotaging sessions with my cynicism.

Just when I was reaching the point of total despair at finding the right kind of help, I received a call from a psychiatrist who had been highly recommended by a manic-depressive friend whom I deeply respected. Dr. H had space for a new client.

Would I like to come in?

In Which I Meet a Real Doctor of the Soul

Shepherdstown, 2001—Dr. H greeted me when I came into the empty waiting room. He was a tall man in his mid-fifties of unassuming elegance, thin-shouldered, his light ginger hair conservatively cut, and he wore a suit that hung too loosely for someone who cared. He invited me into his office, which was sparse and comfortable, gesturing for me to sit in a rather comfy leather armchair with reclining options. Dr. H then sat in a chair a few feet away from me. His recliner was angled so we could share a view out the window if that's how I wanted to spend my time, or, with a slight turn, converse with each other. When he spoke, his voice was soft and genuine.

He began our hour by asking if I could review the intensity of symptoms that I had told him on the phone. Being rehearsed at intake interviews, I spoke in the academic tone of a PhD student: I could not sleep at night yet found it difficult to get out of bed in the morning; when I was able to sleep, I often woke in a night terror; I no longer had the willpower to work out, something I had always relied on for my mental health. I had recently gone on an antidepressant that was doing nothing but making life harder. I had been on anti-seizure medication for five years but discontinued it before we left England. I had two children who filled me with joy, but the confidence in which I parented sat in total contrast to the feelings I carried inside.

I could spend an entire day feeling a moment away from losing them, like something awful was about to happen. It was a physical feeling, like pins in my stomach. And there were times when being inside my head for a minute was so excruciating, it felt like torture, yet hours could pass without any sense of time spent. If I interacted with the outside world or socialized, it was just hard work.

Dr. H asked what life was like before I had started to feel this way.

I told him about our move from England, that we downsized our lifestyle to focus on raising our children. It had been a good decision, and the right decision for our family. But since arriving in the States, I hadn't been able to work. I was the sort of person who needed big projects to calm me, but I barely had the energy to get through a day in my own home. I was exhausted. If it hadn't been for my husband, who was waiting for me in the lobby, I wouldn't have been able to drive the hour and half it took to get to this meeting. I added that my husband and I shared childcare, but recently we had to rearrange our schedule so I could sleep longer hours.

Dr. H asked more questions about my husband and children, which prompted the first visible emotional reaction I had felt since entering his office. Once I began to speak about my feelings for them, my heart started racing. I became teary. I had everything: an ideal marriage, two beautiful children, financial security, no major health problems.

He asked me if I could tell him what my childhood had been like. I shared I had grown up with two parents with middle-class privilege. That things had not always been easy at home—my strong personality hadn't made things easy for my mother. My parents had been very young, my mother over-whelmed and also experienced serious depression.

He asked if I enjoyed being a mother.

I told him I had been terrified of becoming a mother for years, because I had seen what it had done to my mother, and I was afraid that someone was going to attack or murder my children, that they were going to die.

I had known this man for less than thirty minutes, but somehow I felt safe with him. Compelled to share my secrets. So I went further. I said I was hearing my mother's voice in my head. And my fear was—if her voice was in my head, then I might be a danger to my children. This terrified me the most. I would rather kill myself than risk any chance that I might hurt my children.

"Why do you think you might hurt your children?" he asked.

I felt physical pain at the question. I didn't know how to respond. I didn't have an answer.

"Have you ever fantasized about hurting your children?"

"No."

"So why do you think you are in danger of hurting your children?"

"Because my mother lost control with us at home, though I don't believe she ever meant to hurt us, and I believe it was that she was emotionally overwhelmed."

"And you believe that you might act like your mother?"

"I am scared because I don't know why my mother behaved as she did."

"Or it might be that you do know why your mother behaved as she did, but that you don't want to accept it. And you are afraid, because you're depressed, that you will act like your mother?"

"Yes," I admitted. That sounded right.

"Why?"

"Because she was severely depressed at times. And clearly, if I am hearing her voice inside my head, I have no control over my thought processes at the moment."

"Is she telling you to hurt your children?"

"No." It was the lowest moment of my life, putting myself in the hands of a professional who would have to ask me such a question.

"What words do you hear her use?"

"She's telling me I'm selfish and I've always thought my emotions are more important than anyone else's. That becoming a mother hasn't made me any different than the self-centered manipulator I've always been. I'm pathetic, and if I am as miserable as I claim to be, I should kill myself."

"I don't know how your mother behaved at home, or the reasons for her behavior, but you do know there is a difference between experiencing the symptoms of depression and violently hurting someone?"

"Yes," I said, "but they both start in the same place, both stem from the inability to control behavior. Prisons and mental asylums were the same institution for centuries."

"Can I tell you, you are very different than your mother. We might not know the causes of violence, but we do know this. If you have reached the age of thirty-eight and have no history of violence, I can say with confidence you are not in danger of hurting your children. Your problem is very different from your mother's."

And with that, he possibly saved my children from losing their mother, and my husband, his wife.

Over the next several months, I drove an hour and a half each way and met with him three times a week. He would not keep notes of our sessions to protect my privacy, nor would he speak to my husband or anyone else about my health, which helped alleviate the discomfort that I felt in divulging fears that I myself did not want to face. The sessions were not inexpensive—they cut into our savings, but we were fortunate to have some cash left over from selling our house in England.

Our first priority, he suggested, should be to reestablish my sleep patterns, so he prescribed a sleeping pill, which was one of the biggest gifts I had been given in years. He then suggested I was experiencing rapid mood cycling, which is something that can happen when some patients take an antidepressant without a mood stabilizer, and that I immediately go back on the sodium valproate. Within a couple of weeks, I started to feel stable.

After Dr. H and I had worked together for a short time, I learned my physical symptoms, including the seizures, were in line with someone suffering from complex post-traumatic stress disorder (PTSD).

By far the most difficult material to approach over those months was my relationship with my parents. It felt disloyal and triggered a degree of shame, going back to my childhood. What's more, I felt I had just found a way of being with my parents. I had tried to forgive Mom, and because of that we were experiencing family happiness. It felt immature to revisit my youth, and I was scared it might put our current relationship at risk. It was like I had parents for the first time in my life, no doubt the result of the marital therapy they had invested in.

Dr. H explained the value of our sessions—that if I left the emotional coping skills I learned as a child unexamined, I would continue to use them as an adult, when they were no longer necessary. And only more extensive work in therapy would give us the opportunity to look at how they might be limiting my day-to-day functioning. He was fully confident that after this episode was over, I would again be able to enjoy my marriage, my family, my career, my health. I hadn't lost any of these things. I just needed to get better.

We went through events of my childhood and adolescence. For the first time in a therapeutic environment, at least since working with Robin at the age of fourteen, I recounted in detail my experience of the violent crime in Omaha. Dr. H reflected that he was awed by my level of resiliency. He suggested the reason I had survived the kidnapping was a mastery of the skills I had learned in living with my mother—that children growing up in destructive homes learn to adapt to survive violence.

And Dr. H relieved me of my anxiety by suggesting that he didn't see the benefit of revisiting my memory about that night further. It was what happened at home, both before and after the event, more important to examine.

A few months passed, and the Christmas season arrived. I told Dr. H that Dad had called to ask if we were joining them for the holidays. I had confirmed we'd be leaving for Indianapolis in several days.

"Remind me why you are going home?" Dr. H looked truly stumped.

I paused. It hadn't occurred to me I had a choice. It was our first Christmas in the States as a family.

"You have worked so hard to regain your mental health, it seems an odd choice to go home at this time," he observed. "It is no coincidence this episode began when you moved back in close proximity to your parents. As long as you lived in England, you didn't have the challenges they pose. You do under-stand your mother is the same person," he said gently. "When empathy is not in the wiring, medication can't help. She might be able to calibrate her behavior, but it doesn't mean she has changed. And there's nothing you've shared that suggests she is interested in facing the truth that would allow you to reconcile your relationship in an honest way."

I sat quietly. I found it difficult not to want to hear more of what he had to say, but also found my loyalty to my parents making me defensive. Dr. H had never offered an opinion like this. And to suggest that my parents might be connected to my emotional problems, at the age of thirty-eight, felt too simple—silly even. Dr. H almost read what I was thinking.

"May I go on?" he asked. I nodded.

"I'm concerned that your mother isn't your real problem. I think you know she hasn't changed. It's your father who poses your moral dilemma."

I stiffened. This felt heavy, harsh even, a judgment of me, not my father. I had to remind myself that Dr. H had my interests at heart.

"I see I have upset you, but there is one more thing I'd like to say. You, of course, may disagree with me."

This conversation was pushing against a deeper instinct, for self-preservation. But I asked him to continue.

"Kathleen may be Jim's wife," Dr. H continued, "but he has no right to insist that you have a relationship with her." His use of my parents' first names was jolting. "You have always talked about your home as if it were your mother's house, and your father the well-behaved visitor. And I understand it, because you've built your identity on the fantasy that he's saved you. And you've needed that fantasy. But perhaps you can now let it go. It's your blind spot. It's as much his home as it is hers. And he has no right to ask you to bring your children into it. More important, you are a wife and a mother with a family to protect. And unlike Kathleen, you are a real mother to your children. She may have played a role biologically, but she was not a mother to you. She is incapable of the maternal instincts required to be a mother. Perhaps if you can't make the decision to distance yourself from your parents for your own emotional well-being," he concluded, "then you could consider your husband and children's need that you be emotionally well. Of your responsibility to them?"

We sat in silence. I was speechless. He waited. I tried to collect my thoughts. Instead, I watched for the minute hand to reach the end of the hour, finishing our session. I stood, thanked him, told him I would consider what he said. And then slowly walked to my car.

In Which I Ponder the Meaning of Family Togetherness

Shepherdstown, 2001—As I drove home to Shepherdstown from my session with Dr. H in bumper-to-bumper D.C. traffic, I felt my family values, including honoring my mother and father, under attack. My parents might have failed me, in grotesquely painful ways even, but surely I shouldn't turn my back on them. I found myself reacting with a fierce protection. How, for example, would I explain my actions to my children when they were older? That the grandparents they had loved weren't good people? That they were so dangerous they weren't safe to be near? Isn't that what Dr. H was suggesting? Or instead, was it that I was so emotionally weak, so psychologically fragile, that I should not put myself near them? There wasn't an easy door to open here.

I looked at my options. Maybe instead of canceling the trip altogether, I'd ask Gayle if I could stay at her house. It was smaller, but we could sleep on a floor, and it would mean more time together for the cousins. Instead of spending a week, we could limit it to a couple of days. We could still see my parents for Christmas Eve, but have Christmas Day at Gayle's for the kids. That way I could see Vivian, who was living with my parents as well.

I couldn't help but think of Genie and where she might be. I knew she was married, I knew she had a son, but she hadn't been in touch with my parents, Gayle, Jenifer, or me for six years. And Jenifer was in Seattle. I knew what she'd say. She wouldn't hesitate in telling me to take the exit road. She'd done it by enrolling in the army right after high school, which gave her structure and financial independence, and it had paid for her college education. At the age of thirty-two, she had done two tours in Iraq as a medevac nurse, was moving up in the officer ranks, and would end up a lieutenant colonel in the air force. She had little patience for emotional games. She hadn't made any formal estrangement announcements, but she rarely spoke to my parents. She was the only person in the world that I could joke with about the extremes of my mother's behavior and never hesitated to tell me to take care of myself first. Ironically, it also meant I wanted to be careful about calling her.

I discussed things with Thomas when I returned home. This was the first time anyone had offered me a break from working on my relationship with my parents. It felt too easy. But it would also require that I change. And it would affect Thomas and the kids. Thomas's reaction was immediate and swift. "Whatever I can do to support you, I'm there."

In Which I Hear the Sleigh Bells Ring

Indianapolis, 2001—It was late afternoon when we arrived in Indianapolis. After having unloaded presents and other sundries at Gayle's house, I told Thomas I was going to duck over to my parents' house to check out the mood and hopefully grab some time with Vivian.

Coming down their street, I spotted the glow of Dad's Christmas display from a block away. The lawn was packed. There was a life-size Santa in a sleigh, pulled by eight reindeer with Rudolph in the lead. Positioned center left, a nativity scene: Mary and Joseph in a stable, looking adoringly down on their baby in a manger, three wise men in the background. The house was wrapped in baubled lights, the trees hung with white glowing icicles. In addition, there were glowing candy canes lining the sidewalk leading to the front door. And in the middle of it all, the American flag, illuminated by a spotlight, which had adorned every one of their homes.

When I came into the house, no one appeared to be home. I snooped a bit and eventually found Vivian lying in bed off the sitting room, a waif of a being. She'd always been healthy and active, but now she looked sickly thin. When she saw me, she lit up like a firefly trapped in a jar. I asked her when she'd last eaten. She said it had been two days.

"Two days!"

"I've had the flu, so have had no appetite or the energy to get up."

"Haven't you told Mom or Dad?"

"Jim doesn't come home until late in the evening, and your mother . . . well, she's your mother."

I asked her if she'd like a cup of tea and some toast. Her gratitude pained me.

When I approached the kitchen, Mom was leaning against the counter, dressed in her nightgown. As usual, she showed no predilection for warmth toward me. She must have heard me with Vivian, but made no effort to greet me. She had just poured herself a cup of burnt coffee from the percolator.

"Where's my son-in-law and my grandkids?" she asked, as if I were hiding them somewhere.

"They're at Gayle's." I said it in as sensitive a way as I could. I didn't want to provoke her, to make the situation worse. "Mom—did you know that Vivian hasn't eaten for two days?"

"She can get out of bed if she's hungry. She knows where the kitchen is."

"Mom, she's sick, and she barely has any energy."

"Yeah, she works it."

I asked if it would be okay to get her a piece of toast.

"Sure thing. Here you go." She dramatically opened the drawer to show me where the bread was.

I made small talk as I put the kettle on. Where only a moment before my heart had been racing with anger, I now felt flat numb. Self-loathing returned. How the hell could I judge Dad for not standing up to Mom when as an adult I was no better?

I took the toast and tea in to Vivian, who mentioned several times how thankful she was. I watched her eat in tiny nibbles. We had spent a lot of time together in my years in Washington, D.C., and she had flown out to visit us in England a few times. I had packed up her apartment and put it on the market after she had cancer surgery, but since she had moved in with my parents, I had avoided calling because I was scared of Mom picking up the phone.

I was worried about Vivian's health, but I was more worried about her depressed mood. I asked her if she was getting out of the house. She looked over my shoulder to make sure the door was closed and then confided that she had asked Gayle to help her find an assisted living apartment and to set up a separate bank account so Mom no longer had access to her money. She said Mom was spending it without her permission. For example, she had used Vivian's money to replace the kitchen, saying it was necessary now that there were three of them in the house.

When I returned to the kitchen, Mom had disappeared somewhere upstairs.

In Which I Meet a Fishy Oracle

Indianapolis, 2001—I drove over to Dad's office. It was located in one of those strip malls. I was welcomed by a well-manicured receptionist named Jessica, who was full of midwestern cheer. Dad came out and introduced me to his five sales reps, then took me into his private wood-paneled office all serious-like, as though he were about to share something deep.

After he shut the door, he motioned for me to sit down on the couch, then took a deep breath.

"I have something to show you," he said thumping his fist on his desk. I jumped. A fish, mounted on a wooden plaque with a brass plate titled BIG MOUTH BILLY BASS, swung its head round and began to sing, in a reggae voice, the lyrics to Bobby McFerrin's song "Don't Worry, Be Happy."

Dad sprang up from his chair, and with his middle-aged potbelly and his happy feet, started doing this side-to-side little elf dance. He had his mischievous smirk on his face and was delighted to see I had begun to crack a smile. The song continued . . . *Don't worry, be happy now / Oooh, ooh-ooh-oOh-oOh-oOh* . . .

Dad wiggled his butt and turned. It was a vintage performance, and after it was over, he came over and put his arm around me, told me how happy he was to see me and how much he had been looking forward to our visit. Maybe I had grown old, but where I had been charmed in the past by my father's humor, I was now murderously frustrated.

"Dad, are you aware that Vivian hasn't eaten for two days and is seriously depressed?"

He stopped, switching to listening mode. I told him about Mom's reaction in the kitchen. He said he knew that things were stressful between the two, but he wasn't aware that Vivian was ill.

"Dad, this is what neglect of the elderly looks like." I tried not to sound lecturing. "It doesn't matter what tension exists between Mom and her. Even if Vivian had *chosen* not to eat for two days, that in itself raises concerns. You might not spend much time at the house, but this is happening under your roof."

"I'm glad you've brought it to my attention," he said, looking genuinely concerned. "I'll check in with Vivian when I get home."

"Dad, that's not going to be good enough this time." I could tell he suspected that I was going to say something about Mom. I felt the weight of it between us already. "When are you going to understand she hasn't changed? You infantilize her. She's the one who should be taking care of Vivian. She's home all day."

"We are not going to discuss your mother." I'd never seen Dad so angry before, even the muscles in his face were tense. But it made me come back harder.

"I'm not talking *against* her, Dad. This is more serious than that. As far as I can see, she still has the same authority in the house she's always had, she's just learned to wield it in a different way. You think because she's medicated and had six weeks of therapy, she's changed? The only thing that's changed is we are no longer children under her care. Can't you see her treatment of Vivian is the same kind of abuse?"

"I hear what you are saying about your grandmother," he reassured me, "and I will check in on her at home. I was wrong to assume she was okay." He then asked me if the drive had been okay, and it was clear the conversation was over.

Thomas and I and the kids made it through the holiday according to plan, but it required amazing acting skills. Two days later, we headed back to West Virginia.

In Which I Reach a Tipping Point

Shepherdstown, 2002—I returned to therapy with Dr. H feeling like I had passed an exam, but barely. I needed to build up the inner resources to start asserting new boundaries. And thus began a lengthy correspondence between Indianapolis and Shepherdstown, as Dad and I began efforts at reaching some kind of compromise in our relationship, one that didn't insist I have a relationship with Mom.

It wasn't the first time my father had been through this process. He had already experienced the heartbreak of failing to save his relationship with my older sister. As for me, I had tried to cut myself off one other time, only to resume our connection as if our family dysfunction was normal. It was right before I left the United States for England, and it lasted just nine months.

For as powerfully as the forces were pushing me away, I wasn't able to sustain the separation from my father, whom I dearly loved—a man who did deserve more understanding, a man who was compassionate and giving and deserved my respect. No matter how logical I was about it, I could not accept that Dad deserved rejection. But I could no longer afford to refute the truth of who my mother was—that while she might suffer from mental health issues, this did not mean I had to abide by her cruelty, her moods, her anger.

So I wrote a letter. To both of them. It was six weeks after our Christmas together. It began with a full disclosure and update of my mental health, which strikes me now as an unnecessary peace offering of sorts. But it provided the lead-in. That my breakdown—and indeed the depression of my teens and twenties—had discernible cause. Where I had been prepared before to dismiss my pain as the distorted symptom of my confused mind, I would no longer do so.

I did my best to be compassionate and respectful. I thanked them for all the positive memories we had built, the ways they had supported my family in the move, but said the power of the pain I was carrying as a result of the issues never dealt with had brought us to a point where I could no longer continue in the relationship. Specifically, and most painfully, I took Dad on, telling him I would no longer allow him to define what kind of relationship I had with the woman who was my physical and psychological abuser, and that I would no longer accept his denial of the extent of her cruelty, both past and present, nor would I stand by while she continued to hurt people I love—my sisters, my grandmother, maybe my children. I said I couldn't engage with Dad as long as he lived with her. I laid down the rules. I said any attempts by Mom to engage would not be responded to. It was an unbelievably hard letter to write. I felt physically exhausted, signed the page, and wrote their address on the envelope.

Dad's response was unexpected and crushing in its concern. He said he was sorry for the pain I endured, very sorry. He wanted to support me in any way needed. He understood that my responsibility was to my husband and children, and that I owed him nothing. He regretted his part in all of this and asked that I please know I was loved by both of them. I lost my resolve and called him. We agreed to keep communication open between him and me.

In May he called me on Mother's Day and asked if I'd like to speak to Mom. I declined.

It pushed me to be more honest in my next letter. I pointed out our problems were not in the past. I again recapped the symptoms of complex PTSD and depression I had suffered from. I said that I didn't hold him responsible for my mental health as an adult, but that he could have done things differently.

People endure loveless marriages without resorting to the violence that Mom used on us. I pointed out that he expected my sisters and me to forgive abuses that he was not even willing to hear occurred. I pointed out that she beat us, terrorized us, and disrespected us. In addition, she had cheated on him and made Genie and me accomplices by threatening us if we were ever to tell him the truth. She told us he'd hate us, not her. I said I would not go back to swallowing the unresolved pain so I could have a relationship with him. It was ripping me apart. In short, I was convinced if he heard all of it, understood all of it, he would view things differently.

A few days later, I received his response. He wrote back that he now understood the enormity of my experience, at least he heard and understood so much more than he had before. "I acknowledge the atrocities and the serious physical and psychological abuse inflicted on you by her. I also wish I realized why you were not happy as kids. Now that I am looking at the issue squarely in the face, I will come to a decision as to how I will resolve it, overcome my denial and the reasons for the denial." Again, he told me how much he loved me and wanted me in his life, that I deserved a life free of pain and despair and craziness, was so very deserving. And then told me to expect to hear from him again. "I want us to communicate, to learn from each other, to share the love we both have for each other in a productive, happy, undisguised way. I want you to be whole and happy and giggly and complete. It took guts for you to enlighten me, and again, I say thanks for caring enough about me to be honest. Much love, Pop." I felt that he had just given me soul-healing balm.

A week later, he sent another card telling me how much he loved me and to please stay in touch. We went several months with exchanged phone calls, no sign of involvement from Mom. And then in July I received a letter that I hadn't been prepared for. It was from Mom, and it was an attempt at mending our relationship, the first attempt in thirty-eight years. She told me how much she loved me and would do anything to erase the pain she caused me. Told me what a beautiful job I'd done with my life. She asked me to forgive her, "not for my sake, but for you. I know what it is like to go through life harboring

resentments and anger toward people and it's not an enriching place to be."
She knew what a deeply caring person I was and how important family was
to me. She promised me if I trusted her enough to open up, I would find the
risk worth it. "If you aren't able to—know that I love you with all the pieces
of my heart and will continue to no matter what. Love forever, Mom."

The letter showed no sign that she acknowledged on any level the lifetime of
abuse she had inflicted on my sisters and me. My response was quick and
curt. I suggested she show some sign of respect for the amount of damage
she had done and acknowledge it was serious. That would be a starting point.

I don't know why I expected that just because I had become firmer in my
resolve, she would suddenly admit to her abuse. But I knew her well enough
to know this wasn't about us. This was an attempt to maintain her relationships with other family members, most of all Dad—thus the "I know how
important family is to you." She had probably shown Dad the letter before
she mailed it.

But I had my integrity and I had my strength, and because of it, I stopped
worrying about what was no longer in my control.

We were approaching late summer. The Blue Ridge Mountains were lush with
deep greens and blues, the humidity was beginning to lift, the crickets were
at full range, and the Potomac River was perfect swimming temperature. We
were now well settled into our community in Shepherdstown. We had helped
found a parenting cooperative that organized family and kids' activities across
the week. My son and daughter were now four and five, their minds bursting
with little-person questions, and they were picking up knowledge as fast as
we could feed it to them, learning skills, becoming more self-sufficient. We
acquired pets—cats, dogs, rabbits, green anoles, frogs, a hamster—the menag-
erie kept growing. We cooked together. We spent time on the weekends as a
family biking, camping, canoeing, exploring Wild and Wonderful West
Virginia. Participated in the town's Easter parade, attended weekly Celtic
music sessions, took part in one of Shepherd University's musicals as a family.
In short, it was the parenting-family dream Thomas and I had hoped to build
together when we left England.

I was feeling great, not quite the version of myself I had been in the past, anxious that it might fall once again, but I felt safe in saying that I was fully back on my feet.

Dr. H and I agreed we had done great work. He wasn't the type to hang on to patients longer than needed, and I wasn't the type of patient to hang on. And I had never gotten comfortable with the dent it was making in our finances, especially since I wasn't yet bringing in money. He referred me to another psychiatrist who was more up to date on pharmacology than he was. But he assured me he'd be available if I needed him in the future.

I began networking again with old contacts in D.C. to look for a job. Thomas obtained a real estate license and bought our small town's local newspaper with a couple of other dads who had also downsized their careers to focus on raising family. They began publishing long-form pieces that investigated regional stories. By October, my breakdown was far enough in the past that it could be consigned to memory.

And that's when the sniper attacks in the Washington area began.

In Which I Sense an Imaginary Creature

Shepherdstown, 2002—In early October, just as the leaves on the trees were turning their fiery autumnal color, John Allen Muhammad and his accomplice, Lee Boyd Malvo, began shooting members of the public. By the time it was over they had killed ten people, and wounded three, in an area less than fifty miles from our house.

The last week they were on the run, it was rumored they were in our area. The playground at our local elementary school went on lockdown. I began checking car windows, checking out every corner. Moved all activities with the kids indoors. I was terrified to stop at gas stations. It was where most of the victims had been targeted.

And then, finally, on October 24, 2002, after almost a month of Washington under siege, they arrested Muhammad and Malvo at a rest stop on I-70, twenty miles from our home, a rest stop Thomas had driven by that morning.

A few hours later, I climbed into the passenger seat of our old Jeep Cherokee, reached for my safety belt, and sensed his presence in the back seat. I looked at Thomas, who was putting the key in the ignition, and heard myself say in a deadpan tone, "He's in the back."

"Who?" My husband asked, as if waiting for a punch line. Talk of imaginary creatures wasn't all that unusual in our family.

"Just drive." I was determined to appear calm.

"Deb?" I noticed my husband looking slightly concerned now.

"Ah-hm." I looked at Thomas, hoping that if I acted as if I hadn't said anything, he would too. It worked. He pushed the stick into drive, and we pulled out. To my relief, he didn't mention it again, and soon we were in Home Depot looking at floor-sanding machines.

The feeling that Mr. K might be in the back seat was an anxiety I had lived with my entire adult life. I had learned to overcome it, as I had many of my fears. And the internal conversation wasn't exceptional either. It was typical of the self-coaching I did regularly—only this time I had spoken out loud, as if my inner thoughts were on high-volume speaker. I felt oddly detached from the whole thing, and was happy to remain that way.

Unfortunately, that's not how the shadows in my mind were interested in playing. The problem was that the ghost of Mr. K began to make more frequent appearances. At first he returned in my night terrors. Then he'd be there before I fell asleep. And then I'd feel him in other rooms in the house. When I turned a corner, he would have just stepped behind the door. He was getting more and more daring.

A week later, I was still struggling to maintain my equilibrium, using all the tricks and tactics I had learned over the years, but my anxiety levels were making sleep difficult, and my reserves were running down. I couldn't get Mr. K out of my mind. One night when I was lying awake hours after we had gone to bed, Thomas touched my arm.

"Are you okay? What's going on . . ."

I immediately broke into sobs. He tried to console me. I realized there was no way I could continue to go on pretending things were normal. It was too terrifying. So I told him I felt like I was hallucinating, that I was sensing Mr. K so strongly I could swear he was in the house.

"Who's Mr. K?" Thomas asked.

"The guy," I said, thinking it was obvious.

"What guy?"

"The man who kidnapped me," I said. I had never resolved the issue of how to address my perpetrator, my offender. No one had ever told me his name. And I never asked.

It might seem odd that after five years of courtship and nine years of marriage, my husband and I had never had one purposeful conversation about the crime, but it was for the same reason, until Dr. H, I never thought to tell the doctors that I had been the victim of a significant violent crime. It felt counter to my survival instinct to dredge up old trauma.

Thomas pointed out that there was good reason for these memories to be surfacing, given the terror we had all just lived through. He could see I was having a difficult time talking about it. He suggested that maybe I should write down what was going on. Perhaps that might give me a sense of control over my thoughts.

"Like a bedtime story?"

Thomas said he was relieved to hear my humor returning.

In Which I Put a Narrative to the Trauma

Shepherdstown, 2002—It took several hours of staring at a blank page to finally start pressing pen to paper. I saw the trail of ink, the fragments began to join into sentences. I wondered why the act of writing felt so foreign. I had never tried to inhabit my inner mind through pen and paper when I was experiencing this degree of pain. How could these words possibly represent a memory when the act of articulating them felt so unreal? I felt no confidence that what I was writing was fact—it came from such a deep foreign part inside me, from the realm of my soul. I felt the sting of thrill and terror simultaneously. I knew it was truth. But not yet fact.

That in itself was enough to deplete the exercise of value. I hated everything about what I was doing. I hardly remembered who I was that long ago. How could the adult me write the memory of a fourteen-year-old accurately?

Once I realized that the pacing was under my command, I began to assert control over the emotional reflex that stopped me. It was only fear. There was little at risk. I needn't share this account with anyone—ever. After several days, I started feeling a little more confident. By the end of the week, I had almost five pages.

But when I read back through it, I started doubting myself again. How much of it was fact, and how much of it was the colorful memory of the child-teen

I was? How, for example, could I have gone to school that following Monday, just five days after the event? And after we moved to Iowa, why didn't I show signs of being a traumatized victim? I worked at the local library, became a cheerleader, joined the marching band, was at ease in relationships with boys, detasseled corn and walked beans in the summer, joined the track and swimming teams. My drinking was heavy in high school, but not significantly different from my classmates.

Did I have the details right? Had I really grabbed his fist when he was holding that knife at my throat? Why was I so convinced he had a gun when we pulled into that gas station—did I see it? Could I have jumped out the door? And why was I so convinced he was going to kill me near the stockyards? And surely there's no way it could have been as cold as I remembered, cold enough to kill me if I hadn't moved?

As the questions rolled in, any gains I'd made in my confidence that this account was true evaporated. But there was one real benefit. I had proved I could go back in history and still stay rooted in the present. The emotional force of it didn't bend me. I hadn't disappeared into one black hole. I had put the fragments into an order that created a narrative line. They were no longer dancing around my head at random, shadowy feelings, looking for a home.

Now, I wondered if it were fact-checked, how much of it would be true. Luckily, I was married to an investigative reporter.

In Which the Octopus Is Rendered Real

Shepherdstown, 2002—Thomas and I agreed that while he read my account, I'd take the kids to the Baltimore Aquarium. An hour later, my son, my daughter, and I were walking around the underwater kingdom, checking out seahorses, jellyfish, urchins, and sharks. Next we sat in the front-row seats for the dolphin show and were soon splashed by their fins as they swooshed by. Listening to my children's giggles and full-body laughter proved the perfect antidote to my anxious mood.

On our way out, my daughter spotted the one tank I had carefully bypassed. "Come on, Momma," she said clasping my hand, "let's go see the octopus." My son was soon joining in, pulling my other arm as I reluctantly let them drag me toward the darkened hall that encaged the gross beast.

We sat down in front of the enormous tank, on coal-black carpet. The kids wrapped themselves around me as our eyes slowly adjusted to the change in light. There it was, before us. A giant octopus—its sack of a head, its mantle with huge shaded eyes, its flowing dangling legs covered with rubbery oval suckers. It was looking directly at us.

My children stared back, their eyes round with curiosity and awe. Silenced by the magnificence of the monster, I checked my own emotions and found myself split. The parent interpreter who so wanted to get this moment right.

The fourteen-year-old me who was horrified at the violent appearance of the beast. The seven-year-old me who was desperate to transform the image in front of me into Dad's fantastical pet.

I was saved from my conflicted feelings when an enthusiastic aquarium volunteer walked over. "Do you want to know about her?" she asked. My kids nodded enthusiastically. The volunteer pointed out how the huge octopus was able to change colors, how its texture went from smooth to corrugated to prickly. She told us how the octopus was as smart as a cat or dog, and just as she was saying that, the octopus pushed up against the glass, and beneath its giant head its tentacles flowed with the water. It appeared to be dancing.

The volunteer said that the octopus was playing, and sure enough it reached for some orange-and-green plastic toys bobbing in the water. We watched as it grabbed one, then two, then three different objects with the tips of its tentacles, waving them around. The kids squealed with delight. And I joined them. It was just so funny.

I felt the inner tension flow out of me, the knot in my heart melted by my children's joy. By the absurdity of life.

We must have sat in front of that octopus for twenty minutes, watching it somersault, pulse through the water, play some more, slowly relax. Finally, I suggested to the kids we go get some ice cream before the drive back.

Later at home, after we'd put the children to bed, Thomas and I sat down at our kitchen table with a pot of herbal tea. He told me he was blown away by reading the account, that he knew it must have been hard for me to write these memories down. Then he took a deep breath, let the moment sink in for both of us. And continued.

He was shocked at the magnitude of the violence and how little he knew. Just for a start, he knew I had been abducted at knifepoint, but it hadn't fully registered that it had been at four P.M. in the parking lot of my church and school, and during an ice storm. He knew a ransom had been demanded, but didn't know there had been police at the house, that the phone was being monitored. He knew I had been dropped off, but he didn't understand the physical shock I must have been in, that it had been record-breaking freezing temperatures, and it never registered I had been dropped off in the dark. Furthermore, he knew that the crime had been important to my relationship with my father, forged an inseparable bond, and now it explained my unshakable loyalty to him. He also hadn't known that Mr. K had worn a ski mask and I could only ever see his eyes, and finally, he knew that my perpetrator had been jailed, but the significance of my never having had to appear in court—well, he understood the real power of that now.

He suggested that it might be time to find out what the actual charges were and how many years of the sentence the man had served. Perhaps the knowledge might give me a little more control.

"You mean you believe my account?"

"I don't understand the question."

"You mean you think I'm remembering it correctly?"

"Of course I do," he said compassionately.

"I don't know. None of it feels real . . . There's something else that keeps bothering me," I said, blowing the steam across my cup. "A year or two after we moved to Laurens, I went into my father's dresser drawer to borrow a T-shirt, and as I was flipping through them, I noticed a letter, hidden, and it was addressed to me. The return address was from Lincoln and it had a prison address on it. I felt guilty for discovering it, then guilty as I opened it, and then horrified after I read it. The guy had written me this creepy letter, like we were good friends. He said I'd want to know he had found Jesus and God had forgiven him and then, even sicker, added a sentence where he told me not to smoke cigarettes and to avoid the fast lane. It was so frightening and its contents so gross and disgusting that I put it back in Dad's drawer."

Thomas asked if my father ever talked to me about the letter.

"No. Why would he? I was fifteen years old. Once I read it, I did everything I could for the next couple of days to push it out of my mind. Just filed it in the box labeled, 'Dad has it under control.'

"And then there's the other weird story. Remember Todd, that friend I introduced you to when we came through Nebraska on Bike-Aid? He told me one of my closest friends at junior high had gone on to work in the Nebraska State Prison. Her name was Kim."

Thomas looked at me blankly. His memory was a running joke in our relationship. At the time we met, he was still recovering from the sixteen stitches in his head, after the hit-and-run in Mexico that nearly killed him.

So I recapped the story for him. That Kim had pursued a criminal psychology degree at the University of Nebraska, in Lincoln, and as part of the degree requirement she had worked in the Community Release Center, where she had unwittingly become friendly with Mr. K. Later she confronted him after discovering his true identity.

It turned into some kind of psychological conversion, as he fell apart and said that he could barely live with himself and he was so glad he had finally been able to face the truth. They paroled him shortly after that. I can't say I received the story well. I didn't want to hear anything about this man. And I appreciated the position Kim had been put in, which sounded terrible, but it felt like hearing there had been a reconciliation process conducted on my behalf. Yet I wouldn't have wanted her to respond any other way. It was a bizarre occurrence.

After I finished telling Thomas the story, he was more adamant about finding out where the guy was, where he lived. He said that as a victim, it was my right to know. And then reassured me that finding the information was a good thing.

"I don't know his name," I said, and added with anxious dread, "We'd have to call my parents."

"Believe me, Deb. They are going to want to help you with this. We can at least find out the charges." I wasn't as sure as he was, but I reluctantly agreed. Of course they'd be helpful.

He dialed. I heard him ask Mom if he could talk to Jim. I could tell she was saying he wasn't available. Thomas put the phone on loudspeaker, explained why he was calling, said it in a way that didn't give too much of my emotional privacy away—just told her I was having a difficult time, and he was curious, did she happen to know what the guy who kidnapped me was charged with?

"Debora wasn't kidnapped," my mother said matter-of-factly. "But the man was charged with rape." It felt like a full-body sucker punch. The confidence that Thomas had just filled me with evaporated. Thomas asked her again if she knew what the man had been charged with? What the sentence had been? She said no, she didn't remember the charges.

I knew I had been right in my instinct not to make the call. Thomas told her it was okay, he could get the information from the FBI if she remembered the perpetrator's name. She asked why the FBI would have the information. The man hadn't been serious about collecting the money. He never showed up.

Thomas sidestepped the argument and asked her again if she knew the name of the man who kidnapped me. She said, oh, yes, she'd never forget that. His name was Goodwin. Charles Goodwin.

Thomas hung up the phone, flabbergasted. "I can't believe that conversation," he said.

I had always been thankful that everything I told the police as a fourteen-year-old girl had been believed, and never more so now. I stood silent, so crushed inside I was afraid to speak. Thomas began to think out loud. "It's not her denial of the facts that is bothering me. It's her emotional reaction, or lack of it. It's just wrong. I'm so sorry." He was saying it like it was my whole childhood he was sick about. "I want to vomit," he said, talking more to himself than to me. And then he came over and hugged me. I felt the tears, in fact, my face was wet with them, but I was afraid if I opened my mouth, if I sobbed, I would go to pieces.

"Deb, do you understand this is no longer just about Charles Goodwin? This is now also about your parents?"

"We should just leave it," I said. I was feeling scarily disconnected from anything real. This had started so we could allow my delusional mind to rest, by reassuring me this man was not anywhere near me. And now, after six months of vacation—Mom was back in my head again.

I had always thought my police statement was irrefutable because it was backed up by evidence. And it was because of that, I never had to go to trial. But now, my mother suggested Mr. K was never charged for kidnapping. I felt sick at the thought this man never served time for the terror he had inflicted on my father, on my family when he threatened my life, for the threat he had made me witness in that phone booth. He was lucky there was no charge filed for attempted murder.

And yet, surprisingly, I realized that I did want to know. I wanted to know if he had been sentenced for kidnapping, and that my work that night with the police had been helpful. I told Thomas I'd appreciate it if he could contact the FBI.

He suggested I try to get some sleep while he made the call.

In Which I Make a Grand Exit

Omaha, 1979—It wasn't memories of the kidnapping that returned as I lay on our couch. Instead, it was images from the days that followed, specifically my last night in Omaha.

The night before we left for Iowa, my friends threw a going-away party for me at Ben Norris's house. Around eight P.M., a group of us stepped outside to start a chugging contest. We'd never had spirits before, but someone had managed to get vodka. I won by downing half the bottle. Not long after, I began to feel dizzy and my legs buckled.

The next thing I knew, I woke up in a strange bed, wearing a hospital robe. I was damp. And then I realized with horror it was the mattress that was damp, my sheets; I had wet myself. Slowly, I made out that I was in a hotel room, and the curtains were drawn. I panicked. My first thought was that Mr. K had somehow found me, had left me in this place, and would be coming back. Then I saw the phone, picked it up, was relieved to get a line, quickly dialed a close friend. He picked up the phone and I started sobbing, describing where I was, tried to piece it together. He asked me to slow down, I could calm down, it was okay. And with a heavy heart, he asked if I remembered anything from the party the night before. The room was almost too fuzzy to bring into focus, let alone recall the night before.

He explained my parents had checked us into a hotel because the movers had packed the furniture from our house. We were leaving for Iowa that day. He recounted the details of the guzzling contest a group of us had. It was a haze, but now I remembered, yes. I had memories of being dizzy as we walked through the snow back to the house. I passed out within an hour and they couldn't wake me up. The mother of the boy who had hosted the party, who was also president of the Parent Teacher Association and had helped with the reward fund, called my father to tell him to come pick me up immediately. When he arrived, I was unconscious. He tried to revive me by slapping my face, but I remained unresponsive. Someone called an ambulance.

I could hear my friend was choking back tears. He had to pause between sentences. He said when the ambulance arrived and they were loading me on the stretcher, he apologized to my father for supplying the alcohol, and Dad took a swing at him, tried to punch him in the face, but missed. I had a sudden flash of being in the emergency room, of having a tube shoved down my throat.

Just as he was finishing the story, and the horror of the whole night was sinking in, I heard someone put a key in the door. My mother walked in and turned the light on. She told me to hang up the phone, then threw a pile of clothes at me. Told me to shower and change. She drove me back to our empty house in silence. I could hardly stand without my insides setting to work once again at convulsions. My father and my sisters were nowhere to be seen.

Mom opened the car door and told me to get out, that I wasn't getting out of cleaning, we were leaving the house later that day. She told me to go up to my bedroom. She appeared five minutes later with a toothbrush and told me to scrub the baseboards. As soon as she was gone, I lay my face down, the smell of that shag carpet up my nose, and thought, I'm not doing too well.

That evening we headed out of Omaha. It wasn't late, it was just dark, no doubt my fault for slowing things up. My parents took the lead in a van, and my three sisters and I followed behind in the station wagon. Genie, sixteen years old now, was driving.

It was snowing hard as we took the Mormon Bridge over the Missouri River into Iowa, on Interstate 80. After an hour, we turned north onto the county highways. Banks of snow lined the single-lane roads. At times it was like motoring through a white canyon. Every once in a while, we'd get a clear opening, and I'd catch a glimpse of snow blowing in great gusts across the fields. Ten miles outside Laurens, the weather was so bad that Dad had slowed down to twenty miles an hour in front of us. We were all bored, tired, and nervous about the move. Jenifer and I were in the back, Gayle with Genie in the front.

To pick up the mood, Genie began singing a show tune, ramping up her performance with a few thrusts of the arm. Instinctively, I grabbed the back of the seat.

"You're scaring us," I told her. "Do us a favor and keep your hands on the steering wheel."

"Oh, really?" she responded. And then, in a show of respect for my back seat driving, she pulled a harmonica out of her pocket and started to play it. "You want me to stop?" And she lifted both hands and let the white nose of the Chevy coast, not dangerously, but with leisurely purpose, straight into a ditch.

"Happy now?" she said, turning to me.

I saw Dad pull the van over and, in the red glow of his flashing taillights, saw the worry on his face. Genie rolled the window down.

"Are you all okay?" he said, panting little puffs of steam from his mouth.

"Oh, we're just fine," Genie responded, bitter at being put in a position of charge. And then she told him she wouldn't drive if I was in the same car. Dad didn't have time to pick it apart, just told me to get in the van and then set about digging the station wagon out.

I trudged over to the van, rolled back the side door, and climbed in behind Mom. We sat in silence for a couple of moments. And then she looked up and adjusted the rearview mirror so she could look at me without turning around.

"You know, no one in this town is going to know you, or your past. Very few people get a chance to start over with a new reputation."

Honestly, I just wanted to sleep. I was still exhausted and nauseated.

"You know your father asked Genie if she thought it was a hoax? The phone call you made? He actually wondered if it was a joke because you didn't want to move to Iowa."

I knew without a doubt that Dad would never seriously suggest to her I might have staged my own kidnapping to get out of the move, that she had taken a fact (I was on the other end of the phone when Dad said he didn't believe me) and twisted it into something that would serve her own purpose. And sure enough, next came the shot I knew she was lining up on the bow.

"Do you know your father was confused about what counted as rape and what didn't?" she said. "So I had to explain it to him? After that stunt of yours last night, I have to tell you, nothing you'd do would surprise me."

Dad, oblivious to the attack at hand, climbed back in the van, and my Pavlovian response to his presence kicked in—I adopted the unthinking mind of a dog. The three of us sat in silence, didn't say a word for the rest of the journey.

This time we didn't have to wait for a real estate agent to greet us when we pulled into our freshly painted, five-bedroom, three-story Victorian house in Laurens. The Mayflower truck had arrived the day before—all the furniture had been moved into the appropriately marked rooms, and assembled for us.

That night, I lay in bed listening to the ominous silence. I looked out my window and thought about this new town of mine with 1,600 inhabitants in the middle of hundreds of thousands of acres of corn, and I suddenly realized I had never seen stars this bright, or a sky as black as a hearse.

In Which Mr. K Materializes

Shepherdstown, 2002—When I awoke two hours later, Thomas was sitting on the side of our bed, sipping a fresh cup of tea, a warm, calm look on his face. I could tell he had something to tell me. He nodded in the direction of another hot cup of tea waiting on the table beside me.

I slowly pulled myself up, felt the familiar stab of self-loathing as I reached over for my cup and took a swig, hoping he couldn't sense how pathetic I felt. I couldn't help but wonder how he had the emotional stamina to support me in the way he did.

"I called the FBI," he said when my eyes started to focus, "and the agent I spoke to was incredibly helpful." He paused.

I nodded, still cloudy.

"Mr. K's name is Charles Goodwin, Charles Mark Goodwin, and he was born in 1961. And Deb?" He waited for me to look at him. "He was sentenced to twelve to twenty years for first-degree sexual assault and *kidnapping* in March 1979."

There it was—the facts established without a reasonable doubt by the State of Nebraska. Justice. I might have been standing in a courtroom hearing the sentence for the first time, it hit me so hard. I reminded myself how fortunate and exceptionally lucky I had been all these years to never have had to appear in court, to not have had to stand trial as a victim. But as my initial reaction of the news began to dissipate, it occurred to me then the relief wasn't triggered for the reason I expected—that I had just received confirmation that Charles Goodwin served time for a kidnapping charge—but instead came from the fact that I was right, despite what my mother had said.

But what had been so bad wasn't the fact that Mom had the facts wrong as much as the instant I heard her say it, I doubted my own reality; I threw my fourteen-year-old self under the bus. I'm the one who gave her that power. It wasn't her fault. It was mine. What a relief we got *that* straightened out. I must have misinterpreted her point. Of course she hadn't meant to imply I hadn't been kidnapped. This was about his sentence. She thought because Mr. K hadn't shown up to collect the money, they couldn't charge him legally with kidnapping. And then the voice of Dr. H kicked in. "You aren't wrong, and you aren't confused. Trust *that* feeling. It's your inner voice telling you something's off." I suddenly heard Thomas's voice over the emotional roller-coaster in my head.

"*Deb—did you hear me?* I said Charles Goodwin is coming up for parole in six months' time."

"What?"

"He's been in prison this whole time—twenty-four years. He has a parole hearing in September."

That didn't make any sense. I had been told by my friend that he had been released in 1986. Nor did his birthdate, which suggested he was just three years older than I was. I had always thought he was in his thirties.

Thomas told me he also called the *Omaha World Herald* and asked them to send us any articles between 1975 and 1990 that mentioned a Charles Goodwin. We were going to fact-check this thing properly.

Need I say the synchronicity between hallucinating he was in my house and finding out he was just coming up for release did not help my already anxious-ridden mind.

In Which I Review the Headlines

Shepherdstown, 2003—A few weeks later, a rather thick package arrived in the mail. There were about twelve articles spanning four months—stories that gave definition to the mystery of the man who disproportionally impacted my life, yet who remained in the shadows for twenty-five years.

There was information about Goodwin's former arrests, time served in juvenile, speculation about motives, and results from his psychiatric evaluation. But the most difficult to read were those detailing the abduction, the ransom demand, and most heartbreaking of all—an article describing my father's experience that day, his helplessness.

Contained in these articles was the answer to why "Charles Goodwin," as I was struggling now to call him, was still in prison. On December 21, 1987, he had been paroled from the Lincoln Community Corrections Center after serving nine years of his twenty-year prison term for sexual assault and kidnapping. The article mentioned he had obtained a bachelor of arts in psychology, and several people at the University of Nebraska, at Lincoln, had testified on his behalf.

He had been free for less than three weeks when he robbed a Union Bank branch in Lincoln, Nebraska, at gunpoint, wearing a pink bathrobe and long underwear. He faked an accent, which led them to believe that he was of either Hispanic or Middle Eastern descent. He ordered two female employees to lie on the floor in the back room, where he bound them with tape and then forced a third employee to take money from the vault and help him load it into his car. He walked away with more than $250,000 in cash, which made it the largest-ever cash bank holdup in Nebraska.

But his itch for fancy cars got him. The same afternoon he robbed the bank, Goodwin went out and bought a Trans Am, in cash, paying extra to have it painted red. The owner of the garage, suspicious at that amount of cash, called the police. Goodwin was arrested soon after, with the weapon he used to rob the bank—a pellet gun.

Five months later, on June 3, 1988, Charles Goodwin, while still in the local jail awaiting trial, faked a knee injury. As they were moving him to the hospital for an X-ray, he jumped out of the van and managed to run several blocks before being tackled by an officer, at which point he pulled a knife out of his pocket, made from a toothbrush and razor blade, and sliced the officer's thumb before finally being subdued. He was charged with escape, second-degree assault, and use of a knife to commit a felony. So in addition to having the privilege of finishing his time for crimes against me, he now added time for bank robbery—another federal crime—and assault of a prison officer. And that was why he was still in prison.

As the outline of Mr. K began to take the form of Charles Goodwin, I found my emotions slowly evolving into something I had never had to deal with before. This "guy" was a real human being, and his name was Charles Goodwin. I couldn't bear to say his name without feeling I was giving him more respect than I cared to. So I preferred to call him the Fucking Asshole for a while. It was permission I had never given myself before.

In Which I Fact-Check

Shepherdstown, 2003—The articles did a lot to assuage my doubts about my own ability to perceive reality and recall history. They also had a punch. If my memory was correct about the abduction, it meant my memory was likely as a whole to be reliable. Trustworthy. And there was a lot of childhood material back there that I'd prefer to think I had wrong.

Now that I felt more confident in my own story and had learned Mr. K's name and that in fact he was a seventeen-year-old punk, I needed to know what happened to that fourteen-year-old me. When, for example, did my father contact the police? Why did Goodwin plead not guilty and then switch to a plea bargain? Why was it I never had to go to court? Thomas suggested that if we got a hold of the police records, we might find the answers. They'd have witness statements and other evidence records—but procuring these would be difficult. They might have been destroyed by now.

I thought of my childhood friend Kate Shugrue. She was working as a senior lawyer for Child Protective Services, in the Nebraska Attorney General's Office. Our connection had never weakened, and I knew I could always call her.

Once I got in touch, she was immediately supportive and thought it was natural that now that I was an adult, I'd want answers to what had happened

that night. She asked about my parents, and when I told her, honestly, I was
nearly estranged because of difficulties with Mom, Kate said she wasn't
surprised. She remembered my mother as a taskmaster, and that she seemed
distant and uninterested in me and my friends. "She used to push you and
your sisters so hard on the housework!" Kate said, thinking more about it.
"And we'd never hang out at your house, always at mine. Now I understand
why you always seemed to take such a shine to my mom." It was clear to her
the Monday I showed up at school, talking about the kidnapping in the
same tone as about what I had for breakfast that morning, that I was not
getting the support and love I needed and deserved at home. She said she'd
help me find out the full story in any way she could. There was a good chance
that the police reports might no longer be on file, but she would see what she
could do. Several days later, another large envelope arrived.

I opened it to find a complete copy of the court files. The report included
witness statements from people who had been involved that night—the gas
attendant, the woman who rescued me and helped me into her office,
the undercover officers who waited with my father, the friend of Charles
Goodwin who had turned him in—all the pieces of that horrific night, all
the parts of the story I had never heard.

Most chilling of all was Goodwin's original testimony, given right after his
arrest. He had been happy to brag about the whole assault, in extremely foul
language, confirming not only every single fact as I remembered it but with
a violence that leapt from the page. This is when I learned that the railcar he
left me by was next to a loading dock, and that after he left me, he drove to
the Center Shopping Center open-level parking garage, where he saw my
father and parked the van on the third level. He said in his statement to the
police that when he left the vehicle, he noticed what he thought were undercover police. No problem, cool as a cucumber, he asked a stranger if he could
borrow a dime to make a call, fake-dialed someone, hung up, and walked off
to a McDonald's to have a hamburger. That detail still gets me. If there had
been any question of whether Goodwin had been treated unfairly by the court
system, pushed into a plea bargain, this eliminated it.

Near the bottom of the stack of pages, I found the hospital reports and the
description of what had been done to me in medical terms. I had no idea of

the history of my own fourteen-year-old body. After fighting back waves of nausea, I sealed the reports back in an envelope, never wanting to lay eyes on them again.

The most difficult report for me was the last one, which listed the evidence gathered from the van. In addition to a sample of my blood, which they had identified from a piece of carpet in the back of the vehicle, there was another piece of evidence found: irrefutable proof of the personal cost, my cross necklace.

In Which I Solve a Psychological Riddle

Shepherdstown, 2003—Now that I had all the articles, the witness statements, and the police records, I spent hours, with Thomas's help, fitting the pieces together. After we were done, I felt strung out, but I knew this time that it wasn't anything sleep couldn't sort out.

Three months had passed since Thomas had contacted the FBI. Meanwhile, Mr. K's parole loomed. Though I tried to dismiss fears that he could be a danger to me or my family, it wasn't that easy. I had learned enough in therapy to know the antidote to anxiety is not logic; the antidote to anxiety is noting it and letting it pass. But in this case, my mind was exploding with variables, and I couldn't fight the analytical part of my brain that was wrestling for order.

For example, I couldn't put to rest my fear that Charles Goodwin would try to contact me after his release. It wasn't simply a question of would he or wouldn't he contact me. It was a question of chance. What were the chances he would appear in my life—the percentage of probability?

That there was a probability at all, I wouldn't have even been thinking had it not been for the letter he sent to my Iowa address in 1980 and the freak coincidence of his meeting my friend Kim Haller in prison, in 1986, eight years after the crime.

What I could say with confidence was that it was unlikely he spent the same amount of time thinking about me that I spent fearing him. If Thomas hadn't thought to investigate the reasons for my hallucinations, I wouldn't have known he was still behind bars. Learning of the timing of his parole was coincidental; unfortunate in terms of timing, but that was all.

I drew a diagram on a piece of paper so I could see it visually, separate the two.

> (A) The sniper attacks triggered (B) hallucinations/PTSD symptoms. This was *based on memories of past trauma.*
>
> (C) New information of his reincarceration and parole timing triggered (D) appropriate levels of anxiety *based in present time.*

Was it any wonder I was overwhelmed? Identifying the variables and giving them order certainly helped the picture look less fragmented. One set lived in the world of memory, the other in my world today.

It struck me this equation had striking similarities to the work I had just done with Dr. H with regard to my childhood.

> (A) My children reaching the age at which I first had memories of the abuse triggered (B) Mom's voice in my head and intrusive flashbacks/PTSD symptoms. This was *based on memories of past trauma.*
>
> (C) Our move back to America put me back in proximity with Mom, which triggered (D) present anxiety and distance concerning my relationship with her, *based in present time.*

I was still hoping that time was going to produce some sort of resolution, at least a new arrangement that could salvage my relationship with Dad.

In both cases—the relationship with my mother and the relationship with Mr. K—I was trying to separate current challenges from the legacy of trauma they had left me.

Turning my attention back to Charles Goodwin and putting my mother aside, at least for now, I began wondering what the chances were that he was actually rehabilitated. He was a violent rapist, and a repeat violent offender. Having spent twenty-five years in jail, what were the chances that he had changed?

While researching the recidivism rates of violent offenders, I came across the concept of restorative justice. In an effort to address the shortcomings of the criminal legal system, some prisons were facilitating dialogue between victims and offenders.

This allowed victims to ask questions that are left unanswered in the wake of a crime. Some do it because they haven't been able to move on with their lives, some because they want answers to questions. Some had managed to reconcile with their offenders. A few even established ongoing relationships. Just imagining that made my stomach curdle.

I was now an adult making decisions for my fourteen-year-old self, no longer under the custody of my parents. Would gaining a better understanding of the forces that shaped that day put my fears to rest? Despite the serious depressive episodes, the seizures, the dark current of anxiety that had been a part of my inner world for as long as I could remember, I had refused to let this crime define me. Would reopening the door to my unresolved childhood trauma really help anyone?

Every time I thought of calling the Nebraska State Penitentiary to see if they offered such a program, I felt my heart rate quicken. I'd be breaking unspoken boundaries that my parents had set years ago. There must be statutes of limitations on something like this. It felt slightly perverse, like I was stepping into dangerous territory just by making the call. Adolescent even. Like I was fourteen years old and disobeying Mom and Dad.

I decided to make some notes—a process that always slowed my mind. But one of the questions I wrote down threw me—"Was the dog wagging the tail, or the whale tagging the dog?" Just the fact that my brain had dished up a spoonerism threw a chink in my new armor. Was any of this a good idea given I had just recovered from a mental breakdown?

In Which Charles Generously Provides His Services

Lincoln, 2003—Charles found himself feeling more and more elated. He was at the last stop in his incarceration, the Lincoln Community Corrections Center. For the first time in over twenty-four years, at the age of forty, he was beginning to let himself think like a free man. It could even be argued he had been in prison longer than that. He was fourteen years old at the time of his first arrest and had spent his youth in and out of juvenile facilities.

His parole hearing was two months away in September, and the state couldn't hold him much longer. The recidivism rate was much higher for offenders who left prison without a period of supervised parole, so it was unlikely that they would require him to serve the full twenty-five years as it meant he wouldn't be under observation.

He was trying not to get too cocky about it because you never know what might go wrong. This time, he wanted to do it right. He had decided he really wanted to live a life outside prison. Since moving to the Lincoln Release Center, he had successfully held down two jobs in the community for a couple of months. He was still being escorted back and forth to his job sites, but he was able to put money in an account for the first time in years, and was accumulating cash for a deposit on a place to live. The telemarketing he enjoyed enough—his boss was impressed with the easy manner he had with folks and said he was a natural (his boss had a sense of humor). But hanging drywall was better pay, the hours flew by faster, and he enjoyed the team aspect of the work.

Besides the adjustment to being around the general population, including women and children, and the social graces he needed to start practicing, he was discovering all sorts of other adaptions. Just the other day he had encountered an automatic flushing toilet, which freaked the hell out of him. And mobile telephones, so many people had them these days. Being the social man he was, he was getting one of those as soon as he could.

And just to show he wasn't presuming anything about release, he signed up to be one of three prisoners on a panel to answer questions from about thirty or forty staff trainees. His parole hearing was coming up in September and besides a break from the monotony of work, he'd get points on his record for being cooperative.

And then—why the hell did this keep happening to him? There he was, just being Mr. Helpful, and some chick in the audience starts asking about the kidnapping and sexual assault charges. He tried steering the conversation back to the robbery, that's what he'd signed up for, but she wasn't having it.

So he admitted to the kidnapping. And then she asked him, in front of everyone, would he admit he was a rapist? Where was this going? He finally offered up that he was surprised when the girl had started crying. But the chick wouldn't leave it. She asked the question again in front of the whole room. Asked him if he could admit he was a rapist—she wanted to hear him say the words, so he did just to shut her up. What the hell? It was enough to make a guy paranoid.

In Which I Contemplate a Stimulating Conversation

Shepherdstown, 2003—After a month of thinking it through, I took the next step, called the office of Victim Services at the Nebraska Department of Correctional Services, and spoke with a calm and gentle-sounding woman named Jill. She confirmed that yes, Nebraska did offer a Victim-Offender Dialogue program. But after she heard my story, she grew more cautious. They had never before facilitated a case that involved a severe crime or a repeat violent offender. Before we entered dialogue, and to ensure my safety, Goodwin would need to be evaluated by a prison mental health professional. And then he would have to agree to participate. I thanked her for the information and sat on it for another month.

When I reached out again, she was, for lack of a better word, glad I called. There had been a further development, but she didn't feel that she could invade my privacy by contacting me. After my previous conversation with Jill, Goodwin had volunteered to speak on a prisoner's panel for a staff training she was conducting for Victim Assistance. But apparently he had been caught off guard, thinking that he had offered his services as an experienced bank robber, not as a kidnapper and rapist. When pushed about the kidnapping, he volunteered that he had dropped me off on a country road; and when pushed further about whether he was a rapist, he offered that he was surprised when I had started to cry. Jill raised her hand from the audience and asked him if he could say the words "I am a rapist."

She said he did so, but reluctantly. This might have been because he was in a group of thirty people. The reason she shared it with me was because it suggested that he had never come to grips with what he had done.

I hung up the phone wanting to vomit. What was I doing? What could I possibly hope to achieve? It was an abstract battle I was fighting here, and perhaps I could better take care of myself by disengaging. And suddenly it struck me. What if Mr. K/a.k.a. Fucking Asshole/Charles Goodwin said "yes"? That he was prepared to speak with me? I was totally unprepared. I had no idea how the process worked, how to evaluate it, or what kind of training Jill had.

I went back on the internet and found a mediation training program in Austin, Texas, based on the principles of restorative justice. The man who founded the program, David Doerfler, facilitated encounters between the families of murder victims and their offenders.

I spoke with David over the phone, explained that I was contemplating making contact with my offender, and we discussed the dangers in cases of severe crime such as mine—retraumatization, being manipulated, physical dangers, false hope that there could be a happy ending, or a fantasy that some kind of healing would occur that would remove the pain. Our minds worked so quickly together that he asked if I would be interested in going through the training myself as a mediator. Given the violence of the crime we were talking about, it might be a good strategy. He'd let me participate in the course for free if I thought I could swing the airfare. I'd learn about the process and find ways to assess each and every stage I was at, so I could feel more in control.

I dropped Dad a quick email, briefly introducing the concept. He wrote back interested in hearing more, asking me to provide a link to David Doerfler's work. Told me how much he missed Thomas and the kids, and asked if I could send some digital pictures.

And then I asked him about the letter that Charles Goodwin had sent to our Iowa address and whether he still had it. And that was the beginning of what I hoped would be the conversation I had waited for all my life. He didn't respond.

Two weeks later I flew to Austin.

In Which I Chase Nickels

Shepherdstown, 2003—A week after I returned from Austin, Texas, I was still waiting to hear if Goodwin would consent to an initial meeting with my victim advocate. I had plenty of time to re-question the process I had embarked on. Why had I put myself in a precarious position where I had handed him decision-making power in my life? As each day passed, I resented my situation more. When the phone rang at last, Jill told me he had agreed to Victim-Offender Dialogue, that we could move ahead. I felt a mixture of sweeping gratitude and relief, and then anger that I should feel thankful, and then elation.

Jill framed what we might achieve, careful to contain my expectations. She reminded me that only a few months ago Charles Goodwin had denied being a rapist while serving on the panel in order to help prison staff trainees. After all these years, I didn't need an admission of guilt, though. I knew he, Goodwin, was looking at the door to freedom and wasn't likely doing this for personal growth reasons. I wasn't hoping for truth and I wouldn't have to meet him. I wanted to rid my brain of the image of that ski mask and to see the human with the eyes. I wanted to establish that the person who attacked me was not an evil monster lodged permanently at the back of my head like that blade he had pressed into my skull. I wanted to dispel the ghost of him in the same way Dad had taught me when he offered me a nickel to look under the bed all those years ago in Maine. Granted, it might sound like a sledgehammer approach to treating hallucinations.

I began to focus on what I wanted out of the dialogue. We would communicate through Jill—I wouldn't have to see him. I wanted to know how much of the violence of those four hours he remembered, if what he had done to me was important enough for him to remember. That was also a catch-22—that he might be walking around with that memory in his head wasn't a rosy idea either. I had his police statement from the night he was arrested and was so horrified at the brutality of it, I wanted to compare it to the version he would tell today, to hear the word choices he'd use. I hoped to get an idea of how self-aware he was, of his ability to reflect on the chain of events that led to his becoming so out of control. I was also curious to know who he was, what kind of background he had, who his family was, what motivated his violence against me and my family. Had he targeted me?

I also wanted to know specifics surrounding the crime, how far in advance he had planned the kidnapping. Why me? Did he know my father? Had he been following me that day? How much of that story he fed me about his grandmother—about his belief in God—were lies?

And then there was the deeper layer of questioning. I wanted to know whether I was right about my instinct, that he had intended to kill me, and if so, what changed his mind. Kim told me he said in their meeting that day in prison that he couldn't kill me because I kept talking to him about God. I wanted to know if he came back for me. It wasn't in the police report. I wanted to know what happened when he went to meet my father. I already had answers from the newspaper articles and police reports, but I didn't know it from his first-person point of view. I had no idea if it was right to ask him these questions, but Jill assured me there were no rights and wrongs. I was the victim. He could choose not to answer the question.

The day the meeting was scheduled moved excruciatingly slowly. Goodwin couldn't meet with Jill until after he was back from work.

The phone finally rang. Jill spoke with more energy in her voice than her usual measured tone. The meeting went better than she expected, he answered all the questions, and she thought I would be pleased to have the answers. She'd write up the notes and have them over to me by the next morning.

When the email came through the next day, both Thomas and I were aston-ished at the answers. Goodwin's account mirrored in detail the one I had struggled to write at my desk. We compared his answers to the police report when he was seventeen. The adult Goodwin, complete with his psychology degree, recounted the day's events with astounding clarity. He admitted to being grossly out of control, to having a gun, even to his murderous intent. He said that he had changed his plan to kill me after a temporary moment of compassion in recalling our conversation about God, and even felt a pang in the thought that he had hurt a friend. And then, to settle the question of the nature of his violence, something rapists are often blind to, and by far the most painful thing to hear, so painful I winced—he said I had "gone so limp" after the assault, he thought I had died. On hearing it, I thought his choice of wording noteworthy—he thought "I had died." It made his role in the act sound so passive—not like he might have killed or murdered me.

There was a stark change of tone between the two accounts; he spoke with a different vocabulary. The police statement of December 3, 1978, was given by a rage-filled seventeen-year-old, consumed with vengeful hatred of every-thing my father and I represented in his world, who bragged about the way he terrorized my father and about his violent assault against me. Most of all, the difference in his self-awareness was striking. I was stunned. What had I expected?

Reading over the account, I couldn't believe how quickly my fear, anxiety, and rage disappeared, how deeply grateful I was that he had verified the truth of my memory. And even then, even when I was flooded with the impact of hearing my memory of twenty-five years recounted in exact detail by Goodwin, voiced with an awareness of its devastating impact, I found my thoughts turning in an unwanted direction—to my mother. What a gift it would be to my sisters and me if she would do the same. But she would never hold herself accountable. Why should she when Dad was giving her a total pass?

I read through the notes again, and that's when I caught something I'd almost missed. Goodwin said he was surprised that I hadn't displayed any fear when he abducted me. It struck me as remarkable. I'll never forget the moment—the deafening loudness of that silent scream, grabbing his wrist as he had the knife to my throat, then fighting, kicking against him as he shoved me into the van. He confused my lack of submission with a lack of fear.

Again, there were similarities with Mom, in Mom's perception of her actions—the way she described her knife attack on my father with no shame, no thought as to the fear he experienced in wrestling the knife from her hand. And whatever that was, that emotional blind spot, it was the same thing missing in her that left my sisters, Dad, and me at her mercy, and her present denial of what she had put us through.

A few days later the tape cassette of Jill's interview with Charles Goodwin arrived in the mail. Thomas and I sat at the kitchen table and listened to it together. I was afraid of how I might react, but my imagined fear was quickly dispelled. Instead of sending a chill down my spine, we were both surprised at the pleasantness of Goodwin's voice, how soft-spoken he was, like one of those trained meditation experts, almost.

It was hard to believe this was the man behind the mask. How ironic that of all the people in the world to confirm in exact detail the truth of my memory, he proved the reliable narrator. And with that thought, with the feeling of catharsis, I pushed the stop button on the tape recorder.

Thomas and I marked the passage by pausing to make a cup of tea. Before putting the paperwork away, we ran through the list of questions once more, imagining regrets of the future, thinking about anything I might have missed before contact with Goodwin was finished for good. That's when I identified two more crucially important things.

I wanted to see him without the mask, so I could replace the intrusive memory and flashbacks with a real human face. I wanted one more interview on film, video, where Jill would ask him about the letter he sent me, and how he obtained my address. I submitted my request in one last email.

Several days later, Jill called back. Goodwin had refused my request. It seemed we had reached the end of his generosity. He was not willing to be filmed, concerned that I might release it to the public. And he denied writing the letter, even though he had admitted to writing it when Kim and the members of the prison staff asked him how my Iowa address had made it into his file. Instead, he suggested I had been the victim of a horrible prank, or maybe his defense attorney had obtained my address in order to send me something. His explanation might have been worth entertaining had I not read the letter myself.

I tried my request again, this time through a handwritten letter, detailing my reasons for having him filmed, the issues I had with PTSD, told him again how helpful it would be to me, assured him the videotape would be destroyed. Pointed out that once released as a sexual offender, his photograph and address would be available to the public anyway. I offered up the stories of sexual offenders whom I had just met in Texas who embraced the challenge of entering back into the community as ex-prisoners, by knocking on the door of their neighbors, providing them information about their rehabilitation and ongoing treatment. The guys talked about how important it was to reducing their chances of recidivism.

But he just said no.

That left me with a problem. He was lying. And he was refusing me the most honest thing he could do—show me what he looked like without the mask, the thing that had given him the most power over me. Suddenly, the dialogue process felt a sham. In my desire to believe he had changed, had become one of the good guys, I had relaxed my guard too much. Thankfully, I had shared none of my story with him, revealed nothing of myself other than the benefit to me of seeing his true image. Maybe there was a different way to think about it, a way that would salvage the good that had come out of the process. I did finally have so many answers. He was no longer an unnamed knife-wielding masked man who seemingly stepped out of a fold in the air. Perhaps I could grant that he had acted on a higher impulse by agreeing to the dialogue. Just enough that it wouldn't cost him.

His parole hearing was now ten days away. I was angry, and then angry that I was angry. I wanted to close the door. But now, I felt a duty to let the parole board know who they were releasing on the streets. Before I did anything I might regret, I thought a reality check was in order. Thomas supported me as I spoke to our family and friends about going to Nebraska to testify against Goodwin's release. No one was in favor of it. In fact, the older generation of my family in England was adamantly opposed to it. Why take unnecessary risk? I also received an unsolicited letter from an expert who had heard my story through a friend. She dealt with violent sexual offenders and advised me that establishing contact was dangerous.

But how was I meant to convey the level of anxiety I had been living with all my life, and the fear—the weight of it on my inner world—to this circle of people who loved me? Honestly, the idea of inaction, of being frightened into passivity, scared me more. And there was the community of Omaha; shouldn't the police at least be alerted?

I remembered then our friendly small-town mayor, who I'd often stop and talk with on the street, sometimes on the way home from the gym in Shepherdstown. We'd compare notes on the progress of our bum knees. He happened to be a long-time corrections counselor currently employed at a county prison in Maryland, with years of valuable experience in the penal system.

In fact, in 1989, he had been at the Camp Hill prison in Pennsylvania when a riot broke out and numerous prison staff and officers were held hostage. By the time the Pennsylvania State police had regained control of the institution, many buildings were on fire and were in various stages of destruction. I knew he would honor my confidences with discretion if I asked for his advice. Still, it wasn't an easy conversation to initiate on my own—I found it extremely difficult to talk about this traumatic experience—so Thomas volunteered to be with me, support me, while I had the conversation.

The mayor was watching a television documentary with his wife when we knocked on the door. He guessed this wasn't a social call from the look on my face, so he ushered us into the kitchen. I took a deep breath and told him the whole story in ten minutes, after which he didn't hesitate to give his thoughts. "I'm going to make this clear as possible for you," he said with a smile. "There are people who commit crimes because they make mistakes, and there are people who commit crimes because they are just awful people. Those people don't change very often, if at all, in my experience."

We talked about the Victim-Offender Dialogue process, and how the timing with the parole hearing may have influenced Goodwin's decision to participate. The mayor suggested I go to Lincoln. He encouraged me to exercise my power, assuring me it could be healthy but the decision was mine. He said the parole board would take my words seriously about possibly paroling Goodwin. Particularly if I flew all the way to Nebraska to tell them how the brutal crime was continuing to affect me. Hell, they'd appreciate having the additional information that could influence the outcome. Victims, understandably, rarely attend these hearings.

"If you need permission to go to Lincoln, give yourself permission to go to Lincoln . . . with guarded optimism," he said, walking us back to the front door. "Letting that criminal know the consequences of what his behavior did to your life might not change him, but it may change you."

He paused, looked into my eyes intently, checking in, like he was reading my mind. "Seems pretty clear to me. You need to do this." And with that, he wrapped his big bodybuilder arms around my shoulders, giving me a huge bear hug.

In Which I Assess an Algorithm of Risk

Shepherdstown, 2003—I notified Jill of my commitment to testify in Lincoln before the parole board and hoped my courage would follow, fear being my dominant emotion. Jill suggested that she approach members to see if they would meet with me privately the day before the hearing. It would protect my anonymity. It wasn't within normal protocol, but the chairman of the parole board, James Morrison, and one member of the panel, Rachael Selway, agreed there was legitimacy to my request for anonymity, and the meeting date was set.

Jill helped me prepare and forwarded dozens of documents to the parole board ahead of time. The first was a victim statement. I described the crime in detail, the impact on my family, and the long-term price I had paid with my mental health. I assembled the neurology reports, the psychiatric assessments in my hospital records for the past twenty-five years; I asked all the mental health professionals I had worked with to write statements. I couldn't begin to estimate the financial costs.

I managed to track down Kim Haller, my close friend from junior high school who had worked with Goodwin in prison before his first release. We reestablished our friendship immediately and her sense of humor couldn't have arrived at a better time. When I told her the plan, she said that there was no way she was letting me do this without her. She'd be with me in Lincoln and said she would be happy to share her experience with the parole board if it would be helpful, and then offered to organize a party for me with a group of our old friends.

Kate Shugrue, my childhood friend who worked in the attorney general's office, was all in, too. She wanted to be of support in Lincoln as well and volunteered to witness proceedings at the actual parole hearing in my stead.

The only important person on the list I was hoping to find, but couldn't, was my teacher Kent Friesen. He had made such a point to stay in touch after we moved, even driving up to my high school graduation in Laurens and then in the years after. But he had disappeared in the last four years. He had been so pivotal in his support for me—even told me when I saw him in 1987 that he and his wife had gone down to the place where Goodwin left me to die near the stockyards, because they had to know what happened to me. Something my parents never deemed helpful or important.

I wrote an email to Dad explaining that I was going out to Lincoln to testify against Goodwin's parole, and asked if he and Mom would be willing to write letters to the parole board. And not only that, empowered from having embarked on the Victim-Offender Dialogue with Goodwin, I collected the courage to ask him if he and I could talk about not only what happened that night but of the cruelty my sisters and I had endured from Mom while under her care. I suggested we do it by email, which would give us time to consider our responses. It would give us the opportunity to pace it. He said he'd do anything to help me.

A week later an envelope arrived with two statements enclosed, both from Mom. In her cover letter she said that she hoped they fulfilled my purpose and finished with an "I do so hope this works for you. Love you always, Mom."

The first witness statement was a four-page, single-spaced document that explained as "well as possible the effects of that experience on our family." The account began at the point Mom returned home from work to find police in our house, the phone being monitored, and a neighbor in the kitchen. There were no mobile phones then and nobody had been able to reach her at her new place of employment. She was told I had been abducted for a ransom, that Dad was with the police. She described the phone call from the hospital asking permission to conduct a forensic medical exam for court purposes. "Understanding what this meant," she collapsed on the floor. "This was one of the worst fears of my life—that one of my daughters would be raped." She went on to say she believed the move to Iowa was bad for me. And that of all her children, before the assault, I was the only one to have a solid faith in God. She wrote that prior to my assault, I had attended church regularly, and that the loss of my faith had been a dear cost to me. I sat for a moment before moving to the second letter, wanting her regrets for me—the move, the loss of my faith—to be real.

But her next letter was odd, the reasons for separating the information unclear. This one detailed Mom's bewilderment at my older sister's reaction to my kidnapping. After reading it, I wondered if she did so because she was concerned I might also have asked Genie to write an account of events that night—because they differed.

In one of the final exchanges Genie and I had before she distanced herself from the family, she shared the nightmare of that night at home. She confirmed, albeit vaguely, that the question had been raised as to whether the ransom demand had been my idea; my revulsion to what she had said was instant, even if she was just repeating what she heard, so I insisted she not share this part of the story.

She then said when the phone call came in from the hospital, Mom went hysterical, started to shriek, and Genie thought I had been murdered. When she pleaded with Mom to tell her what happened, Mom turned at her with flailing fists. Genie watched horrified as the police officer standing by the phone in the kitchen shut the door so he could finish the conversation with the hospital. But that's not what Mom wrote in her letter. Mom wrote in her letter, "My oldest daughter kept yelling 'what happened'—she looked at me and said 'no, don't tell me' and ran upstairs to her room."

Genie also told me Mom hadn't given her a choice about my sleeping in her room, and though it was no fault of mine, she had been further traumatized when I told her the horrendous details of what had occurred. Mom verified she had asked Genie if I could sleep with her and concluded with, "I don't think any of us got much sleep that night."

A week after the arrival of Mom's letters, a Fed Ex package arrived from Dad containing two legally notarized letters. The first verified the contents of the letter that Charles Goodwin had sent to me at our address in Iowa, and my father's decision soon after to destroy it. He explained it wasn't until I requested the letter that he understood I had ever seen it, that he'd never discussed it with me, in an effort to protect me. While I was deeply frustrated not to have the original letter, this was legal proof to verify it as fact.

The second letter was an account of what Dad had gone through that night. He had been working in his basement office at home when the telephone rang. "At first I thought Debora was putting me on. It quickly became clear to me that she was in real trouble, and was scared to death." He then described how a male voice came on the phone, gave him the demands, and that "I begged him not to harm my daughter." He went to our neighbor, who called the police chief directly. Dad was instructed by the police to comply with Goodwin's demands to carry a bag as ordered, but empty of the $10,000 in cash. He was told there would be a police presence at the shopping center. He could see a plainclothes policeman and sensed others. "Later I learned that the kidnapper, with Debora, were indeed at the shopping center parking lot, but at a different level."

Then followed a powerful account of how he felt as he stood there for that half hour, the trauma of the experience building in his mind, and the toll it took on me, as well as our family. His letter concluded, "I personally have relived the events countless times. The anger that I have felt toward the perpetrator has been consuming numerous times. How anyone could harm a precious, innocent young girl like he did is beyond imagination. The impact of it has caused my family great pain and anguish, and still today it places unwanted demands on all of us."

There it was. In his own words. After twenty-five years. While I was crest-fallen to read his account, I had to read it a second time to assure myself of a factual error. He said I had been discovered by the police in the van at the Center Shopping Center parking lot. What bothered me wasn't that he had gotten the detail wrong, it was the new understanding that he never knew—he never knew that I had been dropped off blindfolded and tied by the Omaha stockyards or that it was from there that I escaped, or even that Goodwin had left me there to die. I was a parent now. I couldn't imagine not having checked every detail of what had happened to my child.

The reason Dad didn't know came from the same weakness that left him blissfully ignorant of my mother's duplicitousness. I tried to square this with the generous, compassionate, devoted father I knew him to be. He never ducked from emotionally supporting me, but how or why was it, when it came to violence, he'd stick his head in the sand? Wasn't this gross emotional neglect? Could there be any excuse?

I wrote him an email. Thanked him for his statements. Decided I would no longer hold back from sparing him the facts, to stop protecting him. I told him what I'd never told him before—that I hadn't been found by the police in Goodwin's van, but had been left to die near the Omaha stockyards. And that it was because of his love for me that I found my courage that night, that my desire to save his life had been what saved me. He responded immediately, apologized for never having understood the danger I had been left in, or how much I had feared for his life. He encouraged me to tell him more. I asked if it was time we made this a bigger conversation, one that included Mom's crimes as well, made him assure me he would not share my letters with her. I needed his confidence. He promised. If the openness between us had not been there in the past, it could be now. He apologized for never having made the opportunity to really listen to me and listed the emotions around his previous reluctance: "fright, awkwardness, longing to continue denial, anger, fear, regret, hurt, uneasiness, embarrassment, confusion, and a lack of understanding or the ability to understand what devastation rape imposes upon a woman."

I wrote back. I said everything I had always wanted to tell him about the reality of living with Mom when he wasn't there. And I ended with this: "I have to ask, how can you say you can't begin to imagine what it must be like for a woman to experience rape? I was so grateful you shared your personal story with me last year. You were also in a life-threatening situation and were severely violated at a young age. Perhaps one of the reasons we've talked so little about my trauma is because you are carrying so many emotions yourself about the sexual assault that happened to you."

I must have hit a raw nerve. The letter that came back was powerfully worded.

Dad replied that only now had he understood how Goodwin's violence compounded Mom's "treatment." He said he wanted to handle me delicately, yet at the same time shake me and yell at me "to get over it, stop being a victim and punishing everyone around you for what happened, flush the damn pills and cancel all future appointments with shrinks and well-intended intellects and hang out with trailer park people who have basic survival instincts that keep them going." He was angry at the way things turned out. Angry that Mom saw fit to treat us as she did, angry for what she did. But "I do see her as she is today and believe there is a difference, a huge difference."

It was the first time I ever felt a political/cultural divide between us. His use of the term "trailer park people," with this proclaimed respect for their stoic work ethic, was bizarrely out of character.

I thanked him. Changed the tone of my email. Told him Thomas and I had a lovely weekend camping with the kids. That I didn't have the time to respond properly, but I appreciated his honesty and the fact that he had shared his emotions.

He wrote back—and thanked me again for writing. Said he had been uplifted at the news of the dialogue between Goodwin and me. "My prayer is that both of you find solace in the process. I salute and recognize the work—and the toughness that it has taken on your part to bring it to this point. God Bless you and keep you as you proceed. Love, Pop."

In other words, his head was back in the sand. He appeared to have missed the point entirely—I was going back to Nebraska to testify against Goodwin's release. And with that round completed, and this peculiar blessing, Thomas and I flew to Nebraska for my meeting with the parole board members in Lincoln.

In Which I Return to the Cornhusker State

Nebraska, 2003—Two days later, I was sitting alongside Thomas, Kate, and Kim at a huge conference table in a room with laminated wood paneled walls at a municipal law office near the Lincoln courthouse, meeting with Judge Morrison and Rachael Selway.

The conversation ran several hours, after which Judge Morrison and Rachael Selway had to explain with deep regret and a heavy sense of responsibility that their hands were tied when it came to Goodwin's release. He had served twenty-four years of a twenty-five-year term, and it was safer to have him serve a year on parole at the end of his full sentence than to release him straight into the community without monitoring.

I raised the issue of the sexual offender registration—noting that Goodwin should have been included on the database before he had been released in 1987, even if he had only been on the streets for ten days before being imprisoned for the next crime. Rachael said she would personally see to it that the database was updated with his details, that he would be registered for life in accordance to his sentence. I left feeling thankful my efforts might at least make it easier for law enforcement to have a reason to know his address, as the sexual offender registration has been proven to reduce recidivism rates.

Three hours later, we were back in Omaha at the party Kim had organized with the friends from Lewis and Clark Junior High School, the group I had never wanted to say goodbye to. It was a stark reminder of what I had lost when I left Omaha. The news of Goodwin's impending discharge, which I had received that afternoon, was troubling. Though I knew it to be morally right that he be released—he had served twenty-four years—rationally or not, I felt I had let these friends and the Omaha community down by not being able to prevent it.

I tossed and turned all night. The next morning, Thomas and I drove back to Lincoln with Kate and stopped at Denny's to discuss logistics over eggs Benedict and coffee. The plan was for me to remain at the restaurant while Kate and Thomas attended the parole hearing at the Lincoln Community Release Center, which was down the road. That way we wouldn't have to rely on hearsay to know what happened at the proceedings, and Thomas at least would be able to see Charles Goodwin. But as the two of them stood to go, my confidence in our decision wavered. It didn't feel right. The whole journey to Nebraska had been triggered because Goodwin refused to allow himself to be filmed on video. And now, when I had the opportunity to actually see him without the ski mask, I was going to read a newspaper instead? At the very least, I could look in from outside a door. After all, I wasn't the only victim to live in the shadow of a legitimately dangerous offender. It was a terror that spouses of domestic abusers lived with, victims who were stalked, reporters and social justice activists who exposed criminal activities—they all lived with continued risk and had to get on with their lives. Charles Goodwin might be dangerous, but I was so tired of living in fear, and I had already taken the risk in provoking him when I told him he gave me no choice but to testify against him. This was my last opportunity to see him in a safe prison setting.

I shared my thoughts with Thomas and Kate. I could always sit in the car if it turned out not to be a good idea, but they were both supportive. Thomas pointed out that Jill could provide another reality check. So with that, after the breakfast bill was paid, the three of us left together.

In Which I Drop In for a Surprise Visit

As we walked into the lobby of the Lincoln Community Release Center, I put my sunglasses on in an effort to hide—which was a bit ridiculous given the conspicuousness of my business attire.

Jill, who was already waiting, expressed a pleasant surprise at seeing me. Thomas told her the plan had changed. I was relieved when she agreed I wasn't being rash. She warned us that the door would open in a minute and pointed out that if I walked in with her, Goodwin would know for sure who I was. I reassured her it was what I wanted to do.

The doors opened and we filed into the cafeteria with the rest of the families and visitors. There were about fifty round tables circled by blue, red, and yellow plastic chairs. The room was as light as the lobby, more windows emitting powerful prairie sun. I spotted Goodwin immediately, sitting at the table by himself.

"That's him," I said to Thomas, my heart pounding in my throat with an odd exhilaration—a mixture of fear, anger, and wonderment that Goodwin was in fact real and not a specter of my hallucinating mind.

Thomas, sensing my reaction, brought me back to earth by nudging me with the *Omaha World Herald* he had been carrying under his arm. "Where?"

I nodded my head in Goodwin's direction.

Jill steered us to a table about twenty yards away from him and we sat down. If he was aware of me, he gave no sign of it, as he continued to look around the room with his quiet equanimity. I was delighted with this new feeling of empowerment, high with it, as a matter of fact. And it was then I realized: no one would stop me if I approached him, which I realized was exactly what I was going to do.

I turned to Thomas, to Kate, to Jill, and apologized for another change in plan, but I had to talk to him. Jill said she'd let the guards know, and she'd be there the second I signaled her. And with this, I turned to Mr. Goodwin. I'd never been so determined to connect to a human soul as I was at that moment. When I reached the table, I found myself asking confidently, yet in a friendly, businesslike tone—

"Are you Charles Goodwin?"

"Yes." He looked up at me, and I knew he recognized me for the same reason I would never mistake him. And there we were, for the first time since he had left me to die twenty-four years ago, in a cafeteria on a bright sunny day in a community release center in Lincoln, Nebraska. I held out my hand. Introduced myself. He stood up, extended his arm for a friendly handshake. My mind started moving in a hundred directions with all the things I wanted to ask. We stood for the longest two seconds in history.

"Do you mind if I sit down?" I asked, my heart beating so rapidly it was difficult to hear my thoughts. "I'd like to ask you a few questions about your plans."

"Sure," he said in a polite manner, offering me a chair. Somehow I put aside my feelings about his refusal to be videotaped, I put aside that just yesterday I had testified against his release at the parole board, I put aside my fears that he was still lying, and I became intent on finding the good in him. Our rapport felt instant; his amiability made it that easy.

The first thing I did was thank him for agreeing to the Victim-Offender Dialogue. I told him the timing of my request so close to the parole hearing had been unfortunate, but until six months ago I hadn't even known his name. He told me his friends and family were concerned when they heard I had approached him and told him not to agree to it. But he felt it was the least he could do. I'd unpack that later, but at the moment, it felt so good to feel like we were playing for the same team, I didn't want to disrupt the equilibrium.

I next asked him if he could tell me what kind of support he'd have once he got out, whether he had people to support him in the transition. He said he had a special relationship with the father of a young prison inmate who had died of a brain aneurysm while serving time. The man had all but adopted him. They attended church together, and Charles stayed with him on weekend furloughs from prison, part of the transition program to release.

"He's financially set," Charles shared. "Not that it's important to me, but he has said he will be there if I ever need help."

"So you don't need to rob a bank to get by," I joked, not able to help myself.

"Yeah," he laughed, a little too enthusiastically. "No more of that! He's even helped me get a car."

I asked him if he could tell me about his more recent rehab program. He responded without hesitating that he enrolled in every rehabilitation program offered, including cognitive therapy and a sex offenders support group. "Most important, though, I have this lady psychiatrist who is there for more than just the paycheck. She's good. I've been seeing her once a week, but that's going to change to once a month. There's not many out there like her. I'm really lucky."

"Yes, I know how tough it is to find the right therapist. I've had a few myself over the years." I left it to him to draw the connection, which I don't think he did. "You know," I continued, "there aren't many people out there who think violent offenders can change. It's a pretty hostile world, and there's very little faith in violent offenders turning their lives around because recidivism rates are so high."

He listened, then paused before speaking. "God has sent great people into my life, though." He told me he was a member of a good church. The head minister had even written a note of support for him for the parole board.

I had no interest in returning to the subject of God with him, and quickly moved on to asking about his family. He said he had lost both of his parents in the years he served in prison. While he wasn't specific about the cause of death for his father, he offered that his mother had died of cancer. He added that he had two brothers. They were decent people, were well respected in the community, and he didn't want to make their lives hard again.

He was also proud to report that he had two jobs—one hanging drywall, the other telemarkteing. Told me his godfather said he didn't know how he could do the telemarketing, deal with all the rejection, but Charles laughed. "It just slides off me." I told him telemarketing was a good job. I'd done hundreds of hours of phone banking myself during elections, and respected the work.

When it seemed as if we had established what felt like solid ground, I asked if I could say a few things to him. He nodded, saying, "Yeah, sure," like no problem, I'm listening.

"I'm not sure you understand the damage you did to my life that night," I started. "I'm not saying this because I want to make you feel bad, but I need you to understand the long-term consequences of your actions. You not only terrorized me that night, you traumatized my father by threatening my life and making him stand there waiting for you. You changed my mother's and my sisters' lives forever. And then there were my friends at school, and at church and the Omaha Community." The words came from a deeply broken place, yet filled me with a calm, peaceful strength.

"I did nothing to you." I wanted him to feel something of my pain—without shame, without judgment. "And it didn't end that night for me.

I have had to fight against the terror you inflicted on me every day since." I felt no anger as I spoke—I felt a release in my soul, the chain of horror I had been carrying for years, the weight I had carried disintegrating. "The damage doesn't go away. You cannot take it back." I paused, waiting for him to catch up.

"I want to say I'm sorry," he said, glancing up and then looking down again, "but it sounds so empty." He appeared to be fighting back tears.

I told him I hoped he would make something of his future, find a family, happiness. And I meant it. I wanted it because I understood now the evil I had experienced could only surface in the absence of human connection.

"Thank you," he said. "Thank you for sharing those words." Then another pause, a strange shift in energy. Perhaps he was gathering thoughts.

"Can I tell you something else, something I never told Jill?" He looked to me for approval to go on. "I told her about what happened to me when I was fourteen— in the holding jail in Douglas County. That's when they broke my jaw. I was always proud of my smile until then." He laughed in a self-deprecating way, as if to ease the tone. "In fact, I think I might get cosmetic surgery now that I'm out." He paused. "But I didn't tell her that I was raped in prison, by a guy, a racist."

He was in real tears now, sniffling, wiping his nose, not looking up. Holding his head in his hands. "I'm sure it had something to do with what I did to you."

If he was hoping I would feel sympathy for him, he was mistaken. Instead, I raised the meeting with Kim. "Did you come to terms with your trauma before or after the session with Kim?"

"Kim Haller, your friend?" He was so surprised by that, his eyes grew wide.

"Yes."

"Did you get to talk to her?" he asked.

"Yes."

"Now, that whole thing freaked me out," he said, leaning to the side of his chair, as if to get out of the way. "Did she tell you about that whole thing?"

"Yes, but I'd like hear your story. She said you were a big help to her while she was working in prison."

"Yeah. Well, this isn't easy for me to tell you. She was working at the release center and we got to be friends. To be honest, I had a crush on Kim. And it's not easy for me to tell you. That's before I found out she was connected to you in any way. So when I found out that she was one of your best friends, I felt sick, you know. I had really terrible nightmares for a long time, and after that, every time I met or had to work with a white woman in prison, I was afraid because I thought that woman was going to turn out to be you."

"But then you went and robbed the bank after that. And you terrorized another three people, three people who aren't at this table today."

"And I've offended more. I hope to honor you by never hurting another human being again."

I felt awkward. "And how about honoring yourself?"

"Yes," he said, looking down.

He relaxed back in his chair.

"You know," he began, "all my friends were asking me why I would want to talk to you, why I would want to go back into that, when I've changed. They said they couldn't imagine what your motivations would be. I told them I was doing it because it's what God would want me to do."

Uninterested in hearing of God's personal plan, I moved the conversation on. Asked him if there was anyone he felt close to, a guardian angel of sorts? He smiled like I'd just hit the jackpot, looked straight at me.

"I had a girlfriend when I was a teenager. But she committed suicide when she was fourteen. An overdose. Alcohol."

"I'm really sorry," I said, genuinely.

"Yeah," he said, looking down. "She was a good friend to me." Then he looked me square in the eye. "She had hair like Farrah Fawcett."

My stomach tightened. The night before, when I had been with my group of old junior high school friends, they had all teased me about my Farrah Fawcett hairstyle, about the ever-present comb in my back pocket.

"I'm glad I came to see you," I said and stood up, wanting to thank him for proving he was an asshole. I looked over at Thomas, thought it might be a good idea for the two of them to meet. I asked Charles if he'd like to meet my husband. He said sure.

Thomas came over. Charles extended his hand. My husband clearly didn't want to take it, but I nodded in encouragement. Just then the court clerk called the name Charles Goodwin.

"Good luck," I said to him.

The four of us attended the hearing. I couldn't help but think as I listened to the speech he delivered to the parole board how much I wanted to believe him:

"It is important to me to be honorable, not because I want to get out of here. I didn't have a bunch of people come, I didn't have a bunch of people write letters or anything along those lines, simply because for me this is not a game anymore. There was a point in time when there was a game about getting out of here. I got out and I failed because it was a game to get out of here, it wasn't about staying out. It wasn't about going out of here and doing the right thing. I was a very very young man. I was a child at the time. I acted like a child. I spoke like a child. I am a man now and I choose to act like a man. And I make my decisions like a man. I have chosen wise men to be good guides because I know my decisions aren't always the best decisions. My choices aren't the best choices. So I speak to wise people to get guidance. And I will very much so continue to try to do that. I will honor any regulations, any stipulations that the board would set here. And very much so, I will continue to honor my job obligations, and more than anything else, I will continue to honor God, and I will honor the people that I have harmed in the past by not harming other people. That's the best I can do for the people I have harmed in my past."

What a rousing speech.

As we walked out of the building, I realized that Charles Goodwin was no longer a monster of evil proportions in my mind. But clearly he was the human who had committed those gross acts of violence against me, my family, and the community I lived in. And he was about to be released again with his rights to live among the rest of us. He had taken his punishment. He had gone through treatment. He had served his time.

I made one last check that he was registered as a violent sexual offender before setting off, and began counting the days to his next offense, hoping he'd prove me wrong.

In Which I Consider What I Learned about Human Nature

Shepherdstown, 2003—A week after I returned to West Virginia, my email inbox pinged. "What's up?" It was Dad. I emailed him back, excited to share the news. I was exhausted, but happy and grounded and recovering from an incredible high. Thomas called it a week of miracles, and that's how it felt. So much love from so many people I had connected with from those years. I told Dad I wish he could have been with me. I told him the parole board had been incredibly supportive, beyond my wildest expectations. After the parole hearing, Rachael Selway made it a point to walk me through the lobby and lent such heartwarming soulful words for my journey ahead that their power remains with me today. And Judge Morrison even walked us to the car and gave me a huge hug before I left. And best of all, Kent Friesen called me from Colorado the morning of the hearing.

What I didn't tell Dad was one of the most invaluable lessons of that day— that I had an opportunity to see my own defensive reactions at play. No one watching me approach Charles Goodwin that morning would have guessed our history. Despite the adrenaline flowing through my system, the bold aggressive impulsiveness of my move, I pulled up a chair as if we were old friends. I sat there and played the role of support, asked him how he felt, ran through the checklist, showed care, concern for his future. Told him how he had damaged my life, and in the following sentence, wished him the best life had to offer. I'd like to think it was the better part of my nature, but if I evaluate it at a more primal level, it was more basic. I was scared of him. I didn't display an ounce of rage, of anger, of judgment that would have been appropriate to the situation—because it might have pissed him off.

What's more, there's only one other person who could do that to me, induce that familiar trancelike dissociative state where I could disconnect from my feeling brain. And that was Mom. I'm not saying I was conscious of it. But I saw it clear as day when I was sitting in Shepherdstown looking back. I'd learned the coping mechanism from an expert—Dad. He'd adopt the same trance around her. He'd go silent, not argue, become submissive when he should fight. He was her mood handler.

Goodwin and my mother might be two completely different people, but there was something about their nature that evoked the same response in me. And I was tired of allowing their violence, past or present, into my inner world. I couldn't deny that Mom, like Goodwin, had learned new behavior—that she was trying her best to exercise her new skills. And I still had a fear that I was making a monster of her just to free myself of the emotional inconvenience of her. But it was a healthy fear and one I could live with. I was not going to let her gaslight me anymore. I would no longer be receiving either one of them in my personal world.

Dad and I continued to be in touch by email and post. He liked sending me cards with puns. And before long, Mom made her next move. She copied me on an email to Gayle and asked me what Christmas presents my son and daughter would enjoy. I called Gayle for support, and she told me she'd let Mom know the gifts weren't appropriate.

Two weeks later a UPS truck pulled up in front of our house with a refrigerator-size box, which the child minder signed for. The kids were putting the wrapped presents under the Christmas tree by the time I got downstairs. I noticed my mother was listed as the sender and the contents were insured for one thousand dollars.

Thomas called my father. Dad apologized for the situation. Gave us a UPS number and suggested we call the driver back. He'd tell Mom. My son and daughter, four and five years old, cried as they watched the driver take the presents away. I felt horrid, a failed mother. I'd just displayed to my children that gifts could not be trusted. How could this be a good example to set for them? It was a great game, this game of my mother's. She won if we accepted the gifts. She won when they were sent back.

I wrote her an email. I asked her to accept the reality of our situation. I wasn't trying to punish her, shame her, judge her. I wasn't angry. But it would not be possible for us to have a relationship until she recognized the nature of her past and present abusive behaviors. I didn't expect that to happen. But I did want a relationship with my father. And I hoped I would be able to see both him and Vivian after Christmas.

I received a letter back. She said that she would not get into a war with me over relationships with Dad, Vivian, and Gayle, but warned me to not continue my campaign against her. "It is not within your power to erase the reality that I am your mother, biologically and emotionally. I did give everything I had to give in raising you. I know I made some major mistakes in parenting but I NEVER intentionally, or with malice, did anything to harm you or your sisters." She told me she would continue to send tokens of love to her grandchildren whenever she saw fit.

How I wish I could have explained to her that whether or not she did anything with malice had little to do with it. It was her lack of perception or concern for my pain, or anyone else's, that allowed her to behave so violently in the first place. And her insistence that I had it wrong was only adding further injury. She concluded the letter with the following:

"I hope that someday, you can find the desire to find out who I really am and understand that I do love you very much and know that I had a lot to do with the woman you are today. You are made of good stuff and capable of becoming a loving compassionate person who can make a big difference in her world; the energy spent on trying to get rid of me as a member of your family is energy that could be spent on loving the rest of your family. Love, Mother."

This was classic Mom. She made the problem me, she denied her abuse, and she claimed my successes for her own. I wasn't going to win by responding.

I received an upset call from Vivian next. A number of the returned gifts had been carefully selected and wrapped by her. I explained what had happened and apologized for hurting her. I told her Gayle had made it clear to Mom that the presents wouldn't be welcomed, but she sent them anyway. Then Vivian shared some hard truths with me. She had moved out of my parents' home two weeks ago. Now, having just settled into her new apartment, her body wasn't adapting well to dialysis treatments and they left her feeling sick. She would really like to see me, Thomas, and the kids. We agreed by the end of the conversation we would see her the first weekend after the New Year. I wrote to Dad and told him. And said he'd be more than welcome to see the kids at Gayle's house, but Mom would not.

Dad wrote back and said it was time he let me know how he truly felt about me "dissing my mother." He said the communication we had wasn't serving him well, and he felt dishonest with his life partner. He could not understand why the core issues could not be brought to the surface. People go on Dr. Phil with problems like ours. He and Mom were open to seeing anyone, spending any amount of money to reach resolution. He would not be included in a visitation with the caveat that my mother wouldn't be. He was enraged that we had returned the gifts, that I could intentionally hurt my own mother like this. She had done something generous.

It was another swing.

I tried one more time. I told Dad I had made it clear almost a year before that I would no longer continue in a relationship with Mom. He had promised me my boundaries would be respected. I pointed out my trip home wasn't planned with the intention to hurt Mom. In fact, I had to plan the trip to rectify the situation she caused by refusing to respect my wishes.

Several weeks later, Dad wrote back. He said he wanted to drive down to see me. He'd be happy to stay in a hotel. There was no overt or covert reason for coming. He simply missed me and wanted time with me. He signed, "Love, Pop."

I wrote back and told him I couldn't see him until he got help. I suggested he take my last letter to a psychiatrist and have it explained to him.

He wrote back at the end of January. Said he had taken my letter to a healer who advised him that I was in obvious pain. "I have a wife. I plan to continue having that wife until I die. She is complex, but making good progress in terms of better understanding herself, the implications of past actions, and what options she has open to her today for going forward. I will continue to search for answers that might be worthwhile. It would please me a great deal if I could have a relationship with you, and therefore, my son-in-law and grandchildren. Jim."

I wrote back two days later. "We've reached an impasse."

That was all. I'd hit that wall. I either allowed him to command my gratitude and forgiveness, or I made the break for reasons of self-preservation. All I could hope for was that time might present different options. I told myself over and over and over again, it was the right thing to do for me, for my family. The fight for Dad was draining my soul. Perhaps most painful of all, I would have to stop denying that what saved me that night alongside that railcar was not my father's love for me but my love for him. My need to save his life. And now it was time to grieve what wasn't, so I could claim my freedom.

Over the next year and half, I stayed close to Jenifer and Gayle. Mom's drinking didn't take long to pick up, which became hard on Gayle. Not only did she live across the street, but she also worked in the family business.

It was around this time that Gayle met the husband I'd always wanted for her. Rob was a commercial airline pilot. After six months of dating, they came to Shepherdstown and told us they'd be getting married. They both understood we couldn't be at the wedding. Gayle called up after and told me Mom got drunk at the reception, then climbed in behind the wheel of a car and started backing out of the driveway before she had some kind of stroke. The wedding celebration ended with Mom being taken by ambulance to the hospital. She lost what was left of her hearing.

Months later, when my mother went into surgery for a hearing implant, she died on the table and had to undergo open-heart surgery. They inserted a pacemaker and said she was good to go. A few weeks later Gayle called again. She was worried about Dad. He had started working at home because Mom needed lots of help. The only way anyone could communicate with her was by pencil and paper because she couldn't hear. But she had no problem speaking. Gayle said Mom was threatening Dad with a divorce if he didn't stop working, but Dad wasn't ready to retire. That the situation had gotten so dysfunctional that Gayle was pleading with Dad to leave her.

But he said he wouldn't, or couldn't, until he found the "right solution"— whatever that meant.

In Which a Choice in the Road Is Taken

Geneva, 2006—We were on our way to Switzerland for a ski holiday with Thomas's parents. The train hurried south toward the Alps. It would have been about two P.M. our time—eight A.M. Dad's time. He was intending to go to Bible study group, but instead his mind was making a U-turn.

Our train rounded the bend and slowed as it pulled into the snowy village of Aime. We found a cab and chased the sun up steep switchbacks to the fir-lined glaciers. When we arrived at the chalet, I thought about borrowing my father-in-law's mobile phone to call Dad—it was one of those moments in life that felt so good I just wanted to share it with him. Over the years I had made so many calls like the one I wanted to make to him now. It would have been as easy as that. But things had changed, and I didn't make that call.

We ate a late lunch, then went out to rent skis.

My father, meanwhile, left his king-size bed. My mother was sleeping in the room next to him. Maybe he went to the bathroom sink to get a drink of water. I wonder if it was the mirror that spooked him. It happened to me at the worst times. I'd look at my eyes and see a complete stranger. The psychological term for it is dissociation. It's not a good place from which to make big decisions.

He was sixty-seven and in perfect physical shape. He had recently returned from New Orleans, where he spent a month helping people rebuild homes after Hurricane Katrina. The motorcycle had been traded in for a new RV that was parked and waiting for more adventure. The horses were long gone. He had sold his million-dollar business to Gayle, who had been his top saleswoman for years. It had been three weeks since he had seen my mother through her major surgeries. One week ago, he had showed up at his four-thousand-member Methodist church in flippers and a scuba diving outfit in order to recruit volunteers for the summer Bible camps he was running for the church.

Dad had spent the previous day chopping wood with his fifteen-year-old grandson, whom he had helped raise. The previous night Dad had called Gayle to make sure she had made it home safely from her business trip. He went to bed early so he could get a good night's sleep for the computer skills workshop he planned to attend the next day.

But then he looked in the mirror. I imagined his hazel eyes and his head of full brown-gray curly hair. I wonder if he ran his hand down his pointed chin, the one I inherited from him. He had one of those smiles that included everything—the eyes, brows, and dimples.

That morning he was meant to start taking Wellbutrin, but instead of reaching for the pills that would save him, he reached for the sleeping pills that would help him die.

In Which I Play Hamlet

Indianapolis, 2006—Thomas and I flew back to Indiana for the funeral. My mother had aged in the few years since I'd seen her last. She appeared feeble. She had lost all hearing and was now learning to hear with an implant and processor, but you could talk with her and it seemed better than when she needed a paper and pen. She'd say "eh?" and put her hand up to the side of her head.

The house was full of mourners. I didn't know most of them, but I greeted a few of Dad's good buddies from the Lee Valley days. I noticed Mom had a Scotch in her hand, but no longer cared. I couldn't blame her. But it looked to me like she was enjoying the party. How I loathed the person I became in her presence. I searched again for something I could give her, a more generous thought to override the rage I felt for her not being devastated as I watched her from across the room. Couldn't she be a little less herself?

When I asked her how she was doing, she said she was sad but "doing okay." Then she said she had something she thought I might like. Suggested I follow her upstairs. I looked at Thomas, gave him the secret code look for "it's cool," and followed her. She took me into her office, where she had been going through pictures. Evidently she had a few of me. She handed me the envelope. I couldn't help but smile when I flicked through them; I genuinely thanked her. There was a picture of me with what looked like lobster claws in the snow, a series of photo booth shots of me at age six where I'm showing fangs, Arlo and me at the Breeze Cottage in Maine, the school picture of me taken on the day of the kidnapping. I thanked her again. And then I asked her if she could tell me what happened with Dad. She said that four months earlier he had started drinking quite heavily and became depressed. A week before he had gone to see a psychiatrist, who prescribed him Prozac. And after five days, Dad called back and said he didn't trust the way he felt, so they agreed he should switch to Wellbutrin. He had picked up the new prescription on Friday and was supposed to start it on Saturday.

She continued, telling me Dad had come to her Friday night and said he thought he should go to the hospital. "I asked him what for? So he could sleep? He complained that's all he did last time. You have no idea what these hospitals charge." She took a slurp of the Scotch. "And you know what? When he took the sleeping pills, he took mine. Why do you think he'd take mine? He had his own. He could have taken those." There wasn't pain expressed in the question, no suggestion in her tone that she was struggling with guilt. She was curious. Did I have an opinion?

"I don't know, Mom, maybe he was afraid he didn't have enough."

"Oh no, he had plenty."

I experienced a sick feeling in the pit of my stomach, the same one I had in Nebraska when I wondered if Charles Goodwin was intentionally manipulating me. I looked at her. Why, with all the people in the world she could have had the conversation with, why did she have it with me? What was it with sociopaths?

But I couldn't let this little heart-to-heart get in the way. I needed something from her. I asked her if Dad left a note, scared to know the answer. She hadn't seen one. I asked if it would be helpful for me to look, if she would be comfortable with that. She said no problem—go ahead.

I went to the basement, which he had turned into an office, and began searching. Aren't you supposed to leave a note if you're going to kill yourself? What does it mean if you don't? Was he really going to leave without saying goodbye? I went through the top of his desk, the drawers, the bookshelves, fanned the pages of every book he had.

The only thing I found that could shed any light on his state of mind was a piece of paper on his desk, with the name and number of his psychiatrist, and a list of symptoms:

- racing thoughts
- can't sleep
- lack of appetite
- can't concentrate
- thoughts of suicide
- anxiety

That was it. At what point did that list of depressive symptoms turn into a series of actions? I moved to the bedroom. I started with the table next to his bed. Went through the drawer. Medications of various sorts, pens, a few other items. Next to the lamp on the bedside table was his Bible. Underneath the Bible was a notebook. It was a stenographer's notebook, with a white plastic spiral binding along the top. I had seen it before. When I opened it up, I remembered why.

It was the journal he had kept of the time he had come to visit Thomas and me in Oxford. He had shown me some of the pictures he had drawn of our back garden, and of the book bindery across the street. There were stories for each day with his signature humor: his "enrollment" in our vegetarian cooking school; his "man on the street" interviews—a bus driver, the Italian owner of the greasy spoon café around the corner from our house; his trip to a grocery store; an epic punting trip in which he flipped himself twice into the River Isis by losing control of the pole; our bicycle rides; lunch, when he would play with my in-laws' leaf blower; and his last view of us as we ran after the bus when it was pulling out to say goodbye. I closed the notebook. Sat against the wall and wept, overcome by the poignancy of the gift, made more powerful by the panic of almost not having found it, a spiritual fantasy that he had led me to it, as I struggled to find a way to connect with him.

After I collected myself, I walked into the garage. I looked around, imagining myself him. I wanted to know what he'd seen as he was about to die and there it was, on the wall in front of the car—his hat with the moose ears, the one he wore when he was telling us about the Civil War and the ghosts, his head bobbing as he directed our looks to the various historical sites, making us laugh so hard it hurt our sides. Next to it was another hat: a reindeer with antlers. It was too Dad. Did he really sit himself in front of that kind of absurdity and say goodbye to the world?

Did he feel close to Katherine and Arlo that morning? Was he thinking of anyone? Was he thinking to hell with everyone? Was he scared? Was he just tired? Did he cry? Was he numb? Did I even cross his mind? Did I have the right to ask?

And then I spotted the industrial vacuum cleaner without its hose in the corner. Gayle had told me he had used it to connect the tailpipe to the car— ran it into the back window and duct-taped it so it was air-tight. Swallowed a handful of sleeping pills for added insurance, closed his eyes, and that was it.

A vacuum. And I remembered that's where Dad had started with the story of his getting kicked out of theology school and making the decision that defined his life—using a vacuum for cleaning up his vomit. And with a rage I'd never given vent to before, I impulsively picked up a sledgehammer next to the machine and rained down enough violence on it to make the steel cylinder crumble with the blows.

Jenifer and Gayle, hearing the commotion, came out to the garage. After I had exhausted myself, we stood together and shared a cigar.

In Which I Meditate on Violence

England, 2020—I spent a lot of time pondering the reasons for writing this story, asking myself what was to be gained. I suppose I hoped that putting the fragments in order, looking at the narrative threads, moving the pieces around, might offer some therapeutic effect. But at times, it felt more like self-harm. Yet I continued, because I felt like there was too much in my shared life experience with my father to leave unexamined. Too many of the social forces that acted on our lives are those also shaping lives in America today. The levels of national violence we are required to adapt to are unprecedented. And the toll on mental health, the levels of anxiety we live with, and the long-term consequences to victims are immense.

In June 2001, after living in England for a decade, Thomas and I returned home to the United States with our two young children. Three months later, Osama bin Laden and his followers hijacked one of the world's great religions and used it to justify their heinous acts. Though I was fortunate not to lose a loved one in this violence, my proximity to this barbarity erased my body's sense of past and present. The region where we lived, just outside Washington, D.C., went from comfortable stability to unpredictable terror with a speed that echoed the way the Omaha community of my childhood was turned upside down. At the time, I didn't see the connection, but I knew these events demanded of me more than I wanted to give. I carried little patience for the depth of anxiety it triggered, for my own reaction. I was not prepared to accept the idea that my body had a genius my mind did not and that I was not in sync with the history it carried, a history I had repressed, a pain I was still denying. Instead, I adapted to the new physical sensations of generalized anxiety, ignored the warnings they were, and staved off the emotional reckoning.

One year later, as I have recounted, the sniper attacks began. Muhammad and Malvo targeted their ten murder victims for no other reason than they were going about their day. This time the symptoms of post-traumatic stress disorder, something that I still didn't know how to name, were enough to bring me to a grinding halt. I was brought straight back to that split second when Charles Goodwin pulled up in front of me in a stolen van, jumped out wearing a ski mask, and put a knife to my throat, turning what once had once been a place of assumed sanctuary, my church and my school, into a life-threatening danger zone.

I am thankful I survived that night, especially given that the majority of children who are abducted by strangers, a crime that is fortunately rare, do not. I hate to mention these children as a statistic, when each one deserves to have their individual stories heard, each one had a family whose lives were shattered.

I could not have dreamt in 1978 that children at schools would become the repeated target of mass killings. Who could have? The morning of Goodwin's parole hearing, Kent Friesen, my junior high school teacher, called to give me some support, speaking of the horrific violence he'd survived after our parting. Ten years earlier, Kent had been teaching students in a chemistry lab at Columbine High School when Dylan Klebold and Eric Harris entered the building and shot and killed twelve students and one teacher.

That this teacher, who had played such a vital role in ushering me through the aftermath of the kidnapping and made such a positive difference in my life, would be placed in a situation where he would be protecting sixty-three students from gunfire while trying to save the life of his colleague Dave Sanders still makes me rage. It belies comprehension that this has become a way of life in a nation that has professed itself capable of progressive change.

Three years and six months after our meeting at the Lincoln correctional center, Charles Goodwin was arrested in Omaha, despite the promises he made to me and countless others that he would never hurt anyone again. He received a sentence of seven years in prison plus four years of supervised release for conspiracy to commit extortion. I refuse to recount the details of his felonies here, as he is no longer a part of my story.

But before I move on, I must note the early choice I made as an author to not differentiate the humanity of Charles Goodwin and myself by race. This was not a simple decision, as we live in a grossly racist society that is not color-blind, and I do not feel it right to deny him the oppression that shaped his external world. Yet to suggest the kind of devastating pain Goodwin inflicted is the fault of society is to err grossly.

Criminals often justify their behavior by claiming they are uniquely abused by society. Goodwin was not uniquely abused, but has proved himself to be uniquely violent. I therefore made the decision to let his rage—which he explained as originating in the trauma of racist violence—emerge in the story as he told it.

———————

The domestic violence I experienced at home, while it belongs to a different sphere than my kidnapping, was equal, if not more devastating, in its traumatic consequence on my life, coming at the hands of the woman who biologically has claim to being my mother. Child abuse is such a hard thing to process, because the criminal is the parent who shapes and constructs your inner self, and whom you are hardwired to love. And it is the twisting of this precious love that makes a parent's violence different than any other.

Like Goodwin, my mother claimed her mistreatment by the world as unique, viewed her inner rage as the fault of society, of a society that pushed her into a teen marriage because of an unwanted pregnancy, that denied her an iden-tity, that oppressed her because she was a woman. She suffered from depression and psychotic episodes. But this did not preclude her from feeling empathy or concern for others, or from acknowledging her cruelty, or from seeking help to change her behavior. Just as the vast majority of victims of violent trauma do not go on to hurt others, a vast majority of those suffering from mental illness do not hurt others. There is no excuse for her actions.

I have seen my mother since my father's death. A few years ago, I flew out to spend time with my dear childhood friend Kate Shugrue, who was dying from cancer, and realized that Mom was living just an hour away. I had no interest in seeing her—the thought of it made me deeply anxious. But she had some-thing which remained important to me, my father's ashes, and she had made clear the only way to get them was to pay her a visit.

So I called my sister Gayle and asked what she recommended I do. Gayle, braver than me, generously placed a call and laid the groundwork, telling my mother when and why I would be stopping by and asking her to prepare a container. I climbed in my car and drove the sixty miles to where she lived, in a fifty-five-and-older community on the outskirts of a major city. When the door opened, I was met by a stranger who barely resembled my mother, a frail, elderly, harmless woman whom I hardly recognized. It was clear that it pained her to share Dad's ashes. Though she recognized me as her daughter, she seemed genuinely surprised to hear me talk about her husband as my father. The confusion may have been the result of early dementia, but more likely it was a reflection of the pathology I grew up with.

And then there is the third act of violence, my father's self-inflicted murder, which has brought with it anguish of a whole different kind.

Dad had serious flaws, but he was a good and decent man. Anyone who had the privilege of knowing him knew his capacity to empathize with other people's pain. And I know without a doubt he carried mine. When he took his own life, Dad proved that he lacked the self-worth necessary to survive. As a consequence, I have been hypervigilant in educating myself about suicide prevention. Tragically, the journey I had to take to free myself of mental anguish was one he couldn't undergo.

My sisters and I never understood why he wouldn't leave my mother after we all left home. Knowing him as I do now, I believe that he felt not only complicit but guilty in his failure to protect us—in a way my mother will never feel. But my father's crimes were in no way equal to my mother's. His betrayal of me arose because he lacked the inner stamina to stand up to her will, and he had too much pride to leave her. As he slowly relinquished the health of his own soul, he increasingly turned to a conservative male move- ment that reinforced the belief that men are appointed by divine force to be kings of the domestic sphere, a script that reinforced his illusion of control. I strongly believe he would have been better served by recognizing that while the body has a biological gender, the human spirit has none. He was the natural nurturer in our family. The mystery of why good people remain in abusive relationships, harmful to their self-preservation, is not an easy one to resolve.

And Dad and I shared similar pain. Both of us had wounds left from inade- quate biological mothers. He tried to mend his hole by making sure his daughter, conceived out of wedlock, wasn't given up for adoption. I mended my hole by not having children until I was in a secure position to do so. Both of us were child victims of sexual assaults. My father steered me through my aftermath in the way he survived his own—by never speaking of it. And for a long time that approach served me well, until my body took over for me and I was forced to acknowledge that trauma will work itself out, whether acknowledged or not.

The truth is, Dad's love did keep me alive on November 22, 1978, and our bond gave me the resiliency to cope with my mother's cruelty. I left his house knowing without a doubt that I was deeply loved, and because of that, I had the self-esteem to be discerning about my choice in a life partner. The man I married is proof of that.

This does not excuse my father's failure to accept responsibility for the level of violence in his own home, for closing his eyes to it rather than addressing it. But when I view my parents together, and then imagine them apart, I see the relationships in his life much healthier and happier without her, but I cannot imagine the relationships in her life healthier and happier without him. The fact that she's estranged from all four of her children speaks louder than words. And that, to me, puts my father deservedly in a separate category.

Where Dad's and my paths really separated was around the issue of truth and reconciliation. He mistook the act of forgiveness for a willingness to forget, to deny that the violence ever took place. While he was correct in asserting there must be a willingness to move beyond acts of violence, it must be accompanied by an acknowledgement of the truth of the offence, of remembering and honoring the victim's emotional reality, as well as a recognition of both the short- and long-term costs of trauma. When the emotions following the wake of a crime are dealt with honestly, they don't have to be denied—they can be healed. Despite the Hollywood expectations and fantasies of forgiveness, there is a large group of us who don't get the happy endings. My mother has never acknowledged her abuse. Charles Goodwin's display of remorse was false. But I can only wonder how things might have been different had Dad been with me on that trip to Lincoln. I wish he had seen me face Charles Goodwin, claim my strength, and walk away with a redefined sense of self. Might that have led him to take a different path?

I still wish, with all my heart, that we could have reached resolution—that my children would have enjoyed their grandfather, that Thomas would have enjoyed his father-in-law, that Dad and I would be free to enjoy life without the pain that wracked both our inner worlds. I'll never know. This book is a way of reconciling myself with that. Even writing this closing chapter, I'm still wanting to save him.

On his visit to England all those years ago, Dad, Thomas, and I took a road trip to the Lake District. On our last afternoon, we stood at the base of the rugged peaks overlooking a lush glaciated blue-green valley: distant waterfalls cut white lines into the rocks, clouds sailed overhead as the sun intermittently shed brilliant light on Lake Buttermere and Crummock Water. Dad wrapped his arm around me and said, "This is truly heaven." And he made me promise that one day, after his death, I'd return and spread his ashes on that spot.

Shortly after my last visit to my mother, Thomas and I returned to the Lake District. As we were walking to find the perfect spot, we passed a small parish church where we met a pastor in the garden. After chatting, he gave us a tour of the church, shared its history. And when I told him what we were there to do, he gave us his blessing. Five minutes later, I released Dad's ashes in a stream and watched as they bloomed into the water and slowly faded away.

———

In writing the scenes in this book, I was reminded of how terrifying we humans can be when empathy ceases to exist. That we are only as strong as the human connections we build. Fate doesn't arrive with a personal name, but we make our fates personal by our response to life's most challenging events. I have my own beautiful family now, my extended family, as well as a huge loving tribe of friends around me. And I have become fierce in my love of life.

In reaching the end of this story, I can't help but remember the octopus Dad conjured up all those years ago. How he had taught me the skill of pretending, real pretending, the kind of pretending that can turn a scary monster into an imaginary game.

There is no need now to pretend.

ACKNOWLEDGMENTS

I would first like to thank the people who not only were involved in saving my life, but who brought Charles Goodwin to justice for the crimes he perpetrated against me and my family. In particular, Jeanette Hansen, who was working at the South Omaha Fruit Market on November 22, 1978, and brought me out of the cold and into safety. Lieutenant Robert Olson, who immediately galvanized the Omaha police department, Sergeant Dennis K. Howard, Officers Farmer, Greg Thompson, and Edward Hale, who staked out the area and protected my father. The staff at St. Joseph Hospital, who treated me with such sensitivity. Officers Bovasso, Tostenson, and Wryaxz. The *Omaha World Herald*, for their extensive coverage before Charles Goodwin's apprehension. And Judge John Murphy and Judge Elizabeth Pittman, who administered justice.

Enormous thanks to all those who provided support to me in Omaha, Nebraska. The Lewis and Clark Junior High School Parent Teacher Association and those companies and individuals who contributed to the reward fund that led to the arrest of Charles Goodwin. The members of First United Methodist Church who supported me in the days and weeks after the crime, in particular Floyd and Bonnie Morehead, Mel and Harriet Olson, and Amy Kuehl. Also, my neighbors George and Carolyn Ireland and Fran and Jo Bushey. The friends and staff whose support at Lewis and Clark Junior High School proved critical to my mental health and recovery, in particular: Todd Cushing, Sheila Tobin-Anderson, and David Van Meter.

Special thanks to: Kim Haller, who generously provided her journals and endless hours of interviews, for the years she spent working in the criminal justice system, and her continual support. Kate Shugrue, for her amazing work in child protection services, providing access to the legal system, her wisdom during the parole hearing, and lifelong friendship. Kent Friesen, a national hero whose mentoring at a crucial time in my life helped steer my course.

To those who helped me during the Victim-Offender Dialogue journey: Sara Nelson, Kris, David Doerfler, Jon Wilson, Esther Casmer, Judge Ken Vampola, and Mike Kelly.

To my creative partners, readers, and supporters while writing this book: Jim Auxer, Tom Avery, Marina Bailey, Lucy and Zam Baring, Niall and Kate Barton and family, Jez Butterworth, Sarah Chalfant, Trevor Cornwall, Dr. H, Amanda Harding, Angela Harding, Belinda Harding, Elsie Harding, Frank Harding, James Harding, Michael Harding, Kate Harrod, Andrea Hart, Jane Hill, Rob Hyde, Arjan Keshavarz, Greg Kent, Ella Leya, David Levine, Kani Marceau, Sipan Marceau, Lynn Medford, Ben Morris, Cait Morrison, Morgan Oppenheimer, Hella Pick, Laura Quinn, Gail Rebuck, Gabrielle Rifkind, Anita Roddick, Marysue Rucci, Julia Samuel, Philip Selway, Charles Sweeney, Ellie Thackeray, Nick Viner, Patrick Walsh, Kate Weinberg, Doug Wilson, Adrian Wooldridge, Amelia Wooldridge, Loretta Wurtenberger, and Sasha Yevtushenko.

To Super Agent Anna Stein, who gave me the courage to write this story, for her fierce emotional wisdom and compassion, and her enduring faith in my strength when it wasn't there. A writer could not have a better advocate or protector. To Clare Conville, my UK agent extraordinaire, who got me on my way and who keeps this fun. And to my dream team of editors: in particular, Liese Mayer at Bloomsbury USA, for her unbelievable stewardship and empathetic grace through this colossal process; Helen Conford at Profile Books UK, for her razor-sharp insight, and Andrew Franklin, publisher, for his steadfast care. To those who have worked with me at Bloomsbury USA: Marie Coolman, Nicole Jarvis, Laura Keefe, Tara Kennedy, Grace McNamee, Laura Phillips, and Valentina Rice; with special thanks to Barbara Darko for her patience, and to Ellis Levine for his discerning eye and legal expertise. And to those at Profile Books: Elizabeth Hitti, Nathaniel McKenzie, Niamh Murray, Hannah Ross, and Valentina Zanca. Thanks to Darren Biabowe Barnes and Dorcas Rogers at C&W Literary Agency, and a very special thanks to the most excellent John DeLaney at ICM Literary Agency.

To my sister Gayle, who carefully read the manuscript numerous times and kept me authentic to my true self and who is basically just a heroine of epic proportions. To my nephew Taylor Robinson, whose deep insight, intelligence, and connection has shaped this material. To my sister Jenifer; her Amazonian strength has always helped me keep perspective (whether it be rolling east or west).

My daughter, Sam, whose grace, trust, wit, and humor have helped me survive the writing of this book. What you can do with Post-its and your magic quill is a thing of beauty. I love you.

My son, Kadian, whose unquenchable thirst for life, and cheerful and charming ways, not to mention profound intelligence, continue to light up my days. It sucks you aren't here. You know how ridiculously much I love you.

And to my husband, Thomas, it was in the inner universe of our marriage that this whole project happened; I love living life with you. Thank you for your unwavering faith and strength, you are very very funny.

A CONVERSATION WITH DEBORA HARDING,
AUTHOR OF *DANCING WITH THE OCTOPUS*

What inspired you to write the book?

I began writing the book several years after the catastrophic loss of my fourteen-year-old son, Kadian, in a sudden bicycle accident. You might say it became imperative to my survival that I separate the existential questions left from the trauma of my childhood—from the task of learning to cope with the sudden tragedy of having lost my gorgeous son. I barely survived being murdered at the age of fourteen. On top of my grief at Kadian being suddenly taken from us, the paradox of losing him at the same age seemed cruel.

When I started writing again, my brain, my emotional compass—none of it worked the way it once had. I literally had to learn how to put sentences together again. Additionally, after spending two years in heavy grief I found myself reemerging into the world at a time when the political landscape was rapidly changing, when a network of social safety, which had been established in a progressive political era when decency and care and concern for your fellow citizen was a kind of presumed starting point, was being destroyed. It felt familiar, like the dysfunctional and threatening environment I had grown up in. Donald Trump and my mother are very similar in personality. And watching his dismissal of assaults on women as irrelevant was mortifying.

I returned to thinking about the issues of mental illness and violence that complicated the long-term aftermath of the crime. This wasn't my first attempt at writing about this subject. But I was compelled to look at the forces that came into play with a wider lens. I had to arrive at place of total irreverence for my past pain to find my true voice and what I felt to be a storytelling structure that could encompass the social and political conflicts that acted themselves out, not only in my journey but in my parents' journey, and in that of my attacker, Mr. K (Mr. *K* for *kidnapper*). Today, the question of what enables a person to inflict savage acts of violence on others seems as pertinent as ever. And the devastating increase of domestic violence cases we've seen during the coronavirus lockdown only makes it more urgent.

What literary role models did you look to in writing this book?

It was on my journey back to the world, after I hadn't been able to pick up a book for several years, that I came across the *Essays* of Michel de Montaigne. A sixteenth-century French aristocrat might seem odd company to choose, but his material was a perfect match for my mood. He combined wit with erudition, while maintaining intimacy with his reader, and wrote about philosophical themes of his day. As I continued to read it occurred to me that I recognized something familiar in the special perspective from which he viewed life, and I discovered that he had written his first draft while suffering serious grief after multiple losses of key relationships in his life.

While there lay great contrast in our social and political backgrounds—he a sixteenth-century aristocrat, a man of letters with an extraordinary intellect; and me, a twenty-first-century woman with my humble background—we shared the task of finding our way home. So that was the initial inspiration and the reason for the title structure: "In Which I . . ." It helped me focus on the theme at hand. His humor also gave me permission to adopt an irreverent attitude to my material.

Toni Morrison—*Beloved* is a genius of a novel, especially in her treatment of the legacy of human cruelty and trauma and the way it can revisit and terrify its victims. But it's Morrison's essays and lectures that served as my moral compass in helping to make choices about how to deal with the issues of racial identity in the book.

Vivian Gornick also helped influence choices I made about structure. Her memoir *Fierce Attachments* works as much on the level of essay as it does an incredible portrait of a challenging mother-daughter relationship and a 1940s immigrant neighborhood in the Bronx.

I also looked to Truman Capote's *In Cold Blood*, but for different reasons. I've always identified with Nancy Clutter, the sixteen-year-old who was murdered. As a victim of a severe crime myself, I have often wondered how she might have told her story. Part of my motivation for stepping into Mr. K's point of view was to demonstrate what a recalibrated scale of empathy for a violent offender in a true crime story might look like. And I suppose I hope that in doing so, people might think a little harder about the victims missing from these stories.

In the telling of the story, you have written episodes leading up to the crime and episodes after the crime from your kidnapper's point of view. This had to have been difficult as a victim. Can you speak about this decision?

This book, for me, is an interrogation of violence and mental illness. More specifically, how we reconcile ourselves to the complexity of relationship issues that follow acts of human cruelty.

There's an unspoken assumption if you are a victim, writing a memoir about a crime, that it must come from some therapeutic need to share; that you are offering your subjective experience in the case it may be helpful for others on the same journey. There's a sort of pressure for victims to stay in our lane, and I wasn't interested in that. I've endeavored to tell the story of four characters and their relationships to one another, from a detached objective viewpoint.

I had a rare set of journalistic sources. And with forty years of distance from the crime, a multilayered perspective, and something important to say about violence levels in America for those with a professional or emotional stake in the issue. And I wanted to do it in a literary way. I was sorely tempted to hide behind fiction but decided, given the times, it was important to claim this story as truth. I also wanted the story accessible for a reader, something they could pick up at the end of the day. This is a dark story—but I wanted it to feel light, even funny at times—something with the pacing of a psychological thriller.

Each of the vignettes from my kidnapper's perspective is crafted from witness statements, police reports, newspaper articles, and the journal taken by a friend of mine who unwittingly worked with him in prison. I didn't have this information before I entered the Victim-Offender Dialogue, twenty-five years after the crime. And it proved incredibly helpful in dispelling the power my attacker had over my life. I think the veracity of these sources provides an important power for the reader as well.

Later, when I imagined bringing my kidnapper to life in this book, it no longer felt like the story belonged to just me. And I liked that. Perhaps the best way to see it from a storytelling perspective is to imagine what would be missing from the narrative without my attacker's point of view. I felt it important to show, not tell, how extraordinarily ordinary violent acts can be. And having grown up with a violent parent, I am used to detaching myself emotionally from situations in order to survive. That skill served me well here. Writing those sections wasn't easy. I felt nauseous the entire time I was doing it. But I felt what I was doing important enough to carry it through to the end.

In the book, you explore idea of forgiveness through a wide range of relationships, from your mother and father to your attacker. Do you think forgiveness ought to be the goal?

In some cases, having forgiveness as a goal can lead to devastating impacts, especially when dealing with individuals who have a proven track record of violence. It can also be used to dodge more difficult feelings like anger, rage, deep sorrow, and grief, which can have long-term mental health ramifications.

One of the things demanded of a victim, a victim of any crime, is that they try and make sense of a moral universe that allows them to continue in life in a meaningful way—in the society in which they must act. To make peace with forces that have personally annihilated the self is no easy matter. It demands that you step back from your viewpoint and see where the crime fits in the larger societal picture. And it is not an easy path to walk. But it is where healing grace lies. This, to me, is forgiveness, but in a much more objective sense. To understand how deeply impersonal being a victim is, one has to learn to hold the darkest side of human nature in hand with the most sublime. And to accept the whole.

Did your ideas about forgiveness change over the course of writing the book?

As I moved through the story, what became clear to me was that the breakdown of communication between my father and I was primarily about differences in our approach to forgiveness.

He viewed forgiveness in the biblical sense. For him, Jesus's last words—"Father, forgive them, for they know not what they do"—meant unconditional pardon as well as unconditional love. He acknowledged that my mother's violence when we were growing up was real, even though he wasn't around to see it, but he could not acknowledge that what enabled her violence in the first place—her inability to see other people's pain—was a here-and-now problem. He insisted she had changed, when all signs in her relationship to my sister and my grandmother, and with him, pointed to something different.

He therefore saw my taking action to protect myself and my children from my mother as being motivated by anger, bitterness, and judgment, an unwillingness to let go of the past. As an act of aggression even, not one of self-preservation and for my mental health. It kept us locked in a repeated cycle of miscommunication, with no way to reconcile the relationship and an ultimately devastating ending.

We all have inclination to want justice when we have been wronged, but you had the rare experience of working through this within the criminal justice system. Your participation in what is often referred to as "restorative justice" through a Victim-Offender Dialogue program gave you the opportunity to hear directly from your kidnapper—not only about the crime, but also about his circumstances and experiences. Do you think this changed your perception of what justice is?

The gains that the restorative justice movement has made changed my life as a victim. Without the theoretical foundations that have accompanied the movement, the Victim-Offender Dialogue (VOD) program would not have been on offer in

Nebraska. It allows the state legal system to acknowledge the crushing psychological aftermath of the journey and the long-term impact that victims are left to deal with after a crime.

One of the difficult things about being a victim of a crime perpetrated by a stranger is the who, the why, and the how. Being able to not only give a name and face to the man who attacked me, but also to understand how he came to attack me, proved pivotal to my recovery from PTSD. It helped put to rest the existential anxiety and terror that would return to me every night in my dreams. Though it wasn't a part of the VOD process and didn't happen by plan—it took place after I testified against him being paroled and for good reason, he wasn't considered safe—I found that meeting my offender face-to-face was empowering.

It's important not to minimize the role of prosecution and sentencing for the victim, which is a critical component of justice. I have had an unusual experience as victim in both prosecution and sentencing—the man who kidnapped me was a stranger. I was a child. He was arrested and charged ten days after the crime. I never had to appear in court. It was the State of Nebraska that brought the case against him. He served what I felt a sentence fitting the crime. Thankfully child kidnappings by strangers that end in sexual assault—and, more often than not, death—are rare. But there are many victims and families of severe crime who experience the further trauma of miscarried justice—when the state fails to bring charges or prosecute those responsible for violent crimes. And when justice fails to bring to account those that hurt other people, it inflicts a whole other level of suffering.

Ironically, Mr. K was the one who unwittingly shone the light on another violent abuser—my mother. There are few cases in domestic violence where the perpetrators are brought to justice. They prey on family members, and often don't cross the line into the public realm, so it's difficult to hold them into account. Without being aware of it, Mr. K confirmed my memory and instincts, which enabled me to make the much more difficult choice to protect myself and my children from my mother.

You made a choice to not reveal the racial identity of your kidnapper until halfway through the book. And then at the end say this was not an easy decision as we don't live in a colorblind society. Can you share your thinking behind this?

America is a violently racist country. I'm deeply concerned with the quantifiable rise of violent incidents connected to white supremacy in the States, especially since Donald Trump has come to power. These groups are considered the number one domestic terror threat in America today. They are violent criminal gangs who prey on our communities. I am extremely fortunate that my whiteness insulates me from the harm of daily structural racism, though knowing we are failing to protect others and are making little progress toward changing systemic racism is a low-level pain.

As I considered the potential ramifications of revealing my attacker's racial identity in today's political environment, it was enough to sidestep the issue altogether. How important was his racial identity to the story? Then I considered omitting every mention my offender makes of his being violently attacked by racists, one of the few allusions to his racial identity in the story, and the consequence of that wasn't good either. To view crimes outside of their political and social context is to make it appear as though violence springs mysteriously from nowhere, and that's just not the case.

My challenge was to write responsibly about a violent criminal acting within a deeply racist society; to dodge the racial elements in the story would be to err on the wrong side of the issue I try so hard to responsibly address: that human beings who commit monstrous acts of violence do so not because they were once victims, but simply because they do not care that they hurt other people. The stresses are always a contributing factor—but never the cause.

I wrestled with this question for a year, reading eloquent authors on the subject— James Baldwin, bell hooks, Ta-Nehisi Coates, Reni Eddo-Lodge, Ibram X. Kendi, to name a few. Toni Morrison, in particular, was hugely helpful to me. She suggested that to make an issue of racial identity in a character at the beginning of the book is to immediately limit the moral universe the reader perceives them to operate in. They will no longer be granted the same range of agency, of free will. And they will become cardboard characters rather than fully fleshed human beings.

Eventually, I identified three people who made decisions about the importance of Mr. K's racial identity and how it affected his actions.

First, there was the violent criminal himself who claimed it was responsible for a good deal of his choices. He told me the racially motivated sexual assault he experienced in an adult prison holding tank at the age of fourteen was a contributing factor to the rage he let leash on me. And for years after his imprisonment, he claimed that kidnapping and sexual assault charges lodged against him were a complaint from my racist father, who couldn't stomach the idea that we were in a romantic relationship. He was believed by many, as the details of police records are kept confidential, even from prison staff.

Second, there was me—did I view him as having less moral agency as a human being because of his racial identity? No. And I would invite anyone who suggests he does to reexamine their reasons for thinking so, because it has implications for every other citizen struggling with the injustices that racism against Black people creates in this society.

Third, there is the reader—the reader being both the person who has the book in their hand, and the society in which the book is received. In the end, I decided to let the issue of his racial identity emerge authentically, in the manner it actually did, and let the reader consider the issues it may or may not raise for them.

My mother co-opted the feminist narrative in the same way my offender co-opted and falsified his own. She claimed she labored under a societal oppression that made her violent. As an anti-racist and a feminist, I hope I've done the job responsibly. I would not let these two violent oppressors use political narratives to hide their cruelty. I would not let them trump my right to tell this story.

Mental illness and violence are part of your family history and you have experienced the physical manifestations of unprocessed trauma. Do you see any links between these experiences?

The human body's somatic response to chronic stress is genius. And its ability to take over the controls when we are out of alignment with our emotions can be terrifying. I was extremely skeptical of the idea that my partial seizures were the result of unconsciously programmed responses to a sensorial perceived threat, and that it was my body's way of pushing the reset button. They were shaming and humiliating. And my debilitating depression and the other sudden manifestations of PTSD were the same.

It's hard to be interested in the emotions of your inner world when you are functioning at a high level and are genuinely happy in other areas of your life. Especially when you have survived severe trauma. It's completely counterintuitive to want to reexamine the narrative you've told yourself to keep functioning. Life is hard enough as it is.

In my case, it was easier to tell myself that my mother's mental illness excused her violence and psychological cruelty than it was to accept the fact that she was comfortable with her behavior, comfortable with who she was, and, despite my father's claims to the contrary, had not changed. My mother experienced psychotic episodes and depression, but the treatment of these symptoms did not cure her of her lethal lack of interest in the emotions of others. My continuing to engage with her, as well as offering her a relationship with my family and children, set off my symptoms of PTSD and depression.

And then I went on medication and internalized the dysfunction of my relationship with my parents, rather than do the real work I needed to do, which meant adjusting my relationships and environment. That's not to say I'm not thankful for medication—it's still in my life—but I no longer see it as the cure for my mental health challenges. Instead, it lightens the load.

You now have a family of your own and have worked through past trauma to create a loving and supportive environment for both yourself and your loved ones. What advice would you give readers who have experienced abuse or trauma to overcome the obstacles attached to it?

I don't think we have enough stories out there that portray "victims" realistically. Human resiliency is an amazing thing. My healing was encumbered by my dysfunctional family, but even as a child I had enough people in the community to get me through the most painful phases of growing up. So I suppose I'd say take risks in vulnerability. And know you aren't alone. There are so many of us—high-functioning, emotionally intelligent, resilient survivors and caring individuals—who know your pain. And there are innumerable tools and people to help. It takes time and tinkering and failure to get emotional balance right—you're building a multilayered system of support. Don't underestimate the task at hand, learn self-compassion, and never let go of hope.

This Q&A evolved out of a conversation between author Debora Harding and Bloomsbury USA in June 2020.

AUTHOR'S NOTE

Almost all of the quotations and thoughts and feelings attributed to Charles Goodwin are based upon police reports, court documents, newspaper articles, other documents in the Author's possession, the Author's recollections of his assault upon her, her interview with him many years later, or Kim Haller's notes of her meetings with him. However, in certain instances quotations and thoughts and feelings attributed to him by the Author were based upon what the Author believes are her logical conclusions based on the foregoing events or documents.

A NOTE ON THE AUTHOR

DEBORA HARDING spent her childhood in the Midwest prairie states of Nebraska and Iowa. At the age of nineteen, she dropped out of university to work for Senator Gary Hart's presidential campaign before relocating to Washington, D.C. to run an environmental nonprofit. Fed up with politics, she cycled across America, where she met her English husband, author Thomas Harding. She then joined him in the UK and worked at an award-winning video production company that focused on the counterculture protest movement in Europe. Later, she cofounded the UK's first local television station in Oxford and gave birth to two children, Kadian and Sam. Wanting the children to enjoy the great outdoors, the family moved back to the United States, and Debora trained as a restorative justice mediator and ran an independent bicycle business. She is now a full-time writer and activist and splits her time between the United States and England.